W9-BJO-128

SCRIPTURE I

# The Mystery
# of Jesus of Nazareth

**General Editor: Sister Loretta Pastva, S.N.D.**

**BENZIGER**

Encino, California

Series Editor: Sister Agnes Ann Pastva, S.N.D.

Consultants: Reverend Thomas H. Weber, S.T.L., S.S.L.
Professor of Scripture, St. Mary Seminary
Cleveland, Ohio

Reverend Paul Sciarrotta, S.T.L.
Director, Educational Center for Catechetics
Notre Dame College of Ohio

Reverend Maurice A. Hofer, S.S.L.
Pontifical College Josephinum
Columbus, Ohio

Nihil Obstat:
Reverend Timothy Broglio
Censor Deputatus

Imprimatur:
Most Reverend James A. Hickey, J.C.D., S.T.D.
Bishop of Cleveland
September 21, 1979

The nihil obstat and imprimatur are official declarations that a book or
pamphlet is free of doctrinal or moral error. No implication is contained
therein that those who have granted the nihil obstat and imprimatur agree
with the contents, opinions, or statements expressed.

Scripture passages are taken from *The New American Bible,* copyright ©
1970, by the Confraternity of Christian Doctrine, Washington, D.C. All
rights reserved.

Copyright © 1982 by Glencoe Publishing Company, a division of Macmillan, Inc.
All rights reserved. No part of this book may be reproduced or transmitted in any
form or by any means, electronic or mechanical, including photocopying, recording,
or by any information storage and retrieval system, without permission in writing
from the Publisher.

Benziger Publishing Company
17337 Ventura Boulevard
Encino, California 91316

*Printed in the United States of America*

ISBN 0-02-655820-3

7    8    9        87    86

# Contents

1 | Jesus the Mystery | 6

2 | The Real Jesus | 26

3 | To Proclaim the Good News | 48

4 | Old Testament Expectations | 70

5 | The Beginning of Fulfillment | 84

6 | The Time Is at Hand | 106

7 | Jesus the Person | 122

| | | |
|---|---|---|
| **8** | Jesus the Teacher | 140 |
| **9** | Jesus the Healer | 162 |
| **10** | The Paschal Mystery | 182 |
| **11** | Rejection and Covenant Love | 202 |
| **12** | All Is Fulfilled | 220 |
| **13** | He Is Risen | 240 |
| **14** | Who Is Jesus? | 264 |
| | Handbook: The Times of Jesus | 289 |
| | Acknowledgments | 314 |
| | Index | 317 |

# The Mystery of Jesus of Nazareth

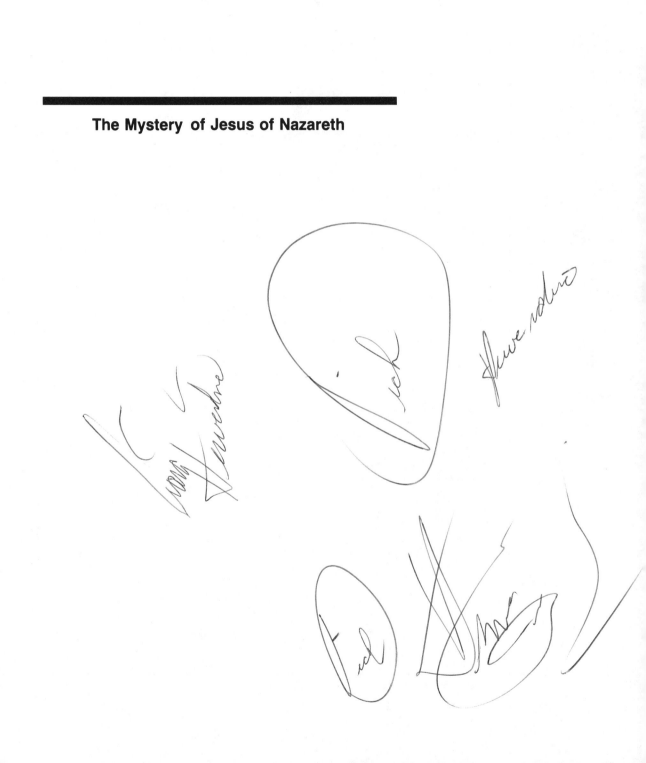

# ONE

Is every person's idea of Jesus unique?

Is every person's relationship with Jesus different?

How is knowing Jesus different from knowing about him?

Are you a mystery?

How is Jesus the mystery who lights up the great mystery—God's plan and your place in it?

*Once we were shadows*
  *groping in the darkness of our sins,*
  *prey to the fears and evil of night.*
*But you, Lord, have sought us out in our dimness,*
  *enfolded us in your strong and tender love,*
  *drawn us toward the warmth of your heart,*
  *and opened our eyes to the brilliance*
  *of your presence among us.*
*You teach us to see our world, our lives*
  *in your changeless light.*
*Snatched from the false security*
  *of anonymous darkness,*
  *we have pledged ourselves to live in light,*
  *to do works of light,*
  *to bring your light into the darkness of our world.*
*Your love guides us, your love impels us, your love sustains us.*
*Light of our life, Lord of our hearts, we thank you.*

(Sister Mary Denis, S.N.D.)

# Jesus the Mystery

God has given us the wisdom to understand fully the mystery, the plan he was pleased to decree in Christ, to be carried out in the fullness of time: namely, to bring all things in the heavens and on earth into one under Christ's headship.

(EPHESIANS 1:9)

## MEETING THE LORD

But you've studied the life of Christ before! Why should you go through it again?

One of the reasons is that you are in an important stage of your development. Your teenage years are among the most exciting in your life, a time when you burst the bonds of childhood and take giant strides into a new and different world. Your body is in a period of accelerated growth, your mind is reaching its fullest development, and your emotions are stimulating your life with a multitude of new sensations. Wonderful as all this is, it is your emerging power to be aware of others and to enter into deep relationships that mark your journey from adolescence to adulthood.

For example, have you recently recognized that someone you thought you knew well seems a little different now? Perhaps you notice a new kindness around the eyes or a certain graceful way of walking that previously had escaped you. From that small revelation you go on to discover other traits that seem to create an entirely "different" person.

Actually, the person hasn't changed. You have. You have a new ability to perceive and appreciate many of the factors that contribute to the "mystery" of another human being.

■ Think of a friend. When did you first meet him or her? How has your impression of your friend changed? Do you think it will continue to change? Why or why not?

Jesus Christ has been a friend of yours from way back—for so long, in fact, that you may feel you know him very well. But do you? Do you *really* know him? You've just seen that your viewpoints concerning other people change as you get older. And now that you are entering the world of adulthood and its relationships, you may want to take a closer look at Jesus. You may find yourself noticing things you never noticed before.

## IMAGES OF JESUS

Look at the photos of Jesus on the chapter-opening pages of this book, in which he is portrayed by various artists in different situations of his life. Each person's image of Christ is unique, so if you aren't satisfied with any of these pictures, bring your favorite one to class.

■ Which picture comes closest to being "your" Christ? Share with the class your reasons for choosing the picture you did.

■ Through the ages, no two artists have created identical paintings or sculptures of Jesus. Why do you think this is so?

Please study carefully these statements made by students of different ages and faiths:

The most important reason for believing in Jesus is that I have faith. There is no real reason for my faith, but I have it. The Bible helps back up this faith, as does my Catholic background. My belief in him affects my whole life because everything I do relates to him. *(Joe Vontorcik, Grade 9, Ohio)*

Jesus is God's Son. He is our Savior. He is God and man and he came down to earth and died on the cross. He rose and performed miracles and taught. He had the first Mass with his twelve Apostles and he is our brother and friend. What does he mean to me? A lot! *(Kelly Holobert, Grade 9, Ohio)*

Whenever I think of Jesus, everything seems bright and colorful and not all gloomy and dark. I've always associated Jesus with all that is good and can think of nothing wrong being connected with him. *(Pat Flowers, Grade 10, Pennsylvania)*

When I first learned about Jesus in elementary school, I pictured him as a kind policeman who might help you find your way back when you got lost. I still see Jesus basically that way, but now I have a deeper understanding of him. Before, Jesus always seemed so far away, but now I know he is always near. I see him in a kind deed and on a happy face. And, of course, I receive him into me in the Eucharist, too. *(Angel Fernandez, Grade 10, California)*

I am confused about Jesus' role in my life because I don't know everything about myself or about him. *(Cathy Griffis, Grade 9, New York State)*

Jesus isn't just a great man who lives in the sky. He is my best friend. He is there to talk to whenever I want or need to talk. In every kind deed or thought, I communicate with Jesus Christ. I tell him that I love him and am trying to be like him. He speaks to me through other people, nature, and everything that happens to me. *(Sheryl Fuldauer, Grade 10, Virginia)*

Now study these statements made by adults of various faiths:

*From Jeremy Harrington, O.F.M., ed., Jesus, Superstar or Savior? (St. Anthony Messenger Press, 1972), pp. 105 ff.*

I began to believe in Jesus when I came across a Bible. I felt the holiness of the book in my hands. The Bible has a profound effect on me. The Word in the Bible is like the Word made flesh. It has a power—you can't explain why. *(Dorothy Day)*

*Dorothy Day (1897–1980) was the co-founder of the Catholic Worker movement and founder-editor of the* Catholic Worker *newspaper.*

Jesus is the foundation of my whole life. He is my strength. If you have Jesus in your life, you know it, you feel it. He's the solid rock you can stand on every day. There's no problem you can't face if you have the love of Jesus to strengthen you. *(Johnny Cash)*

*Johnny Cash is the popular country singer who made* Gospel Road, *a movie about the life of Jesus.*

Christ is the embodiment of the Word of God. He is God's image. Because of Jesus, the Word of God is not abstract; it is flesh and bone. Incredible! You and I, individuals that have been converted to Christ, are called to become flesh and bone like him, to take on his Word, to be what he was. That's a journey of a lifetime. And it all depends on God's grace and our openness to it. *(Michael Cullen)*

*Michael Cullen is an Irish immigrant who founded Casa Maria, a Catholic Worker Hospitality House in Milwaukee.*

He [Jesus] makes it pretty darn tough sometimes. He unsettles me and makes me feel tension and makes me realize how I really don't live up to his example. But at the same time I can take comfort in that unsettling insecurity and sense of failure because even the people he picked to follow him didn't *always* live up to what they thought they should do. Yet he still loved them. He just asked them to gradually grow and love him, and that is what he is doing in my life. *(Ethel Gintoft)*

*Ethel Gintoft is the associate editor of the* Catholic Herald Citizen, *the Milwaukee diocesan newspaper. She is the first lay woman on the Board of the Catholic Press Association.*

■ Which person seems to know the most about Jesus? Which statements second your own thoughts? In a small group, share your observations.

## WHAT DO YOU KNOW ABOUT JESUS?

Answer the following questions in writing as completely as you can.

1. What have you always wondered about Jesus that you would like answered in this course?
2. What is your favorite story about Jesus? Why?
3. What kind of personality does Jesus have?
4. Have you any idea what Jesus looked like? If you do, briefly describe or draw him.
5. What do you think was the most important thing Jesus did in his life? Why?
6. Give any three of Jesus' short sayings, such as: Learn of me for I am meek and humble of heart.
7. Name any three parables you are familiar with. Tell one of them, including as many details as you remember.
8. Give the meaning of these images made famous by Jesus: a pearl, fishes, seed.
9. Rank these religious values in the order of importance you think Jesus gave them, making 1 the most important: poverty, keeping the commandments, concern for others, love of God, trust in the Father, humility, faith.

You may wish to take this quiz again at the end of the course and compare answers.

■ Which set of activities were you most comfortable with—the discussions of the portraits of Jesus, the analysis of other people's ideas of Jesus, the examination of your relationship with Christ in your journal, or this inventory of what you already know about Jesus? Why? It is helpful to understand that there are different ways to know others and each person follows his or her own way.

## TWO WAYS TO KNOW

One day a professor who taught physics at a prominent university and who had written several books on Albert Einstein asked Einstein's wife if she really understood her husband's theory of relativity. Mrs. Einstein just smiled, and then she said, "No, but I know Albert pretty well."

- What is the difference between *knowing* and *knowing about* someone?
- Think of three people you feel very close to. How did you get to know them?

To find out *about* people you can do things like look up their public records, read books about them, ask their acquaintances what they are like, or, if they are historical figures, learn about them in class.

But to really *get to know* people, you need to rub shoulders with them, to enter into a relationship with them. A relationship is an especially close association in which there is a great deal of sharing between two people. The relationship may be natural, as in the bonds among family members, or it may be built on a common interest such as a job, a sport, or a hobby.

A personal relationship involves an intimate meshing of lives and destinies. You somehow perceive the mystery of another person and learn to trust your instincts, as well as the other person's responses, at a deep level. This trust is the basis of communication and leads to fierce loyalty and support.

How is it possible to be friends with Jesus, considering that he lived two thousand years ago? The fact is that Jesus is still present among us. His presence in the world is not the same as that of other figures whose fame makes them live on in our memories. The presence of the risen Christ among us today is unique and mysterious. For believers, Jesus is much more than a historical model. He is a living person who is present in us. And he gives what every true friend gives—the power that enables us to grow as persons.

- Is it necessary to know a great deal about someone before entering a relationship? Cite examples.
- Do people who are already friends want to know more about each other? Is it important for friends to learn about each other's past? About each other's future dreams? Why or why not?

As a believer, you already know Jesus as a friend. You might have touched his reality in a sudden flash of peace during a moment of prayer or when you sensed his forgiveness. This was an expression of friendship.

Intimate friends hunger to know all about each other. They look for information to confirm their instinct that those they love are all they had hoped for. But sometimes "the facts" cause disillusionment, because the person who is loved is found, after all, to be human. Then, the test of affection is whether they can adjust to the new image.

Your years of faith have built up a relationship to Jesus that should not be underestimated, even if that faith has been taken for granted. In the process of maturing, you have formed your personal portrait of Jesus through the examples of your family and friends; by the teachings you have been exposed to; and by the architecture, art, and music that are part of the Christian heritage.

For instance, if someone asked you how Jesus would act toward an enemy soldier who had been wounded, you'd have no hesitation in saying he would be kind—enemy or not. Though there was no war story among Jesus' parables, you have a general notion of his great compassion.

But learning about Jesus can also be disillusioning, not because he has faults, but because some of your ideas of him may not have been correctly formed. For example, you may have pictured the Jesus you received at your first Communion to be a child like yourself. Now that you have learned that it is the risen Christ you receive, you may have to do some adjusting. Letting go of your original idea may involve some discomfort.

Yet, if your relationship is to stay healthy and genuine, there must be a constant testing of your portrait against the real Jesus.

Because Jesus is a living person, you can get to know him in several ways. You can learn more *about* him by reading historical accounts; but you can also *get to know him personally* through Scripture, the sacraments, the lives of others, and your own prayers and goodness to people.

People who live or work together usually get to know each other well, but not always. A relationship requires willingness on both sides to care and to share.

- What things keep people who live close together from really knowing each other? What things promote close relationships even between people who may be separated? Do you think it's important to know something *about* a person you want to have a relationship with? Why or why not?
- Return to the quoted comments on Jesus that appear above. As far as you can tell, which comments reflect a personal knowledge *of* Jesus? Which discuss a knowledge *about* him?

- How is the study of the life of Christ in a religion class different from the study of someone like Napoleon or Caesar? Consider such things as the person to be studied, the reason for the study, and the methods of approaching the subject.
- How will you be able to improve your knowledge about Jesus?
- What can you do now to get to know Jesus himself better? How can you mark the progress in your relationship?

See Matthew 7:20

## YOU ARE SOMEONE SPECIAL

Look at your thumb. Scientists have discovered that the surface of an individual's thumb is unique among the 4 billion persons alive today. Further, since the beginning of mankind no one else's thumb has ever had the exact pattern of lines that yours has.

What is true of your thumb is true of your every cell. Each of the 60 million cells in your body bears your personal trademark, and it is this distinctive genetic pattern that makes you *you.*

But personality is more than heredity. The environment in which you live and the influence of others have a tremendous effect on your personality. And beyond that, at the deepest level of your being, you have a God-given identity that is exclusively yours.

- List in your journal the ways in which you are different from others in your family. Note physical, mental, emotional, moral, temperamental, religious or social differences. Why do you suppose you are the way you are?

*Temperamental* in this sense means a person's disposition, such as cheerful, energetic, thoughtful, or sluggish.

## YOU ARE A MYSTERY

A *mystery* is something so deep and complex that it cannot be fully grasped.

Every so often you hear of people who reject a painting of themselves that they had commissioned an artist to do because they feel it doesn't do them justice. You may have had the same feeling when looking at your photograph or when someone has tried to size you up in a word or two.

When you think of it, no portrait, photograph, or human opinion can totally capture a human personality.

- Why wouldn't your own diary or even a very complete book about you contain the secret of who you really are?
- In what ways are the members of your family a "mystery" to you even though you live with them every day?
- Think of a special friend. What do you feel you still don't understand about this friend?
- In what ways are you a "mystery" even to yourself?

It is truly amazing to consider that of all the trillions of individuals God might have called into existence, he chose you over all other possibilities. By creating you as a "unique mystery," God demonstrated his intention to have you fulfill a purpose in his divine plan that no one else can fulfill.

## JOURNEYING WITH JESUS

Many people who travel keep a record of their experiences. By noting down the landmarks, historic sites, and customs of the people, they become more sensitive to everything on their day-to-day journey. Their jottings also help them to put things in better perspective later, when leisure permits them to recognize patterns and see connections they missed the first time around.

*Both words—journey and journal—are rooted in the French word* jour, *which means "day."*

Keeping a journal of your study-adventure with Jesus in this course can have the same function and be a great aid to building your friendship with Christ.

You may wish to make your journal strictly objective, limiting your notes to the history, person, and objective meaning of Jesus. Or you may prefer to make your journal strictly personal, noting only your reactions to what you learn, the growth of your relationship with Jesus, and your prayer impulses. A combination of these two is a third alternative.

### Your Journal: Why?
1. To clarify your ideas and feelings.
2. To trace the growth in your knowledge of and relationship with Christ.
3. To provide a means for you to voice shaky opinions privately.

### Your Journal: What?
After each class or study period, you may wish to record some of the following:

> Points to remember
> Additional ideas
> Questions
> Personal applications
> Your evaluations and opinions of what you
>     learned
> Personal reactions
> Resolutions

Prayers
Failures
Progress

This textbook will provide suggestions for entries in your journal, but you will probably wish to write in it much more often than is suggested. You may grow in seeing ways to use your journal by noticing the kinds of things you are asked to do. Be as creative as you like. Your journal is between you and your Lord. As a starter, try answering any or all of these questions in your journal.

1. Describe in a few words a person you know who is like Jesus.
2. What type of relationship do you now have with Jesus?
3. What kind of relationship are you searching for?
4. Who do you say Jesus is? What does he mean to you?
5. What is your most frequent or earnest prayer to him?

As this course proceeds, you may wish to check your responses from time to time to observe any changes in your thinking about and relationship with Christ.

## WHO SHOULD YOU BECOME?

You can look at your life and see numerous roles available to you. There are so many, in fact, that at times your future seems confusing and a little frightening. This increases the mystery of your existence, because without fully knowing what you are to become, you must make choices as you go. It's like bicycling in a dense fog.

- Write five questions that from time to time you find yourself wondering about in regard to your future. For instance: Should I go out for sports? Should I become a priest or a sister? How can I fit in with others?
- Explain the various ways in which one of the things you named could affect your future. Who else might possibly be affected by your choice? In what way?

Who and what you become will depend upon a complex chain of gifts and opportunities from God as well as your free response to them. The fact that you don't fully understand how you became who you are at this moment should be encouraging; it shows that someone else is concerned, that someone else is helping. As Shakespeare put it, "There's a divinity that shapes our ends."

*Hamlet*, Act V, Scene 2

Even if you realize that God guides your life, you first have to know God's will before you can respond to it.

- Discuss: How can you know who you are to become? How can you know God's special purpose in creating you?

Thoughtful people have pondered these questions for centuries. In facing the mystery of human existence, wise men and women all over the world have realized not only the importance of the questions, but their inability to answer them without the assistance of their Creator.

## FITTING INTO THE PLAN

As architects build from the blueprint they designed, so God has a plan for his creation. Yet our God is a hidden God, said the prophet Isaiah, a far more hidden mystery than the most complex human being. Who can reach him to discover his plan? "Who, for example, knows a person's innermost self but the person's own spirit within him?" asked Saint Paul. "Similarly, no one knows what lies at the depths of God but the Spirit of God."

Isaiah 45:15

1 Corinthians 2:11

When Moses asked to see the light of God's presence, Yahweh answered, "I will make all my beauty pass before you, and in your presence I will pronounce my name: 'Lord'; I who show favor to whom I will, I who grant mercy to whom I will. But my face you cannot see, for no one sees me and still lives."

Exodus 33:19–20

God is mystery and his plan is also a mystery that has lain hidden, according to Paul, "from ages and generations past." As he told the Corinthians, it could not be discovered by mere human wisdom. This plan might have remained hidden for all time, as some designers jealously guard their secrets of wisdom and eventually take them to their grave. However, God chose to do otherwise.

Colossians 1:26

1 Corinthians 1:21

Our God, who is "the God of gods and Lord of kings," is "a revealer of mysteries," says the Book of Daniel. Beginning with Abraham, he made himself and the mystery of his wisdom known by promising to build a people to whom he would pass the secret of his knowledge. Then, through Moses, he made a covenant with the people of Israel, giving them his laws of goodness as part of his revelation. He made another promise to David: Your descendants will bring the plan to completion in an age of peace.

Daniel 2:47

*Revelation and the plan of God are the same, because in revealing himself God reveals what we are all about.*

Finally, the full plan was revealed in Jesus. Sent by the Father, he was to save all people and bring them God's life of happiness and peace. In Jesus, then, the Father makes known not only his full plan, but everyone's personal role in that plan.

Romans 16:25–26

Paul wrote to the Roman Christian converts who were confused as to how to act when the people all around them lived contrary to the Gospel: "I preach Jesus Christ, who reveals the mystery hidden for many ages but which is now manifested through the writings of the prophets. At the command of God, this mystery was made known to all, that they may believe and obey."

Jesus Christ is the central mystery of the Christian Faith. He is the mystery that solves the mystery of God's plan and each person's place in it. The wisdom of the ages, the infinite riches of the Father, and our own Brother and Savior, Jesus is God's master plan for the universe and for every life.

## JESUS, OUR LIGHT

John 10:10

In Jesus, we have a distinct advantage when it comes to knowing God's will. He became a human being for the purpose of bringing the fullest possible life to all people. He told us, "I come that they might have life, and have it to the full."

John 8:12

Some people erroneously believe that the only life Jesus comes to bring is life after death. Not so. The full life Jesus promises begins now, today, if you are open to it. He also said, "I am the light of the world. No follower of mine shall ever walk in darkness; no, each shall possess the light of life."

John 1:9

Jesus is not some bright spotlight shining impersonally over a dark stretch of land or sea. Rather, he influences people in the secret reaches of their minds. He lights up their world from within. He is "the real light which gives light to every human being," as John wrote.

How he does this is a mystery so vast and deep that no one can completely understand it. But understanding the mystery of how Jesus works within you is not nearly as important as letting him into your life to do his work in you. He taught that people can't make progress toward becoming their true selves or understand the mystery of their lives without him. "Without me," he said, "you can do nothing."

John 15:5

But with him, you can do everything—become your true self, make your unique contribution to the world, and find happiness. Christians are people who live their lives in union with Jesus. They don't just keep the laws of the Church or study her doctrines and participate in the liturgy. Christians center their lives in the person of Jesus. They are personally devoted to him. He is the one who knows the Father and who has come with the power of the Father to bring salvation. He not only lights your way; he can actually bring about a change in you.

*"For all the world, Christ is the answer"* (Eli Stanley Jones).

Jesus always meets people where they are—in the depths of their hearts, at the point of their needs, where the greatest miracles take place. He appeals to rich and poor, to heads of state and ordinary citizens, to the elderly and the young. He heals the sick of heart, mind, and body; he fills the joyful with even greater joy. His friendship makes a distinct difference in people's lives. For you, he still says, "I am the life, I am the light of the world. Come to me."

John 14:6, 8:12; Matthew 11:28

■ Have you experienced the work of Jesus in your life? Describe it in your journal and, if you wish, discuss it with your class or group.

## SNEAK PREVIEW

This book will give you a working knowledge *of* Jesus as his followers came to know him. It will also investigate knowledge *about* him—his roots, his personality, his friendships, his unique teachings, and his mission. As you redefine the meaning of Jesus for yourself, you may personally discover why he has attracted so many friends over the centuries. You may experience a deepening of your own involvement in the mystery of Jesus. This may be the beginning of a lifelong adventure of friendship.

■ Take a few minutes to flip through this book. What aspects of Christ's life that you see presented interest you most?

## SUMMING UP

1. *Words to know:* relationship, unique, mystery, plan of God, revelation, Light of the World
2. What is the difference between knowing about someone and knowing that person?
3. In what ways can a Christian get to know Jesus better?
4. How does the study of Jesus in faith differ from the study of another historical figure?
5. Describe some qualities that make every person a mystery.
6. What is meant by the plan of God? Why is it mysterious? How did the human race learn of it?
7. How does Jesus fit into God's plan?
8. Why did Jesus call himself the "Light of the World"?
9. How does Jesus help a person to understand himself/herself more fully?
10. What are some topics presented in this book?

### Think/Talk/Write

The questions in this section will allow you to reflect more deeply on the ideas in each chapter.

1. Do you know someone who has had an experience of Jesus? What effect did it have on the person's life?
2. If you've ever helped anyone with a doubt about faith, describe what happened and what the experience did for you.
3. How much do you think about the future? What do you see when you think of yourself twenty years from now? How do God and Christ fit into this picture?
4. As you go through life, your love for Christ either grows or withers. In your journal, write about whether or not you are increasing your knowledge both of and about him.

### Activities

These are ideas for activities and research projects dealing with the chapter material.

1. Do a survey of five persons, trying to get a variety of ages and interests. Explain that you are taking a survey about religion and, if they are willing, ask the following questions. You may want to prepare a printed form with these questions on it and take the survey in writing.
   a. Do you believe in God? Why?
   b. Do you belong to a church and participate in its worship? Why?
   c. What does Jesus mean to you?
   d. How important is he to you in your daily choices?
   e. What things do you do to help your relationship with him to grow? What conclusions can you draw about people's religious lives as a result of your investigation? Share your survey with the class. What similarities and differences do you find among your classmates' results?
2. Read and report on an autobiographical account of the meaning of Jesus in someone's life. Here are some suggestions:
   > *Run, Baby, Run*, Nicky Cruz
   > *Clap Your Hands*, Larry Tomczak
   > *Christie*, Catherine Marshall
   > *Tramp for the Lord*, Corrie Ten Boom
3. In his encounter with Jesus on the road to Damascus, Saint Paul was thrown to the ground and blinded. He had to be led by others like a child for three days. Read the account of this event in Acts 9:1–22. What symbolism do you see in this episode? What meaning can it have for any person sincerely trying to find the truth about life? Express your idea in a statement, poem, collage, or drawing.

**Scripture Search**

These short exercises will relate the chapter to God's Word.
1. Light and darkness are universal symbols for good and evil. In John 8:12, what does Jesus promise to those who follow him? What does he mean?
2. Studying Abraham Lincoln's life might inspire someone to imitate his fair-mindedness. What does John 14:5–7 say about the effect of getting to know Jesus?
3. The theme of this chapter is summed up in John 6:40. What does Jesus say is the will of the Father for those who believe in the Son?
4. How does 1 Corinthians 2:6–10 tie in with the theme of this chapter?
5. Read the quotation that appears at the head of this chapter. What is God's ultimate plan for all things that he created?

# TWO

Is Jesus a historical figure?

Is Jesus still alive?

How does God communicate with human beings?

How did God communicate himself most fully?

How can you get to know Jesus better?

What practical difference does the inspiration of Scripture make to you?

Lord,
  You are close beside me here and now.
  Yet you do not force yourself upon me.
You wait
  for me to make the first step, once you have said,
  "Come to me."
  You wait until I in turn say to you,
  "Come to me, Lord."
Christ Jesus
  Savior, Lord of all, son of the living God,
  To whom shall I go? You have the words of eternal life.
I believe in you
I trust you
I want you
I give myself to you.
Please give yourself to me.

# The Real Jesus

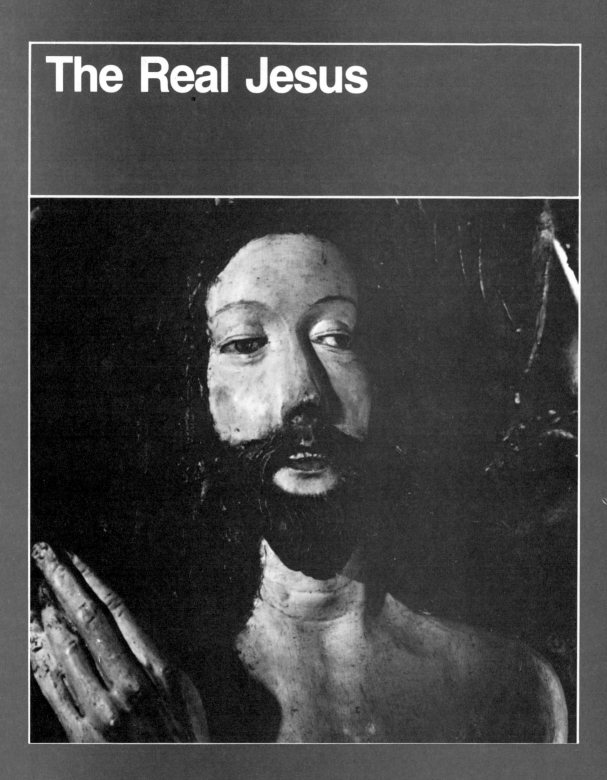

This is what we proclaim to you: . . . what we have heard, what we have seen with our eyes, what we have looked upon and our hands have touched.

(1 JOHN 1:1)

## GETTING ACQUAINTED WITH CHRIST

In the year 2100, how would a person go about proving that you had existed? When you meet a new person and decide that you want to become his or her friend, what things do you do to bring it about?

These two questions can be very helpful in getting acquainted with the real Jesus, since he is both a historical figure who lived in a particular place and time and a living person who is ready to meet you and enter your life today.

## ACCOUNTS FROM ANCIENT HISTORY

If you wanted to get an accurate picture of a famous person like John F. Kennedy, you would compare what different sources of information have to say about him. What would a dictionary tell you? What information would the newspapers of his day give you? What could you find out by referring to the memoirs of his mother and an old political enemy?

*Memoirs* are a person's written reflections on the events of his or her life.

The Bible, of course, is the chief source of information about Jesus. But ancient historians who were not Christians have also left records of who Jesus was, when he lived, and what he and his followers did.

The earliest non-Christian account of the existence of Jesus is found in the writings of Flavius Josephus, a Jewish historian who wrote in about A.D. 95.

> About this time there lived Jesus, a wise man, if indeed one ought to call him a man. For he was one who did surprising deeds and was a teacher of people who accept the truth gladly. He was the Messiah. When Pilate, upon hearing him accused by men of the highest standing among us, had condemned him to be crucified, those who had come to love him did not cease. On the third day he appeared to them restored to life. For the prophets of God had prophesied these and many other marvelous things about him.

■ Do you believe Josephus was describing Jesus objectively?

*Objectively* means in an unprejudiced way.

■ Some scholars believe that this passage has been tampered with by an early Christian. Why would they think this? If insertions were made, what conclusions can you draw about the usefulness of this passage in your search for the real Jesus?

Tacitus, the first pagan historian who refers to the crucifixion of Jesus, does so in an account of the fire rumored to have been started in Rome by the Emperor Nero in the summer of A.D. 64. He writes:

> Consequently, to get rid of the report, Nero fastened the guilt and inflicted the most intense tortures on a class hated for their abominations, called Christians by the populace. Christus, from

*In this case, the "extreme penalty" is death by crucifixion.*

*The "mischievous superstition" is the Christian religion, thought to be a threat to the Roman state.*

*Besides these accounts, Jesus is also mentioned by several other ancient non-Christian writers.*

whom the name had its origin, suffered the extreme penalty during the reign of Tiberius at the hands of one of our procurators, Pontius Pilate, and a most mischievous superstition, thus checked for the moment, again broke out not only in Judea, the first source of the evil, but even in Rome.

Although it was around A.D. 115 that Tacitus wrote about the fire, he had taken the trouble to research the term "Christian," and, having discovered the existence of Jesus, found the official report concerning his death. From this fact we may infer the existence of legal documents pertaining to the executions decreed by Pilate under the rule of Tiberius.

These ancient non-Christian writings from Jewish and Roman historians give two confirmations of Jesus' existence entirely apart from the Bible. Even though they may be garbled or biased, the accounts still confirm that Jesus was a Jewish male who lived in the province of Rome during the reign of Tiberius Caesar. They also confirm that he had been the moving force behind an active group of followers who were different enough from their contemporaries to cause a stir among the government officials of their day. These references, however, do not tell us much about the person Jesus. For a better description we have to look elsewhere.

JESUS

## THE WORD OF GOD
### (A Bible Service)

Use this service in your class or group to focus your prayer on the power of God's Word.

### Introduction

**Leader:** The people of ancient religions had symbols for their gods—golden idols that were made by human beings and could be destroyed by them. Before a burning bush, Moses received the revelation that the true God is Yahweh, eternal and holy and far beyond, yet also living and personal. As a sign of love, this unreachable God chose to initiate communication with the people he was determined to make his own.

And so, not idols but the Word of God became the carrier of God's truth. As the centuries passed, that powerful Word, which was the sole cause of creation, went out from God through the prophets of Israel. God would be faithful to his people forever. Through the prophet Isaiah he promised, "Though the mountains leave their place and the hills be shaken, my love shall never leave you nor my covenant of peace be shaken, says the Lord, who has mercy on you." Isaiah 54:10

*Suggested Song*—"Though the Mountains May Fall" by Dan Schutte, S.J.

### Reading and Meditation

**Leader:** God speaks his Word by his own choice to whomever he wills, and we respond freely and with readiness.

*First Reading*—1 Samuel 3:1–10

**All:** Lord God, we know that you have called us again and again. Sometimes, like Samuel, we have been open to your Word. Forgive, Lord, the times when we have failed to respond. Send out your light and your truth and do not abandon us ever.

*(Silent reflection)*

**Leader:** After centuries of slow preparation, time became ripe for God to draw his people very near to him. To fulfill his promises to the prophets, he sent his only Son, and the Word became flesh. Through human words and human deeds, Jesus showed us the Father. He is the light of the world, full of grace and truth.

*Second Reading*—John 1:16–18

**All:** Jesus, you are the Word of the Father showing us the way. Through your Spirit, give us a deep understanding of what we must do to become the salt of the earth and the light of the world.

*Suggested Song*—"What You Hear in the Dark" by Dan Schutte, S.J.

*(Silent reflection)*

**Leader:** Mary's openness to the word of Scripture formed her pure heart into a worthy chalice to receive Jesus, the Word of God.

*Third Reading*—Luke 1:34–38

**All:** Pray for us, Mary, to the Holy Spirit who worked such wonders in your heart, that we may carry Jesus, the Word of God, to everyone we meet.

*(Silent reflection)*

*Suggested Song*—"In My Name" by Darryl Ducote

## THE GOD CONNECTION

The problem with developing a relationship with God is not only that he is invisible, but also that he is completely different from anything human beings can imagine. God said to Moses, "My face you cannot see, for no man sees me and still lives."

Exodus 33:20

Besides God's invisibility, there is something else that hinders you from knowing God. Just as you can't know the thoughts of a friend unless that friend reveals them to you, you won't be able to know God unless he reveals himself to you.

## GOOD NEWS

Amazingly, God does reach out. Throughout history to the present day, he has drawn human beings to live in close association with him. He began to unfold himself to the prophets of Israel, but God is so deep a mystery that, to fully communicate with people, he willed to actually become one of us so that he could talk our language and act in ways we understand. Jesus is the true mirror of the Father, but even today no one is able to "look on the face of God and live." Therefore, raised now to the right hand of God and made equal to him, Christ continues to reveal his Father to us until the end of time.

*"The hidden God, the mysterious God, is not distant and absent; he is always the God who is near" (Henri de Lubac).*

Saint Peter became so excited when this Good News dawned on him that he was accused of being drunk on the morning of his first sermon:

> Men of Israel, listen to me! Jesus the Nazorean was a man whom God sent to you with miracles, wonders, and signs as his credentials. These God worked through him in your midst, as you well know. He was delivered up by the set purpose and plan of God; you even made use of pagans to crucify and kill him. God freed him from death's bitter pangs, however, and raised him up again, for it

Acts 2:22–24, 33
*Peter's statement is an example of the kerygma which is the basic kernel of faith upon which Christian beliefs have been based.*

was impossible that death should keep its hold on him. . . . Exalted at God's right hand, he first received the promised Holy Spirit from the Father, then poured this Spirit out on us.

Acts 2:39

Peter had known for some time that Jesus was risen, but his excitement increased when he realized that the same Christ was still alive and active even after his return to his Father. "It was to you and your children that the promise was made," Peter told the crowds that pentecost morning. And when the Apostles later performed miracles of healing, he said that their power was energized by Jesus' Spirit working through them. When they preached, prayed, broke bread together, or performed works of healing and instruction, Christ himself was there among them.

## CHRIST TODAY

Acts 2:39

Peter did not stop there, but looked far into the future. "The promise was made to all those still far off whom the Lord our God calls," he said, thinking of all the generations to come. The Father never intended that only the early Church should experience Christ alive. His plan included everyone until the end of time. This means that you can enter into a personal relationship with God in the same way that the first believers did. Because Christ is a real person, as truly alive as you are, you don't have to be satisfied with merely reading about him in history books. You can touch him and talk to him and hear him just as the early Christian community did—by faith and by participation in his living Body, the Church.

*The Church is Christ's living Body because the same Spirit energizes both.*

■ What is your reaction to the idea that Christ wants to be your friend?

If you think about how you got to know your different friends, you will understand that getting to know someone involves a great deal of interaction and mutual self-revelation. It takes many encounters in which you share

*Mutual* means giving and receiving equally.

JESUS

your ideas and sentiments so that your relationship is not just superficial, but meaningful.

The same procedure is applied in getting to know Christ. You are usually introduced to him by your parents. When you are ready, they take you to meet the larger family of his friends—the members of your parish. There, you can listen to Christ reveal the love of his Father through the Scriptures and experience the Father's care for you through the sacraments, especially the Eucharist. He helps you to understand and deepen this relationship through the doctrines of his Church. Finally, when you try to converse with him in prayer, his Spirit fills your heart and you become one with him.

Doctrines are the official teachings of the Church on the Christian way of life.

Along with making the Father known to all his children, Jesus also monitors the direction of his body, the Church. Through Church councils, encyclicals (letters) of the Holy Father to the whole Church, and new insights into moral teachings, Jesus sheds light on the strengths and weaknesses of his people. Then, with the guidance of the Holy Spirit, he teaches Christians how they can better adapt themselves to the will of the Father and thus fulfill God's plan for them.

One of the greatest of mysteries is that when God makes himself and his will known to us (revelation), at the same time he reveals what we are called to be.

THE REAL JESUS

## GOD'S ALL-POWERFUL WORD

Often, people don't realize how much power words have. The child's rhyme, "Sticks and stones can break my bones, but words can never hurt me," is simply not true, because words *can* hurt you. They are extremely powerful. They can communicate love and hate, reassure you, make you laugh, and open your mind to new ideas.

The Hebrew people knew the might of words. To them, a word was something as forceful as action. Words were not just passing sounds; when they were spoken, they took on an identity and a power all their own.

This Hebrew understanding of *word* gives a clue to the way God communicates with his people.

First, God's Word is spoken *in creation*. You have no doubt experienced a mysterious awe at the power of the sea, the majesty of a mountain, or the beauty of a child or a flower. Since the beginning of time, people have recognized the traces of God's presence in the universe.

As various civilizations developed and people became more aware of their identity and beliefs, they were better able to identify God with creation. The world's great religions—Hinduism, Buddhism, and Confucianism—came about because gifted religious leaders penetrated deeply into the mystery of God as he appears in the world. Christians hold the people of these religions and their beliefs in deep reverence. We recognize the gifts God has given to them in response to their search.

Second, God's Word was spoken *in history*. At a certain point in time—about 1859 B.C.—God injected himself into history in order to associate more closely and directly with Abraham and his descendants, the Hebrews. His purpose was to reveal himself to them more

*"Indeed, God's word is living and effective, sharper than any two-edged sword. It penetrates and divides soul and spirit, joints and marrow; it judges the reflections and thoughts of the heart"* (Hebrews 4:12).

**Natural revelation** is the knowledge of God that human beings can gain by their own reason.

**Divine revelation** is God's communication of his very self in words and deeds for the purpose of bringing people to his friendship.

personally than he had been able to do through creation. Through them, he initiated a plan that would draw the entire human race into his friendship.

After his initial breakthrough, God continued to communicate himself to the Hebrew people through repeated calls, promises, saving deeds, and covenants, all of which are recorded in the Old Testament.

Third, God's Word is spoken *through the prophets.* The Hebrews were convinced that the events they experienced were acts of God because God had spoken to them directly and personally through their holy men. By direct supernatural communication, Moses learned God's name and was invited to form a covenant of love between Israel and Yahweh. As the centuries wore on, other prophets experienced similar direct communications with God and were thereby able to reveal God's plans for his people in the form of promises or prophecies.

Finally, God's Word is spoken *in Jesus.* In these "last days," God spoke directly through his Son, who was his Word made flesh: fully human. The Letter to the Hebrews puts it this way:

> In times past, God spoke in fragmentary and varied ways to our fathers through the prophets; in this, the final age, he has spoken through his Son. . . . This Son is the reflection of the Father's glory, the exact representation of the Father's being.

Hebrews 1:1–3

All statements about God, from whatever source, can be judged by Jesus' words and deeds. In an unparalleled way, those who encounter Jesus, the Son of God, encounter the Father. Jesus said, "Whoever has seen me has seen the Father."

John 14:9

- Read the first chapter of the Gospel of John. What feeling does it give you? In light of that chapter, what kind of person do you imagine Jesus was?

## JESUS AND THE BIBLE

Every major religion has sacred books. For Christians, the mystery of Jesus is revealed in the Scriptures (the Bible). The Scriptures are more than a book. The Christian Bible is a collection of sacred books of which God is the principal author. They were written by men inspired and guided by the Holy Spirit, and they contain much of what God has revealed. Because they are *inspired,* the Scriptures are a special way of meeting Christ.

*Inspiration* comes from the Latin root *in-spirare,* which means "to breathe into." Inspiration in the Bible has two sides, one having to do with the people who wrote the Bible, the other having to do with you. Christians believe that God breathed his Holy Spirit into the minds of the sacred writers, influencing them to write what they did. Today, God breathes his Spirit into the Scriptures as you read them, making them come alive for you and thus making Christ truly present in them.

*The word "spirit" comes from the same root.*

■ Some people believe that God dictated every word of the Bible to the authors of the different books and that the authors, like secretaries, took his words down. Others believe the Bible is a collection of writings like any other book, and that God had very little to do with the way they were written. How would you explain the part God played in the writing of the Bible?

## GOD'S INSPIRATION

Today Catholics believe that God did not simply whisper words into the ears of the sacred writers who faithfully wrote them down. They believe instead that the writings of the Bible were accumulated in a step-by-step process.

First, God *revealed* himself to his faithful people, either through mighty events like the resurrection and

38

the Exodus or through the words and deeds of his representatives, the Apostles and prophets. Then God enlightened their minds so that they could unlock the true meaning of his actions. These privileged people *preached* what they had seen and heard, but, in the way of all great orators, they shaped it to fit their audience. From the moment it came to them, their word was as truly their own as it was divine. Finally, they, or others who were part of their community, were inspired by the same Spirit to *write down* what had been revealed in order to communicate, preserve, and safeguard it. During the entire process of preaching and writing, the Holy Spirit was the author, but he still allowed each contributor to express himself in his own way.

*Prophets* are people chosen by God to speak his word.

God did not merely tolerate the particular personality of the author or use it in a mechanical way; instead, he worked through it, making good use of all the writer's powers and gifts, and even his shortcomings and limitations. If a writer was a pessimist, his writing reflects his negative outlook. If a writer was a natural poet, his writing sparkles with his unique talent. The result of this combined authorship is that Scripture is still wholly human even though it is also wholly divine.

A *pessimist* is someone who takes the gloomiest possible view of a situation.

You can find many historical facts about Jesus by studying the Bible. When you read about Jesus in the Bible, however, it is not like reading about him in a history book or an encyclopedia. Something different is going on: God communicates directly with you as you read the Scriptures. The living Jesus is present as you read, working in you just as he worked in Palestine two thousand years ago. It is this ability to unite us with God that prompts a billion people—one-fourth of the human race—to honor the Bible as the greatest book in existence. Even non-Christians like India's Mahatma Gandhi have respected its power for healing and peace.

The Scriptures are nothing less than the living Word of God. They are a liaison with Christ, who is always ready to speak to you and fill you with hope. Through them you can experience Christ as he is: alive, active, and doing all in his power to be your friend. They provide a way for you to know him as intimately as you know the members of your own family.

Christ invites, but friendship is a two-way street. You must be open to allow him free entrance so that you can respond to his call. Before reading or hearing Scripture, many people show their openness by praying for light to understand it and for help to live its teachings.

- Have you ever experienced the presence of Christ as you were reading the Scriptures? Describe and evaluate these experiences in your journal.
- What things might be a hindrance to receiving God's communication?
- What things can you do to make it easier to hear the Lord when he speaks through Scripture?

Book title

# The Second Epistle of Paul to Timothy

Theme headings added by modern editors for clarity

## Introduction

*The authorship and date of this epistle are discussed in the Introduction to the First Epistle of Paul to Timothy. The letter portrays Paul as a prisoner (1, 8.16; 2, 9) in Rome (1, 17), and indicates that Timothy is in Ephesus (4, 12). It reveals that, with rare exceptions, Christians have not rallied to Paul's support (1, 15–18), and takes a pessimistic view of the outcome of his case (4, 16). It describes Paul as fully aware of what impends, looking to God, not to men, for his deliverance (4, 3–8.18). It recalls with affectionate remembrance his mission days with Timothy (1, 3ff; cf Acts 16, 1–4). It points to his preaching of the gospel as the reason for his imprisonment and offers Timothy as a motive of steadfastness his own example of firmness in faith despite adverse circumstances (1, 6–14). The epistle suggests that Timothy should prepare others to replace himself as Paul has prepared him for his own replacement (2, 1f), urging him not to desist out of fear from preserving and spreading the Christian message (2, 3–7). It presents the resurrection of Jesus and his messianic role as the heart of the gospel for which Paul has been ready to lay down his life (2, 8f), not only to express fully his own conviction but to support the conviction of others (2, 10–13).*

*This letter, like the preceding one, urges Timothy to protect the community from the inevitable impact of false teaching (2, 14—3, 9), without fear of the personal attacks which may result (3, 10–14). It recommends that he rely on the power of the Scriptures and on the positive proposal of doctrine (3, 15—4, 2) without being troubled by those who do not accept him (4, 3ff). The epistle observes in passing that Paul has need of his reading materials and his cloak (4, 13), and what will be best of all, a visit from Timothy.*

Introduction by Scripture scholars summarizes and explains important themes in the book

# 1

Chapter

¹ Paul, by the will of God an apostle of Christ Jesus sent to proclaim the promise of life in him, ² to Timothy, my child whom I love. May grace, mercy, and peace from God the Father and from Christ Jesus our Lord be with you.

## Thanksgiving and Prayer

○ I thank God, the God of my forefathers whom I worship with a clear conscience, whenever I remember you in my prayers —as indeed I do constantly, night and day. ○ Recalling your tears when we parted, I yearn to see you again. That would make my happiness complete. ○ I find myself thinking of your sincere faith—faith which first belonged to your grandmother Lois and to your mother Eunice, and which (I am confident) you also have.

Verses

## Exhortation to Faithfulness

⁶ For this reason, I remind you to stir into flame the gift of God bestowed when my hands were laid on you. ⁷ The Spirit God has given us is no cowardly spirit, but rather one that makes us strong, loving and wise. ⁸ Therefore, never be ashamed of your testimony to our Lord, nor of me, a prisoner for his sake; but with the strength which comes from God bear your share of the hardship which the gospel entails.

⁹ God has saved us and has called us to a holy life, not because of any merit of ours but according to his own design—

---

⁵ 2 Tm 3, 14f; Acts 16, 1. ⁷ Rom 8, 15. ⁸ Lk 9, 26; Rom 5, 3. ⁹ Mt 10, 10; Lk 10, 7; Ti 3, 5.

Cross-references locate other Bible verses that are similar in meaning

---

1, 1f: For the formula of address and greeting, see note on Romans 1, 1–7. *The promise of life in him:* which God grants to men through union with Christ in faith and love; cf Col 3, 4; 1 Tm 4, 8.

1, 4f: Purportedly written from prison in Rome (1, 8; 4, 6ff) shortly before the writer's death, the letter recalls the earlier sorrowful parting from Timothy, commending him for his faith and expressing the longing to see him again.

1, 6: *The gift of God bestowed when my hands were laid on you:* the grace of ordination, signified by the laying on of hands; cf 1 Tm 4, 14.

1, 8: *Never be ashamed of your testimony to our Lord:* i. e., of preaching and suffering for the sake of the gospel.

1, 9f: Redemption from sin and the call to holiness of life are not won by personal deeds but gratuitously bestowed through the incarnation according to God's eternal plan; cf Eph 1, 4.

Footnotes explain individual verses and themes throughout the book

## A PRACTICAL GUIDE TO THE BIBLE

### What Is the Bible?

The Bible is the sacred book of Christians who believe that God speaks directly to his people through its words.

The word *Bible* comes from the Greek *ta biblia*, "the books." The Bible is also called Sacred Scripture, which means "holy writings." Other names for the Bible are the Word of God, Holy Writ, the Book of Books, and the Good Book.

*The Church, under the guidance of the Holy Spirit, determined which of the many ancient holy writings should be included in the Bible. This official list is called the canon of Sacred Scripture.*

### Divisions of the Christian Bible

*Testament is another word for the Covenant, or solemn promise of faithfulness, made by God to his people.*

1. *The Old Testament* tells the story of God's relationship with the people of Israel before the coming of Christ. The Old Testament contains forty-six books.
2. *The New Testament* tells of God's new covenant of faithfulness made in the person of Jesus Christ. It contains twenty-seven books arranged as follows:
   a. *The Gospels* (Matthew, Mark, Luke, John) tell the story of God's mighty works in Jesus' life, death, and resurrection.
   b. *The Acts of the Apostles,* written by Luke, describes the activities of the first Christians, especially Peter and Paul.
   c. *The Letters* (or Epistles) were written to explain the mystery of Christ to new Christians and to give them advice and encouragement. There are twenty-one letters. Thirteen are thought to be by Saint Paul. Others bear the names of James, Peter, John, and Jude. The authorship of Hebrews and 2 Peter is uncertain.
   d. *The Book of Revelation* speaks in highly symbolic terms about the end of the world. It was meant to bring consolation to the Christians who were being persecuted at the time of its writing.

JESUS

Books that can be of help in your study of the Bible include Bible commentaries, Bible dictionaries, and concordances. Examine a library reference shelf to find out what they contain. Cite one example of each.

## What to Look For in Your Bible

Ancient scholars divided each book of the Bible into *chapters* and *verses* for easy reference. Chapters are the major divisions of each book. Verses are the smaller divisions, usually of just a sentence or two. The chapter and verse of a book of the Bible are usually cited thus:

Matthew 5:38–42

book    chapter   verses

- What do you discover in each of these Bible references: Matthew 4:23; Mark 1:13; Luke 7:19; John 18:1–2; Acts 18:1–4; 2 Corinthians 2:12–13; James 1:12; Revelation 6:1–2.

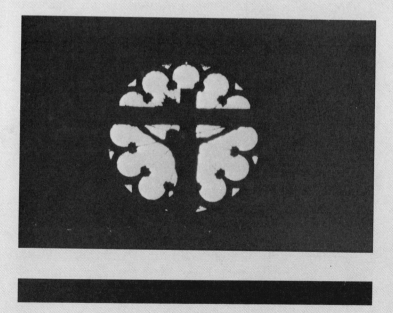

## CAN THE BIBLE MAKE A MISTAKE?

You may have met people who believe that the Bible is a strictly historical record and that it contains no factual errors. This misguided idea is known as fundamentalism. Actually, many biblical statements have been proven inaccurate in the light of modern science and history. Some passages in the Bible are even contradictory. For example:

- The sun could not have been created after the light, as the Book of Genesis declares. (See Genesis 1:3–5, 16–17.)
- King Darius the Mede did not succeed Belshazzar as king of Babylon, although the Book of Daniel says he did. (See Daniel 5:30–6:1.)
- In the Gospel of Mark, Jesus names Abiathar as the high priest of David's time, but in the First Book of Samuel he is called Ahimelech. (See Mark 2:26; 1 Samuel 21:1–2.)
- The Gospels of Matthew, Mark, and Luke state that Jesus was crucified the day after the Jewish Passover began, while John's Gospel says the crucifixion occurred the day before Passover. (See Mark 15:42; John 19:14.)

But if God is the indirect author of sacred Scripture, doesn't it follow that the Bible *must* be true? After all, weren't the judgments of the sacred writers divinely inspired and assisted? The problem is how the Bible can be true and at the same time mistaken.

The answer lies in understanding the main purpose of sacred Scripture: the Bible does not teach science or history—it records and reveals God's presence in the world. Errors in science or history do not falsify the truth of the Bible, because the Bible is still accurate in presenting the truths necessary for salvation. Catholics believe the spiritual truth the sacred writers intended to convey. They do not hold as true all the historic or factual details through which these truths were expressed. Like many of the imaginative stories used to teach a moral or religious truth, many of the factual details serve merely as carriers of revelation.

*Examples of such stories are the Books of Jonah and Daniel.*

Inspiration guarantees that the *original* writings of sacred Scripture are God's truth. Translations from the original are also God's Word insofar as they are accurate. But since they are interpretations, it is possible that a translation may contain human error. Approval of a translation by the living, teaching Church is a guarantee that it contains the truth God wished to communicate. The official approval is shown by means of the *imprimatur.* This word, together with the name of the bishop who gave his approval, appears on one of the first pages of any Catholic Bible.

*Imprimatur* (im-pree-MAH-ter) is a Latin word meaning "let it be printed."

- What English translations of the Bible can you name?
- Compare two different translations of a passage of Scripture (for example, from the *New American Bible* and the *Good News Bible*). How are they alike? How do they differ? Which do you prefer? Why?

# SUMMING UP

1. *Words to know:* Good News, inspiration, Word of God, natural revelation, divine revelation, canon of Sacred Scripture, Bible, Testament, *imprimatur*
2. Who were Flavius Josephus and Tacitus? In your own words, summarize what they had to say about Jesus.
3. What is the significance of having historical records of Jesus?
4. Discuss the similarities and differences between knowing Jesus as a historical figure and knowing him as a person.
5. What problems do people encounter when building a relationship with God?
6. In what ways does God work to overcome these problems?
7. What was the "good news" that Peter preached to the people on pentecost morning?
8. Explain what Christians mean when they say that Jesus is alive today.
9. In what ways does Christ communicate with his followers today?
10. How did God inspire the writing of the Scriptures?
11. In what sense are the Scriptures the living Word of God?
12. What did "word" mean to the Hebrews?
13. In what ways does God speak his Word?
14. What are some names for the Bible? List its main divisions and authors.
15. How can the Bible contain errors and still be considered the true Word of God?

## Think/Talk/Write

1. Tell why you agree or disagree with this statement of a writer from the Middle Ages: "The knowledge of God is implanted in us all."
2. Would you defend or disagree with this quotation: "Christianity is different from all other systems of religion. In them, people are found seeking after God. Christianity is God seeking after people."
3. It has been said that everything is a Word of God. What does the statement mean? What do you think about it?

**Activities**

1. Be a roving reporter. Ask three Protestants: What does the Bible mean to you? Which means more to you, the Old Testament or the New? Why? Ask three Catholics: What does the Bible mean to you? Which nourishes you more, Scripture or the Eucharist? Compare the answers of the two groups and report your findings to the class.
2. If you have an opportunity, ask a Jewish person: Which book of your Scriptures do you like best? Why? Have you ever read the New Testament? What do you think of it?
3. Copy your favorite Bible passage and bring it to class to read. Tell why you prefer it. What truth does it reveal?
4. Make a study of the variety of Bibles available today. Which are Catholic? Which are Protestant? How do they differ? Which are approved for use in liturgy?

**Scripture Search**

Take a moment to flip through the pages of your Bible for a general sense of where the books are.

1. Find where the New Testament begins. About how much of the total Bible is it?
2. The first Gospel is by Matthew. In what order do the other Gospels follow? Which is the longest?
3. The book that follows the four Gospels was written by Saint Luke. What is its name?
4. The last book of the New Testament uses much symbolism. Skim the last chapter to find five symbols. What are the last words of the Bible (just before the complimentary close)?
5. The next to last section of the New Testament contains the letters. The first thirteen of these are attributed to Saint Paul. To which ten groups or individuals did he write?
6. The authorship of Hebrews and 2 Peter is uncertain. Who wrote the remaining letters? Which is the shortest? How many letters are there in all?
7. Everything preceding the New Testament makes up what Christians call the Old Testament. The first five books of the Bible are called the Pentateuch. Genesis is its first book. What is the fifth?

**THREE**

Why were the Gospels written?

How did the Gospels develop?

How are the Gospels different from one another?

*This day*
*is something like*
*a door, Lord.*
*I open it*
*in the hope*
*of your sure presence*
*and the promise*
*you made through your Gospel.*
*I pass through,*
*accepting all the life*
*that waits beyond the threshold.*
*I close the door with care,*
*knowing what I am shutting out,*
*welcoming all I am closing in,*
*and moving forward*
*in peace*
*and with thanks.*
*For you are the door,*
*the threshold,*
*and the beyond*
*of all my living.*

# To Proclaim the
# Good News

These [things] have been recorded to help you believe that Jesus is the Messiah, the Son of God, so that through this faith you may have life in his name.

(JOHN 20:31)

## THE TERM "GOSPEL"

*Mark is the only evangelist to call his book a Gospel. He opens his account, "Here begins the Gospel of Jesus Christ."*

The four books attributed to Matthew, Mark, Luke, and John were called Gospels from the very beginning. The English word *gospel* comes from the Old English *god-spell,* which meant "good news" or "good story." This was a translation of the Greek word *euangelion,* which was also the direct source of the word *evangelist,* a writer of one of the four Gospels. *Euangelion* originally meant either proclaiming the Good News or the Good News itself even before the Good News was written.

■ If a non-Christian asked you what the Gospels are, how would you reply?

The Gospels are not just ordinary books about Christ, as are some books that describe great persons out of the past. In a mysterious way, wherever they are proclaimed, Jesus himself is made present as our Savior. The Gospels are unique because they are the living Word of God. The living Jesus is filled with the power of the Holy Spirit and speaks through them to all who believe.

For Christians, the Gospels are the climax of both the Old and New Testaments. Because Jesus is the Messiah, the Son of God, every person who hears his Word is challenged to the most important decision of life: whether or not to be saved in Jesus. For this reason, the Gospels are the four most important books in human history. Together they proclaim one message: Christ has redeemed you—believe and be saved. This is the Good News.

*Christ is the Greek word for messiah.*

■ What marks of worship surround the proclamation of the Gospel in the liturgy?

## WHAT THE GOSPELS ARE

The Gospels are a new and distinctively Christian form of literature that resembles a portrait, only the evangelists use words instead of color and line.

A portrait artist would not paint an elderly bank executive as aged, wrinkled, and dozing off in his chair. The artist would rather try to re-create him as vibrant, intelligent, and dignified, emphasizing the qualities that gave his life its particular meaning. A painter interprets a person's inner spirit and life role rather than merely surface appearance.

The four evangelists likewise arranged their materials to create an interpretation of Jesus that was neither strictly historical nor strictly biographical. Although they presented many details of Jesus' career, they were silent on several subjects you would expect historians and biographers to include: his family background and education, his physical and mental qualities, his personal habits, the influences that shaped his attitudes, and the chronological sequence of his life. Instead, the

*Theological* refers to how a thing relates to God and his relationship to the world.

Mark 8:31–33

Acts 2:23

*The term* Christ *comes from a Greek word meaning the "anointed one of God." It was an expression that witnessed the faith the early Christians had in Jesus' divinity.*

evangelists were concerned with what gave Jesus' life its deepest meaning—his relationship with God and with us. Consequently, we say that their interpretation is theological.

Just as it doesn't matter whether the banker ever actually wore the particular gray pinstripe the painter gave him to represent his usual business attire, it doesn't matter whether Jesus is portrayed as beginning his public life in Judea, as John tells us, or in Galilee, as the other Gospels state. The purpose of the Gospels is to proclaim the theological meaning of what Jesus did—to reveal the Father's love for us. Thus the Gospels are an interpretation of Jesus' life made through the eyes of faith.

But the Gospels are not merely a collection of the personal-faith views of the evangelists. The disciples were slow to grasp what Jesus said or did while he was alive. Peter could not see why Jesus would have to suffer. But after the coming of the Spirit, Peter preached with conviction that Jesus was the Messiah *because* he had suffered.

Thus the Gospel interpretations are the result of insights given the Apostles by the Holy Spirit, whom Jesus said would instruct them and remind them of all he had told them. The continuing influence of the Spirit becomes clear when you consider that although each wrote his Gospel at a different time and place and for a different audience, all four evangelists agree on one thing: Jesus was the expected Messiah, the Son of God who came to reveal that God is our Father and wills to save us.

So the Good News is not simply a biography or a message about Jesus. It is something like a sermon meant to stir up faith, but a sermon in which Jesus offers himself through the Spirit to all who wish salvation. Although the evangelists wrote separately, their four accounts form but one Gospel: Jesus Christ. That is why we always read the Gospel *according* to Saint Matthew or *according* to Saint Mark.

## NEW TESTAMENT MANUSCRIPTS

You may wonder whether original manuscripts of the New Testament still exist. The answer is no, but we have no originals of any other ancient literature, either. In fact, most ancient works have only two or three manuscripts dating from before A.D. 1000. But there are more than 4,500 copies of the New Testament that are older than a thousand years, some of them almost eighteen hundred years old.

This large number of very old manuscripts shows how widely the New Testament was used, even in times when books were scarce. It also demonstrates that the New Testament wasn't "made up" or added to in later times.

*The oldest manuscript* is known as the Rylands Fragment and dates from A.D. 130, just one hundred years after Jesus. It contains John 18:31–33 and 37–38. It was found in Egypt in 1920.

*The most extensive manuscripts* are the Chester Beatty Papyrus from A.D. 250, which contains most of the New Testament, and the Bodmer Papyrii from A.D. 200, which consists of most of John (1–14, except for 6:12–35) and some letters.

When parchment came into wide use, copies of the New Testament became widespread and many minor variations occurred in the process of hand-copying; insertions, corrections, clarifications. As a result, since the nineteenth century, scholars have been comparing these early manuscripts to trace the "families" of similar variations from the original. Textual critics estimate that 90 percent of the New Testament has come down in the original form. The study of biblical texts for accuracy is called *textual criticism.*

## FORMATION OF THE GOSPELS

Recent advances in language studies and historical and archaeological discoveries have brought new insights into how the Gospels evolved. Scholars agree that they passed through three stages: (1) the historical stage, (2) a period of oral preaching, and (3) the actual writing of the Gospels. During the years between pentecost and the writing of the last Gospel around A.D. 90 to 100—nearly seventy-five years—there was a rapid growth in the Christian community's understanding of Jesus.

> ▪ How long did it take you to fully understand the personality of someone who is close to you? Is the process finished? Why or why not?

### Meeting Jesus the Man:
### The Historical Stage, A.D. 28–30

The first stage in the evolution of the Gospels was the life of Jesus himself. Although Mark and John open their Gospels with Jesus' public life, Matthew and Luke announce the Good News through the story of his birth. From their accounts we learn that the Savior was born of a Galilean Jewish virgin named Mary in Bethlehem around 6 B.C., during the reign of Augustus Caesar. (This seeming discrepancy in dates—after all, "B.C." means Before Christ—is the result of a later mistake. In the sixth century A.D., Denis the Little, the monk who prepared our Christian calendar, miscalculated the year of Herod's death, making it coincide with the Roman year 754 B.C. instead of its real date, 748, about six years earlier. As a result our calendar is off by four to six years.)

Luke 3:1

"In the fifteenth year of the rule of Tiberius Caesar," according to Saint Luke, about A.D. 28 or 29—ancient thinking allowed for broad leeway in computing time—when he was "about thirty years of age," Jesus left home, was baptized by John in the Jordan, and returned to Galilee to begin his public career as an itinerant

*Itinerant* means traveling from place to place.

54          JESUS

preacher. After gathering together a band of followers, he enjoyed a period of successful influence, teaching, and healing in northern Palestine. When he was rejected in his hometown, he made his way south to Jerusalem, where he met severe opposition from the Jewish leaders. Condemned by them on charges of blasphemy, he was turned over for execution to the Roman procurator, Pontius Pilate, at the time of the Jewish Passover around A.D. 30 (the exact date is uncertain). The tomb in which he had been laid was found empty the following Sunday. The historical period of the Gospels ends there.

## Proclaiming the Good News: The Stage of Oral Preaching, A.D. 30–50

After pentecost, the Apostles wanted to win as many people as possible to the faith before the Second Coming of Jesus. Because the first disciples were not well-educated, literary persons, and because writing materials were expensive, they preferred oral, eyewitness testimony to written accounts.

The Apostles were not secretaries and they did not have tape recorders, so they had not set down every word and action of Jesus. However, some people wrote down the sayings and stories of Jesus during the period of oral preaching. As the Gospel penetrated the Roman Empire, between A.D. 50 and A.D. 65, letters, written summaries and sayings, and collections of parables and miracles began to circulate. Thus the entire community of early believers played a vital role in shaping the Gospels. The hymns, creeds, and formulas of the liturgy by which they expressed their faith found their way into the sacred writings.

Through the Holy Spirit, Jesus was alive and working in the community of his followers. Just as he had dealt individually with the people who had come to him during his lifetime, the Apostles adapted his teachings to the needs of particular groups of Christians with different backgrounds and cultures.

1 John 1

*The scholarly study of these units that had been formed during the oral period is a science that began in 1919 and is known as* form criticism.

Acts 11:20 tells us that *all* early Christians worked to make converts, not just the Apostles. This in itself could have endangered the factual teachings of Jesus because it is difficult to maintain unity when many people explain the same topics. Although there were some alterations, like expansions and contractions, in regard to *basic* teachings, the Apostles insisted on faithfulness to what they had really seen and heard and touched. In fact, they repeated their stories and sayings so often that their materials were shaped for easy memorization into something like preassembled units. They are: *Outline summaries.* The synoptics each have four sections: prologue, Galilean ministry, journey to Jerusalem, last days in Jerusalem. *Liturgical formulas.* Fragments of hymns, creeds, and prayers of the early Church. *Miracle stories.* Quick summaries of Jesus' healing power for new Christians. *Conflict stories.* Stories of Jesus used to solve conflicts in the early Church. *One-line sayings with a moral.* Condensations of Jesus' teachings for easy memorization. *Special stories.* Unique narratives connected directly with Jesus.

## Change of Plans:
## The Stage of Gospel Writing, A.D. 65–100

A *generation* is about thirty years.

During the first generations of the Church, the Apostles and other first-generation Christians relayed their eyewitness encounters with Jesus to converts. These personal memories of the Lord generated an excitement that could not have been created in any other way.

It was the spread of Christianity into the more literary Gentile world, the deaths of Peter and other witnesses of Jesus' ministry, and the realization that Jesus wasn't coming as soon as expected that led to the creation of the Gospels. Mark was the first to put the oral and written traditions with which he was familiar into a continuous account, probably around the time of the fall of Jerusalem in A.D. 70. During the next thirty-five or forty years, the other evangelists did the same.

## EDITORS AND AUTHORS

The evangelists can be compared to editors of a school yearbook. If a yearbook editor decides that school spirit will be the theme of the sports section and only glum faces turn up in the photos, the editor may have to change his theme. Editors are limited by the materials of others that are available to them. But like authors who originate ideas, they can also create a theme by carefully selecting photos and adding their own script.

The evangelists were both editors and authors. They surveyed all the materials on hand—written fragments, notes, collections of sayings, liturgical formulas, narratives, anything that had preserved Jesus' memory. They did not include everything in their Gospels for, as John wrote, Jesus worked many other signs besides those he recorded. As a true author, each evangelist also selected, arranged, and highlighted events to produce his own unique faith perspective. (In some cases, it is known that followers of an evangelist may have reorganized or made slight additions to his Gospel after his death.) Thus Matthew, Mark, Luke, and John, the first Christian theologians, each built a separate mosaic. The result is four different views of the same subject, Jesus. Together the Gospels present a rich and varied portrait of Jesus.

John 20:30

A *theologian* is one who organizes a body of opinions about God and our relationship to him.

From a human viewpoint, the first Christians and the evangelists are the authors of the Gospels. As Luke writes:

> Many have undertaken to compile a narrative of the events which have been fulfilled in our midst, precisely as those events were transmitted to us by the original eyewitnesses and ministers of the word. I too have carefully traced the whole sequence of events from the beginning, and have decided to set it in writing for you.

Luke 1:1–3

But from another point of view, God is the true author. He guided the formation of the Gospels during the period of preaching, and he urged each evangelist to write what he did according to his own style. The total image of Jesus that comes to us is precisely what God had in mind to reveal to his people.

You may wonder how the four Gospel accounts were chosen over other writings about Jesus that were in circulation at the time. The Church accepted the four Gospels because each had become recognized as an authentic proclamation of the apostolic faith in one or more of the different Church communities. The universal Church then officially adopted them around the middle of the second century. The same is true of the other books of the New Testament.

## OBJECTIONS OVERRULED

Is it possible that the Gospels were made up? It seems unlikely. Would the Apostles have created stories that would have caused them to be rejected, persecuted, and even martyred? Would the first Christians have accepted and died for a myth? Could four different traditions have resulted in one consistent portrait? It seems improbable that Jews would have substituted simple, uneducated fishermen as their leaders in place of their learned and respected rabbis.

Common sense also dictates that no effect can be greater than its cause. How could the community that eventually spread to the whole world have originated without a great leader? It is not normally a group that forms a central figure. Rather, central figures gather around themselves communities in which their ideas take root.

But the strongest proof of the authenticity of the Gospel is that it seemed to run counter to both Jewish and pagan beliefs. Its claim of a man being "Lord"—that is, equal to God—offended the strong Jewish tradition that God is completely "other" and one. The Chosen People now became the whole human race. Now sinners and outcasts were not only acceptable, they were loved by God. The kingdom was not to be limited by political boundaries.

The Gentile converts who chose to follow Christ had to renounce their easier and immediately more satisfying life of immorality. They were asked to make the radical change from being self-centered and sensual to sharing with their brothers and sisters in the Lord. In some cases they were called to surrender their lives.

No, the Gospel was not made up. Such things could only have come from God.

■ In your journal, write your own convictions about the authenticity of the Gospel.

## FOUR GOSPEL VIEWS

Every person you know sees a different side of your personality, and yet you are much more than what any one person sees. The task that faced the evangelists was even more difficult than summing up the life of an ordinary person. Their subject was the God-man and their purpose was to proclaim something of his mystery.

■ How would five people you know size you up in a word? If they can't, does that make you any less than what you are?

Three of the Gospels—Matthew, Mark, and Luke—roughly follow the same chronological order and include almost the same events. They are called synoptic Gospels or, simply, the synoptics, because, seen together, the Gospel accounts look very much alike. John's Gospel not only begins differently and follows different events, but it also has a unique style.

*Synoptic* is derived from *syn* ("together") and *optic* ("seen").

Sometimes the only person in the family with dark hair emphasizes the blondness of the others. The uniqueness of John's Gospel highlights the similarity of the synoptics. And yet, even among blondes in one family you find that each has a distinctive hair color. Likewise, each synoptic writer makes his own distinctive contribution to the New Testament.

## Mark: The Suffering Messiah

Mark always comes straight to the point in his Gospel. The first Gospel to be written, his account is the shortest of all four, containing only 661 verses. It emphasizes Jesus as a man of action, of strong character, and of suffering.

*Time and Place of Writing.* A.D. 65–70, probably in Rome.

See Acts 12:12, 25; 13:5, 13; 15:37–40

*Authorship.* Probably the John Mark who prepared the room for the Passover (14:14) and whose mother's house served as a center for the first Christians is the author of the Gospel. Possibly also Peter's traveling companion (1 Peter 5:13).

*Purpose and Audience.* To provide evidence that God acted through Jesus for our redemption. To encourage the Roman (Gentile) Christians persecuted under Nero in A.D. 64 to bear their sufferings as Jesus did.

*Style.* Fast-moving, dramatic episodes. Use of unanswered questions. Simple yet profound. Powerful in arousing enthusiasm. Jesus hardly speaks at all.

*Organization.* First half (1:1–8:29)—Galilee: Jesus is the Messiah. Climax (8:30)—(The Jew) Peter's declaration, "You are the Messiah!" Second half (8:31–16:20)—Journey to Jerusalem: Jesus is the Son of God because of his prophecy-fulfilling suffering. Climax (15:39)—(The Gentile) Roman centurion's declaration, "Clearly this man was the Son of God!"

*Theme.* Jesus, the mighty Son of God, redeems us by his unselfish service and by his suffering and death.

*Picture of Jesus.* A man of divine action and suffering. A divine/human whose identity is known to the demons (1:23–27, 34) but hidden from human beings (4:11–12), and only dimly recognized by his disciples before the resurrection (6:52). In fact, Mark shows that Jesus tried to keep anyone from openly proclaiming him as the Messiah (the "Messianic Secret") so that the people would not confuse him with the political messiah they were expecting (8:30). He destroys the powers of evil and establishes the kingdom of God.

- Find ten phrases in Mark that show Jesus as a man of action, either coming or going. What do you think Galilee and Jerusalem symbolize?
- Read the Cure of the Leper (Mark 1:40–45). What is Jesus' motive for curing him? Why does Jesus command him to keep the miracle a secret? How does Jesus show his respect for the law? What is the effect of this miracle on the town? What does the cure symbolize?
- Look up the prophecies of the Messiah as Suffering Servant in Isaiah 42:2, 49:2, 53:1. What do they foretell about him? What does Jesus call himself in Mark 10:45?

## Matthew: Jesus as Teacher

Matthew describes Jesus in terms of someone his Jewish converts knew very well: their great teacher, Moses. In this Gospel, Jesus is addressed as teacher or rabbi more than a dozen times. He teaches a new Law of Love that brings the Old Law to completion. The position of Matthew's Gospel at the head of the New Testament reflects the high regard the early Church had for it. For centuries, it was the most commonly read and quoted Gospel of the four.

*Time and Place of Writing.* Perhaps around A.D. 85, probably in Antioch or Syria.

*Authorship.* Probably based on sources compiled by the Apostle Matthew or on the traditions handed down by his disciples. If the final author had been the Apostle, he would probably not have included 90 percent of Mark, a non-Apostle's Gospel. He did, however, follow Mark's order of events, copy or shorten many of Mark's narratives, improve Mark's style, and, in places, change Mark's theology.

*Purpose and Audience.* To counteract the hostility of the Jews by showing that the Church is the true religion of God and that Christ's Law is fulfilled by inward goodness (love). Tried to make Jewish converts

*Rabbi* is a title meaning "my master"; it also means *teacher.* A rabbi was a Jew over thirty years old who was authorized to interpret Jewish law.

Here *abstract* means lacking concrete images.

The Torah, or Pentateuch, consists of the first five books of the Bible attributed to Moses; they contain the Law.

Matthew is the only evangelist to mention the word "church."

by revealing Christ as the fulfillment of the Jewish Scriptures.

*Style.* Slower paced and more abstract than Mark. Five sermons (discourses) interrupt the story sections. More faithful to Jesus' sayings than any other evangelist. Easy to quote.

*Organization.* To depict Jesus as the teacher of the New Torah, Matthew is carefully arranged into five booklets, in each of which a teaching section is preceded by a narrative section. Balances his prologue of Jesus' birth and infancy (1:1–2:23) with an epilogue describing the New Covenant, the passion and resurrection of Jesus (26:1–28:20), and the commission to preach the Good News universally.

*Theme.* Jesus, the great rabbi, is the New Moses who fulfills the old law and gathers the people of the kingdom of heaven.

*Picture of Jesus.* Jesus is the Messiah who brings forgiveness of sins and entrance into the kingdom to all through the Church. He asks inward goodness, not mere external observance by imitation of his own loving service.

- ■ How does Matthew's epilogue (28:20) match the theme of Emmanuel introduced in the prologue (1:23)? How is the theme in Matthew 2:1–2 repeated in 28:1? What passage in Chapter 3 correlates with Jesus' baptism by blood in the passion? What parallel do you find between Matthew 4:3 and 27:40?

### Luke: Jesus, Merciful Savior of All

Luke portrays Jesus as a most appealing, people-loving person. Sent to all nations (the Son of Adam, 3:38), Jesus was a light to the Gentiles (2:32) and a friend of Samaritans, women, sinners, the poor, tax collectors, and even the Pharisees. A French writer, Ernest Renan, called this Gospel "the most beautiful book in the world."

*Time and Place of Writing.* Between A.D. 70 and 90 in Achaea (Greece).

*Authorship.* Probably Luke, the "dear physician" and companion of Paul. A sensitive man with concern for the Gentiles, the poor, and minorities. Excellent Greek style, historical interests, and cosmopolitan outlook indicate someone who had a good education and had traveled widely.

Colossians 4:14. Luke is known as Paul's secretary.

*Purpose and Audience.* Proclaims Jesus as the Savior of the entire human race. Declares him innocent of political revolution. Tries to convert the Greek-speaking readers throughout the world by showing that the Holy Spirit guided Christianity, which was not only the fulfillment of Judaism but a new world religion of peace and joy.

*Style.* The longest, most poetic, and most highly polished of the Gospels, with many vivid human portraits, especially of Jesus as a loving humanitarian. Describes Jesus' psychological motivation and his concern for all classes of society, stresses prayer and life in the Holy Spirit, portrays domestic scenes, and offers the charming birth and infancy narratives. Half of this Gospel consists of material not found in the other Gospels; the other half is based 60 percent on Mark and 25 percent on Matthew.

*Organization.* Three periods of history: the Time of Israel (Old Testament), the Time of Jesus (Luke's Gospel), and the Time of the Church (Acts of the Apostles). These divisions, together with Luke's arrangement of Jesus' genealogy, establishes Jesus as the center of history and the universal Savior of humanity.

*Theme.* The main theme is Jesus as a universal and compassionate Savior. Luke is also called the Gospel of Mercy, of the Poor, of Women, of Prayer, of the Spirit, and of Joy.

*Universal* means including all.

*Picture of Jesus.* The God-begotten, God-appointed, God-empowered, God-guided man whose mission was to free all people from oppression. God's great compassion for human weakness forms the heart of this Gospel. Above all, Jesus is the understanding, merciful, and forgiving one, even on the cross.

- What parables does Luke place in Chapter 15, which is a central chapter of his Gospel? What does this reveal about his view of Jesus?
- Find one example of each of the themes developed in Luke.
- Find the explanations in the following passages and tell why they are included: 4:31, 22:1, 23:51, 23:56, 24:13.
- Does the Acts of the Apostles, Luke's second book, begin where Luke's Gospel leaves off or does it reiterate the end of his Gospel?

### John: Jesus, Son of God

If you admire people who stand out in a crowd, you'll appreciate John's Gospel. Although it centers around Jesus just as the synoptics do, from the first lines it catches Jesus from a different angle and is written in a different style.

*Time and Place of Writing.* A.D. 90–100, probably in Ephesus.

*Authorship.* Probably one of John's disciples who gathered John's papers together.

*Purpose and Audience.* "To help you believe that Jesus is the Messiah, the Son of God, so that through this faith you may have life in his name" (20:31). To strengthen Christians combating those who denied Jesus' messiahship as well as the Gnostics within the Church who claimed that Jesus could not have taken the form of evil human flesh.

*Style.* Simple and deep. Includes vivid, concrete details, accurate geography and place names, and John's personal meditations on Jesus' life. Hidden meanings are expressed in literary devices, including the following: (1) Figurative language, in which John has Jesus preach in metaphors or figures of speech and then answer a questioner who misunderstands what is being said. (2) Double meaning or symbolism, in which John

The Gnostic heresy holds that the material universe is evil. John shows how Jesus' divinity gave him power to overcome evil.

relates a story as if he were using a stereo system. The symbolic, or sacramental, version is played through one speaker while the historical, or factual, version is played through the other speaker. This technique makes the Gospel applicable to our lives today even though it is relating events in Jesus' time. (3) Dialogue becoming monologue, in which Jesus begins a conversation with one or more people but, as he continues to talk, the audience is forgotten and the speech is directed to everyone, making its message universal. (4) Duplicate speeches, in which the disciple-editor may have heard John develop a topic in two slightly different ways and includes both versions. (5) Contrasting images, which John used to represent the struggle between good and evil—for example, light and darkness (1:1–5).

*Dialogue* is a conversation between two people. A *monologue* is one person speaking to himself or herself.

*Organization.* Interweaving of themes. Two main divisions, or books, preceded by a prologue that sum-

## Summary of Differences Between John and the Synoptics

| SUBJECT | JOHN | SYNOPTICS |
| --- | --- | --- |
| Place of ministry | Chiefly Judea | Chiefly Galilee |
| Subject of preaching | Jesus himself and the meaning of his ministry | The kingdom of God |
| Jesus' language patterns | Long sermons, often controversial | Short sayings, parables, normal conversational style |
| Reason for hostility against Jesus | Jesus' claims about himself | Jesus' liberal interpretations of the Law of Moses |
| Purpose of Jesus' miracles | To point to Jesus' true identity; called "signs" | As works of compassion or to show God's power in action in Jesus |
| Number of incidents | Only seven signs narrated and explained in great depth | Forty miracles described; many more suggested |
| View of Jesus | Jesus is the pre-existent Word of God | Jesus gradually revealed as Lord and Christ |

*Logos* is a Greek word that means the eternal Word who expresses and reveals the Father.

marizes Jesus' life and John's themes and followed by an epilogue in which the risen Jesus returns to guide his infant Church. Book I (1:19–12:50)— Book of Signs: Seven "signs" or mighty works of Jesus that help people to "walk in the light" of faith; John shows that some do not believe. Book II (13:1–20:21)—Book of Glory: To those who accept him, Jesus is glorified by the Father in his death, resurrection, and ascension, and—from this position of glory—gives the Spirit of Life.

*Themes.* Jesus is the Son of God, the Word who gives eternal life to all who believe in him. The importance of the sacraments, especially baptism and the Eucharist, as bringers of God's life. The world is a sacrament (sign) of God; Jesus' humanity is a sacrament (sign) of his divinity. Other themes: faith, light, love, sin, and spirit.

*Picture of Jesus.* Emphatically the Son of God, a term that appears twenty-eight times in this Gospel. He is Son by his unique closeness to the Father (1:14, 3:16, 18), his dependence on his Father (14:28, 5:30), and his work of giving life to the world (5:21, 6:25).This work continues into the present age as Jesus, the Word, speaks and mysteriously acts among us, especially in the sacraments. He is also the Son of Man and the ideal man, or second Adam, as well as the Word (Logos) and Wisdom of the Father "made flesh" (human). John stresses Jesus' presence in the Church as it awaits his coming in glory.

- What is the meaning of the metaphors used in 1:5, 3:4, 6:41, and 10:1, 7?
- What do the following characters symbolize? Lazarus (Chapter 11), the paralytic (Chapter 5), and John himself (19:26–27).
- What double meanings do you find in the action or objects in 2:8–9, 2:19, 3:14, 4:11, and 19:34?
- What two similar ideas are repeated in 8:13–18 and 10:11, 14? Find another one.
- What contrasting images to the following terms do you find in John 1:1–18: uncreated Word, light, natural birth, law?

**Four Gospel Perspectives**

| EVANGELIST | TIME | PLACE | AUDIENCE | THEME |
|---|---|---|---|---|
| Mark (Peter's Secretary) | A.D. 65 | Rome | Persecuted Gentiles in Rome | Suffering Christ |
| Matthew | A.D. 70–80 | Antioch or Syria | Palestinian Jewish Christians | Fulfillment of Old Testament Prophecies |
| Luke (Paul's Secretary) | A.D. 75 | Greece | Gentile world | Universal Savior |
| John | A.D. 90–100 | Ephesus | First- and second- generation Christians of Asia Minor | Son of God |

## SUMMING UP

1. *Words to know:* Gospel, evangelist, Christ, Messiah, Suffering Servant, New Moses, universal Savior, Son of God, sign
2. What are the Gospels? Why were they written?
3. Explain the three stages by which the Gospels evolved to the form we have today.
4. What preassembled units have biblical scholars been able to identify?
5. Who are the evangelists? In what way were they both authors and editors?
6. What are the synoptic Gospels? Why are they given that name?
7. How is John's Gospel different from the others in its order of events? In its presentation of miracles? In its use of words and situations?
8. What picture of Jesus does each of the evangelists present?
9. How do we know the evangelists didn't make up the Jesus story? What one Gospel do they all preach?

### Activities

1. Biblical archaeology: In the spring of 1947, a shepherd accidentally discovered jars containing ancient scrolls when he explored a cave hidden among some cliffs near the Dead Sea. The discovery led to a fresh search that turned up other fragments and archaeological finds. Research the topics "Qumran Scrolls" and "Dead Sea Scrolls." Has our present understanding of the Bible been expanded due to the discovery of these scrolls?
2. Surveying: Go through any one Gospel and jot down any references made to the geography of Palestine. Are there a great many or just a few? What does this tell you about the authenticity of the Gospels?
3. Talk show: You are making a long road trip with friends. On the way, they challenge you with the statement that they can't believe the New Testament because it's just stories made up by the Apostles. How would you answer? Remember, they are your friends.
4. Be a lawyer: Mark's Gospel contains many evidences of eyewitness accounts. Look up these passages and find the vivid details in them: 1:21–29, 4:35–5:43, 6:30–56, 7:24–27, 8:27–9:29.

**Think/Talk/Write**

1. The sacraments don't operate automatically. They require creative cooperation on the part of the people. Jesus personally instructed people like Nicodemus and the Samaritan woman (see John 3:5–21, 4:21–26). Where can people go for help if they feel they don't derive any real benefit from the sacraments?
2. Which sacramental signs are the most meaningful for you?

| baptism | water | new life |
|---|---|---|
| confirmation | oil | strengthening |
| Eucharist | bread/wine | sharing, unity |
| Reconciliation | telling sins | conversion |
| matrimony | pledging vows | union |

3. Is it really possible to be a light that changes the world, or is darkness so thick that it snuffs out tiny flames? Where can teenagers be lights in the world?
4. What did being a light cost Jesus? What will it cost his followers?

**Scripture Search**

Reread the list of biblical "preassembled units" at the end of the section entitled "Proclaiming the Good News: The Stage of Oral Preaching." Doing the following exercises may help you to better understand them.

1. Search Chapters 1–3 of Mark for the transition from the prologue to the Galilean ministry.
2. Where do you think the liturgical formulas given in Matthew 28:19 and James 5:14 originated?
3. The miracle stories usually have three steps: request, Jesus' action, and the effect on the people. Trace these in Luke 5:17–25.
4. What conflicts in the daily life of the early Church do you think the stories in Mark 2:18–22, Mark 2:23–27, and Luke 5:27–32 served as guides for?
5. What sayings do you find in Matthew 10:39 and Mark 9:37? Which others do you know by heart? What others can you find?
6. What unique narratives do you find in Luke 3:21–22, 4:1–13, and 9:28–36?
7. How will a recognition of these units help you in reading the Gospels?

# FOUR

What was the cornerstone of Israel's belief?

How did God show his favor to Israel?

What event almost caused Israel to despair?

Who gave Israel new hope?

Where does Jesus fit into the story of Israel?

*Father, we acknowledge your greatness:*
*all your actions show your wisdom and love.*
*You formed man in your own likeness*
*and set him over the whole world*
*to serve you, his creator,*
*and to rule over all creatures.*
*Even when he disobeyed you and lost your friendship*
*you did not abandon him to the power of death,*
*but helped all men to seek and find you.*
*Again and again you offered a covenant to man,*
*and through the prophets taught him to hope for salvation.*
*Father, you so loved the world*
*that in the fullness of time you sent your only Son to be our Savior.*

(Eucharistic Prayer IV)

# Old Testament Expectations

The Lord your God has chosen you from all the nations on the face of the earth to be a people peculiarly his own.

(DEUTERONOMY 7:6)

## THE GREAT GETAWAY

The Hebrews of the thirteenth century before Christ were under a lot of pressure. The new pharaoh had it in for them. He was afraid that with their large numbers they might successfully organize and join Egypt's enemies during a war, so he gave orders to break their spirit. They were conscripted into labor gangs and forced to work on the building of the new warehouse cities on the Nile delta. However, their spirit remained unbroken and they continued to multiply, so they were reduced to long hours of hard labor in the fields. The Hebrews had, in fact, become slaves, but even this debasement was not enough for the pharoah. He chose to heighten their suffering until it was unbearable by giving the command to have all their newborn sons thrown into the river.

*In training their young to fly, eagles push them off high perches and then swoop down under to catch the young birds on their broad wings.*

Then it happened! God swooped down like an eagle and saved them. It was like having the whole neighborhood troop in to bail you out of trouble. It was like an announcement to prisoners of war just before their execution that the war is over and they are free. Under the mighty Moses, who had been commanded by God, Egypt was plagued with frogs and flies and, finally, the death of their young. At last, under Moses' direction, the Hebrews hurriedly gathered their things together, ate a hasty meal, and made off into the night. Getting away was miracle enough, the attitude of the Egyptians being what it was, but when the waters of the Red Sea rolled up to let them pass and then eased back to drown the Egyptians with their horses and chariots, they knew who was on their side.

*Because this body of water between Egypt and present-day Saudi Arabia is often more like a marsh than a sea, it is also sometimes called the Sea of Reeds.*

Who was this God who favored Hebrews over Egyptians? He was the God of their forefathers, the God of Abraham, Isaac, and Jacob who had revealed himself for the first time to Abraham four hundred years earlier. At that time, he had been identified as the "most high God"—the One mightier than the many gods of the surrounding nations. He had also been a person who entered Abraham's life and promised him a land for the many descendants that would be given him, even though Abraham was already seventy-five and his wife was past childbearing.

This God had made a covenant with his faithful servant and he had fulfilled his part so far. Abraham's aged wife, Sarah, had given birth to a son, Isaac, and the clan had been saved from a famine. After that, the descendants of Jacob had traveled through the desert, successfully avoiding the trade routes where they could have been recaptured.

- ■ Has someone ever broken a promise to you? How did you feel? Angry? Hurt? Betrayed? Shocked?

## COVENANT

God called his people out of Egypt for one reason: to make a covenant with them. You may not grasp the meaning of what was happening to the Hebrews in the Exodus unless you understand what an ancient covenant was.

The Hebrews, like many seminomadic peoples, relied on oral rather than written communication. A person's spoken word had all the binding power of our most formal treaties signed by persons of state. Once solemnly uttered, the spoken word could not under any circumstances be retracted without terrible consequences. To seal their agreement, the covenanting parties usually tore animal carcasses in half and walked between these halves to show what the parties were willing to have happen to them if they broke the covenant.

In the covenant ritual made with Abraham, only God passed through the torn animal because this covenant was not a bilateral contract between equals. It was the promise of a greater party made to a lesser one. It showed that God would be faithful to his promise even if Abraham or his descendants broke their promise.

The benevolence in this kind of an agreement was symbolized by shedding animal blood or partaking of a reverential meal at the time the covenant was solemnly declared. The sprinkling of blood signified an artificial or adopted blood relationship. This method was chosen because blood was the symbol of life. Sharing life was also the symbol of the covenant meal, during which the parties ate and drank in fellowship as one family.

There were duties on both sides. The services agreed upon were to be performed by the lesser party, while the greater party was to protect or avenge the lesser blood brother if his family were ever attacked by enemies. The covenant, then, was far more than a contract or an agreement. It was the establishment of a relationship of loving interaction between the parties. So in freeing the Hebrews from the oppression of the Egyptians, God was protecting them and saving them from their enemies just as the superior party was bound to do.

An *avenger* is one who takes revenge.

## NAMES OF THE CHOSEN PEOPLE

Sometimes it becomes confusing to read the history of God's Chosen People because there were several names by which they were known. Actually, they had *four* names, each acquired during a definite period in their history but carried over to later eras as well.

*Hebrews.* The clan of Abraham from the area of the fertile crescent extending between Canaan and South Mesopotamia were known as Hebrews. In Saint Paul's day, a Hebrew was a pure-blooded Jew who spoke Aramaic.

A *clan* is composed of a number of families with a common ancestor.

*Aramaic* was the language spoken by descendants of Aram, son of Shem (Semites).

*Israelites.* When Abraham's grandson, Jacob, had been tested by Yahweh, his name was changed to Israel. His (and Abraham's) descendants were thereafter known as Israelites. As a nation, Israel was divided into twelve tribes. The only one to endure was Judah.

*Chosen People, People of God.* At the time of the Covenant, the Israelites were called by God to be "my Chosen People."

*Jews.* Before the fall of Israel in the north, this name included only members of the tribe of Judah. After the Babylonian Exile, the "Jews" were those who returned to renew themselves in the practice of the Mosaic law. By the time of Jesus, the Jewish leaders had added many unessential practices. Jesus stirred the anger of these leaders by condemning their hypocrisy. In John's Gospel, the term "Jews" often means the religious leaders with whom Jesus was in conflict, although in Luke's Acts of the Apostles it sometimes refers to Jewish-born Christians.

■ Write one sentence with each name the Chosen People have had, showing that you know how to use each term correctly.

## LOVE OF A PEOPLE

To Abraham, God had only been *El Shaddai*—the "God of the Mountain"—one who towered over the gods of other nations. To Abraham's descendants, he had been the personal God of their patriarchs. When he revealed his mysterious name to Moses, God made his identity better known. He had given the Israelites a certain power over himself by entrusting them with his personal name, Yahweh—"I am who am" or "I am the one who lives," which meant the one who reveals himself and who stays with you. This brought them nearer to God, just as being able to call someone by his or her first name implies a closer relationship.

After bringing the Hebrews out of Egypt and giving them his name, God revealed to Moses the purpose of these actions.

Exodus 19:1–5

> In the third month after their departure from Egypt . . . when Israel was encamped . . . , Moses went up the mountain to God. Then the Lord called to him and said, "Thus shall you say to the house of Jacob; tell the Israelites: You have seen for yourselves how I treated the Egyptians and how I bore you up on eagle wings and brought you here to myself. Therefore, if you hearken to my voice and keep my covenant, you shall be my special possession, dearer to me than all other people, though all the earth is mine."

His purpose from the very beginning had been to draw his people into a close, family kind of relationship with himself.

After reviewing what he had done for them, he outlined their obligations. Unlike earthly kings, the obligations God required were not for his benefit but for theirs. He gave them the commandments—the Law. The first three "words" of this law emphasize their duty to worship him as their one Lord. They were not to be like other nations in adoring false and "dead" gods. Their God was living and personal. The remaining

JESUS

seven commandments outlined the kind of community God wished to create among his people. The words of the Covenant taught them that, in Israel, to be one with Yahweh was to be one with each other, and to be united with each other was to be one with Yahweh. The commandments embraced all aspects of human life—the family, personal life, the lesser covenant between man and woman, property, and relations with neighbors.

By these terms, the Hebrews, a group of desert wanderers who had just been released from slavery, were made "a kingdom of priests," a holy nation in the eyes of their God. Just as priests were set aside from the people for special dedication to God, so the tribes of Israel were to be set aside from all other people as God's special possession.

Exodus 19:6

## A FAITHFUL PARTNER

In the spirit of true covenant love, Yahweh remained true to his promises. He fed and cared for his people and he guided them through the desert for forty years. He helped them overcome the enemies who tried to keep them out of Canaan, the land he had promised to Abraham. His mercy seemed especially visible when, in 1000 B.C., he united them into a prosperous nation under David.

But the Israelites did not keep their agreement. Idol worship, crime, and violence were their response to God's gift of the land. Following their corrupt kings, the people deserted God, preferring to rely on false gods and covenants with foreign nations for military safety. Then, like a parent who reluctantly punishes a child in order to help him learn, God left Israel to its own resources. The result was terror. The people were shocked when God allowed Assyria to capture Samaria, Israel's capital in the north. But when Solomon's magnificent Temple and Jerusalem itself were completely destroyed in 587 B.C. and the people were deported to Babylon, Israel was devastated. God had never before abandoned his people.

The prophets kept repeating that God had not left his people, but was only instructing them in his true identity, and in theirs. He was not on the side of might and force as they had thought. Rather, he was a God of compassion whose power was made clearer in times of weakness. He was closer to them in their suffering, the prophets said, than he had been in the golden days of King David. Even as they mourned the loss of their land, God was preparing them for a new idea—that he is not honored by the sacrifice of animals and mere exterior worship. He wanted a faith from the heart.

Jeremiah 31:31–33

The prophet Jeremiah wrote, "The days are coming, says the Lord, when I will make a new covenant with the house of Israel and the house of Judah. It will not be like the covenant I made with their fathers. . . . I will place my law within them, and write it upon their hearts; I will be their God, and they shall be my people."

Finally, Cyrus of Persia conquered Babylon in 539 B.C. and set the Israelites free, but those who returned to Jerusalem found destruction everywhere. With a new appreciation of their freedom and their faith, the Jews rebuilt the Temple and the city walls and renewed their Covenant, promising with great fervor to be faithful to God's Law. For four hundred years they struggled under the domination of Greek and Roman rulers, some more oppressive than others. Then, in 163 B.C., the Maccabee family led a rebellion against the tyrant who had tried

*Because most of those who returned to Jerusalem were from Judah, the Israelites from this time on were called Jews.*

*The tyrant was Antiochius Epiphanes.*

to impose Greek culture on the Jews. He had suppressed all religious activities and had put a statue of the Greek god Zeus in their Temple, thus desecrating it with "the abomination of desolation." Because the Macabees were victorious, the people enjoyed independence until 63 B.C., when Pompey entered Jerusalem and placed it under Roman rule. These conditions remained until after the time of Christ.

In Israel's history you can trace a regular pattern. A time of faith is followed by a period of infidelity, and with faithlessless comes punishment. The suffering stirs up a faith in the people that is usually purer. They see God and his plan more clearly. God then blesses his people.

## A NEW VISION

During the frightening experience of being torn away from their native land and almost losing their knowledge of the true God, Israel's prophets made sense out of what was taking place. They looked back to the glorious age of David when the kingdom had been a minor world power and the people had enjoyed the freedom to practice their religion in their own land. Since prospects of a return to a monarchy seemed out of the question, the people again asked themselves the meaning of Yahweh's promise to David of a kingdom without end.

Ezekiel, one of the prophets deported to Babylon by Nebuchadnezzer, had a vision of a large plain filled with very old, dry bones. They symbolized that Israel was dead because of its unfaithfulness to the Covenant. God first made him walk among the bones, and then he commanded Ezekiel to prophesy over them. But as Ezekiel spoke the word of God over the bones, he heard a rattling and saw the bones joining together. Muscle and skin began to cover them, and spirit was breathed into them, until finally the dead bones came alive as a vast army. "These bones are the whole house of Is-

*Nebuchadnezzer was the Babylonian leader who destroyed Jerusalem and deported its inhabitants in 598 B.C.*

rael," he was told. The people had been saying, "Our bones are dried up, our hope is lost, and we are cut off." God then promised that their graves would one day be opened and Israel would rise. "O my people!" said the Lord. "I will put my spirit in you that you may live, and I will settle you upon your land."

When the spirit of God was allowed to work within the people, Israel would have a resurrection, but that restoration to life could come only through the destruc-

Ezekiel 37:1–14

JESUS

tion of all that was unlike or opposed to God. It was the same message as Jeremiah's: personal and interior conversion to God, a new heart and a new spirit within each individual person. This was to be the core of the new kingdom.

Ezekiel 36:26

*To the Hebrews, the heart was the mind and the power to make a decision. The spirit was the impulse to put what the mind saw into action.*

But above all others it was the prophet Isaiah who deepened Israel's understanding of the meaning of God's saving action. He told them that their hopes should definitely not center around any political system.

Many in Israel found it hard to accept this interpretation. They were convinced that the prophecy made to David had meant that the reign of God would come through the political clout of one or more messiah-kings born of David's line, and that his reign would last until the end of the world. For this reason it was important for those who belonged to the House of David to keep an account of their ancestry. This future kingship would represent the call of all Israel to be the source of blessings—the messiahs—to the world.

After Isaiah and the Exile, those who closely studied the prophet shifted their hope from an earthly monarchy to a kingdom not of this world. Isaiah had said that God's kingdom had always been a process of "bringing people out"—from slavery to freedom, from death to life, from the darkness of not understanding into the light of truth. The expected Messiah was to be a mysterious king who, like Israel, would have to suffer to bring the people out of their sin and into the promised land of God's reign.

There was to be one more prophet of the Old Law— John the Baptizer. When he appeared and announced the coming of the kingdom, the people thought that at last the Messiah had come. But he said, "I'm only preparing the way." Pointing to Jesus, he prophesied: "Look! There is the Lamb of God who takes away the sin of the world!"

John 1:29

It was the moment for the New Covenant and the final revelation. It was the hour for the arrival of the Messiah.

# SUMMING UP

1.  *Words to know:* Moses, Exodus, Covenant, Hebrews, Israelites, Chosen People, Jews, Yahweh, the Law, Exile, Jeremiah, Cyrus of Persia, Maccabees, monarchy, Ezekiel, Isaiah, House of David, Messiah, Suffering Servant, John the Baptizer, New Covenant
2.  Why was the Exodus such a key event in the history of Israel?
3.  Explain the meaning and purpose of a covenant.
4.  Of what significance are the names by which God revealed himself to Israel?
5.  In God's Covenant with Israel, what did he promise? What were the Chosen People asked to do in order to fulfill their half of the Covenant?
6.  Why was the Exile such a shock to Israel? What lesson did it teach?
7.  Explain the pattern that emerges in the history of the Chosen People.
8.  What was the role of the prophets in preparing for the Messiah?
9.  What do the genealogies found in Matthew and Luke tell us about Jesus?
10. What was the ultimate goal of the covenant relationship God established with Israel?
11. By what names have the descendants of Abraham been known? Which could apply to you?

## Think/Talk/Write

1.  Everybody dreams of a Promised Land. What are some things the advertising world promises? Evaluate the worth of the list you come up with. What are things people search for in life? What do you think brings people the most peace and happiness? What are your happiest moments? Why? Jesus once said that people don't live by bread alone. What does he recommend in Matthew 4:1–4?
2.  Read the account of the Exodus (Exodus 12:1–15:27, 19:1–20:26). What parallels do you find between these events of the Old Testament and what you know of the New? If you need to refresh your memory about the latter, refer to John 1:19–34 and Matthew 5–7. Refer also to the article on Moses in *The Dictionary of the Bible* for valuable help.

3. In some ways each person's life can be compared to a well. When it is drilled far down into the earth, it hits a common underground stream. If we go down far enough into the faith of the Jewish people, what elements can we find that are common to Christianity?

## Activities

1. Trace the origins of your faith. How many of the religious practices of your grandparents or great-grandparents do you observe in your home? How long has the faith been in your family? When and where did the first person receive it? If it goes back through your forefathers to Europe, Asia, or another part of the world, who transmitted it in that country? Where did the missionary to your native land come from? Who was he/she?
2. Only as big as Vermont (10,000 square miles), Palestine is centrally located. For what three continents does it form a meeting place? Providing access to the Great Sea (the Mediterranean), it was the crossroad of empires in three directions. As a result, it became occupied in turn by each of the five great empires of ancient times: Assyria, Babylonia, Persia, Greece, and Rome. Search Psalm 60. Which of the cities mentioned are on the map? Which were friendly to Israel and which were her foes?

## Scripture Search

1. How does Luke show that Jesus fulfilled the hopes of Israel in his announcement of Jesus' birth (Luke 1:26–38) and in his description of the passion (Luke 24:25–29)?
2. Describe what these Old Testament prophecies foretell about the reign of God: Micah 2:13; Zephaniah 3:15; Jeremiah 3:17, 8:19; Ezekiel 20:33; Isaiah 43:15, 24:23, 52:7; Obadiah 1:21; Zechariah 14:9; Psalms 47, 93, 97, 98, 99.

## FIVE

Why don't all the Gospels contain the Christmas story?

Why does one Gospel begin with the birth of John the Baptizer?

Why is the infant massacre part of the Christmas story?

Was Jesus showing his independence by remaining behind in the visit to the Temple?

*My being proclaims the greatness of the Lord,*
*my spirit finds joy in God my savior.*
*For he has looked upon his servant in her lowliness;*
*all ages to come shall call me blessed.*
*God who is mighty has done great things for me,*
*holy is his name.*
*His mercy is from age to age on those who fear him.*
*He has shown might with his arm;*
*he has confused the proud in their inmost thoughts.*
*He has deposed the mighty from their thrones*
*and raised the lowly to high places.*
*The hungry he has given every good thing,*
*while the rich he has sent empty away.*
*He has upheld Israel his servant ever mindful of his mercy,*
*even as he promised our fathers,*
*promised Abraham and his descendants forever.*

(Luke 1:46–55)

# The Beginning of Fulfillment

Rise up in splendor! Your light has come, the glory of the Lord
shines upon you. . . . Nations shall walk by your light, and kings by
your shining radiance.

(ISAIAH 60:1,3)

## A TIME FOR CELEBRATION

O little Town of Bethlehem,
How still we see thee lie.
Above thy deep and dreamless sleep,
The silent stars go by.
Yet in thy dark street shineth
The everlasting Light.
The hopes and fears of all the years
Are met in thee tonight.

For most people, ancient Christmas carols usher in a
time of happiness every year. Even the crowded parking
malls, the endless lines of shoppers, and the commer-
cial Santas cannot quite destroy it. Coins jingle merrily
in the poor boxes and the bright spirit of giving warms
a cold world. At Christmas the most deprived enjoy

some special food treat and the Scrooges become generous.

■ What does Christmas mean to you?

*Scrooges* are people who resemble a character in Charles Dickens' "Christmas Carol" who was too miserly to let the Christ Child into his heart.

The source of all this happiness is Bethlehem, a little town of long ago. In its dark street shines—to all with eyes to see—the Light of the World, Jesus. In his holy name, the hopes and fears of all the years are met. God has come to his people to set them free and show the way to peace. It is just cause for celebration.

*Bethlehem means "House of Bread."*

*Celebrate* comes from an ancient root meaning "to gather together" or "to hold up for public praise." At Christmas, the world gathers to praise God's love in the form of a newborn infant. Jingling bells and lighted trees are a reminder of his earthly nativity, but they are also signs of the rebirth of eternal life that God offers to all. It is this life that brings peace, but only those who let the mystery take hold of them find it hiding in the humility, poverty, and quiet love of the crib.

*Nativity* comes from a Latin word, "to be born." It refers to the birth of Jesus.

So quietly did the great mystery of the Incarnation take place that many of the Chosen People missed their Lord and Savior. In the modern stir of Christmas, many still pass him by.

The *Incarnation* is the mystery of God becoming human.

■ When does Christ come? How do Christians celebrate his comings?
■ Tell or write the Christmas story from memory, giving as many details as you can.

## HOW THE CHRISTMAS STORIES WERE WRITTEN

You would think that in telling the story of someone's life, an author would begin at the beginning. Surprisingly, the infancy narratives—the stories surrounding Jesus' birth and childhood—were not part of the early Gospel. If you think about it, the Apostles had not been companions of Jesus until he began preaching, and the Gospels did not appear until a generation after Jesus' death. By A.D. 65, when the first Gospel came out, most of Jesus' family and neighbors had died. The subject of Peter's first sermon shows that the death and resurrection are the oldest Christian tradition. It was the passion-resurrection events that had established Jesus as Lord.

But as time went on, the Apostles realized that Jesus must have already been the Messiah in his lifetime. They began to see his public ministry in a new light and set about collecting the memories of his sayings and healings. By the time Mark wrote, about thirty years after Jesus' death, he presented Jesus as the beloved Son of the Father at his baptism, the beginning of his public life.

During the decades following the appearance of Mark's Gospel, the Christian community had to resolve the question of whether Jesus *became* God's Son by adoption at his baptism, or whether he truly *was* God's Son from the moment of his conception. Both Matthew and Luke, who wrote later than Mark, show in their infancy narratives what the early Church believed: that Jesus was the expected Messiah from his conception. (John, writing fifteen or twenty years later than Matthew and Luke, reflects the final development of the early Christians' understanding of Jesus' identity. The first sentence in his Gospel proclaims Jesus the eternally pre-existent Word of God who became a human being.)

The meditations of the early Christians, then, gave Matthew and Luke the stories that dramatize the mystery. They use several techniques in the infancy scenes. Sometimes the stage is bright with the powerful, white floodlights of *theology* and *Scripture,* which tell who this child was and how he fulfilled the prophecies of the Old Testament. Sometimes the scene is played in the mysterious blue atmosphere of *prophecy,* which holds in its shadows hints of events to come. The characters—the shepherds, the wise men, and Herod—can be seen as *symbols.* And yet the times, people, geography, and local color surrounding Jesus' birth are set in actual *history.*

*Conception* occurs the moment the male and female cells unite to produce a new human being.

*Local color* is the literary description of the speech, dress, habits, and so on that characterize a certain region.

JESUS

Each evangelist presented his pre-Gospel—the stories that precede Jesus' public life—in his own style, with different incidents and characters, but both express the beliefs of the early Church.

Matthew and Luke open their Gospels with Jesus' conception and the revelation of his messiahship. Each creates a mini-Gospel that dramatizes the message of the whole Gospel: Jesus is the Savior. He is met by two kinds of responses—belief and rejection.

You will see that the age-old Christmas story that captured your heart as a child has something new for you as you examine it more closely.

## GREAT EXPECTATIONS: A GOLDEN AGE

In 27 B.C., the citizens of Rome wanted peace. They were bone-tired after more than a hundred years of war. When the intelligent and cultured Octavian Caesar mounted the throne, a flurry of expectation ran through the populace. Octavian was the eighteen-year-old adopted son of the renowned Julius Caesar. He liked to read and write, and he had the good taste of the educated. He built fine marble buildings and promoted the arts.

The new emperor did not disappoint his people. Almost at once he launched the famous *Pax Romana,* a long era of peace. Given the title Augustus (reverend), the young Caesar was looked upon as a god who would deliver the whole world from its barbarian ways. His reign, everyone felt, would usher in a Golden Age, full of promise. His birthday was declared the first day of the new year. An excavated inscription reads: "The birthday of the god marked the beginning of the good news for the world."

Some of the excitement trickled into distant Palestine, where Herod was king of Judea. The Jewish population there resented Roman domination; they wanted self-government. Jewish expectation had always run

*Pax Romana* ("Roman peace") was a concept promoted by Augustus Caesar to strengthen his empire.

*Barbarian* means uncivilized.

*This is Herod the Great, Antipater's son, not Herod Antipas, the "sly fox" who killed John the Baptizer.*

higher than that of the Roman citizenry; but then, Jewish hopes were not pinned on Roman emperors.

## THE PROMISE OF A MESSIAH

*David had been promised an eternal kingdom; see 2 Samuel 7:16.*

For a thousand years, prophetic rumors of a coming Messiah had been afloat in Israel. Vague at first, and tied to the nation's monarchy, they gained momentum as the prophets offered glimpses of what God had in store for his people. Many self-proclaimed messiahs had already appeared, but all of them had faded into the oblivion of history. Now there seemed to be new grounds for hope. Somewhere, somehow, a savior—perhaps two—would come as God had promised. This new era of peace seemed the ideal time for it. Expectancy electrified the air.

*Oblivion means the state of being lost and forgotten.*

*Some Jews expected a savior priest and a savior king.*

The opening chapters of Matthew and Luke announce the Good News that Jesus was that long-awaited Messiah.

- Skim Matthew 2:1–12 and Luke 1:26–33. What things would people expecting a Messiah appreciate in these passages?
- From the things you read and hear, do you think our world is still looking for a savior? Are you? Why or why not?

## THE CONCEPTION OF JESUS

### Birth Announcements in Israel

Whenever God chose someone to play an important role in the history of salvation, the Scriptures signaled that choice by a story of wonder surrounding his birth. A heavenly visitor told Abraham that his aged wife would have a son. An angel announced the birth of Samson to his barren mother. The childless Hannah prayed to God and conceived the holy Samuel, and Rebekah and Rachel went without children for years

*See Genesis 17:15–21; Judges 13; 1 Samuel 1:1*

*Barren means being unable to have children.*

JESUS

until, as a result of prayer, Rebekah gave birth to Jacob and Joseph was born of Rachel.

The children of these women were regarded as special gifts of God because in each case some obstacle to normal pregnancy was overcome. These birth announcements, in which God is seen to play a more direct role in giving life, were prophetic of the greatness of the ones to be born.

## Joseph's Predicament in Matthew

Saint Matthew presents the birth of Jesus entirely from Joseph's point of view. This Gospel highlights Mary's virginity by emphasizing Joseph's predicament: before they lived together, his young bride-to-be was pregnant. If Joseph made the situation public, Mary would be stoned for adultery. A dream—a direct enlightenment from God—settled Joseph's problem and at the same time revealed the identity of the child to be born. Matthew includes a quotation from the Old Testament (Isaiah 7:14) that would have been familiar to his Jewish audience. It emphasizes Mary's virginity and God's coming, through this miraculous birth, to remain with his people.

*In Israel, betrothal (engagement) required the same faithfulness as marriage.*

- ■ Read Matthew 1:18–25 again. How was Jesus conceived? What picture of Joseph do you get? Who was the child to be? What second reinforcement of the virginal conception is given?

## Two Birth Announcements in Luke

Luke followed the Israelite tradition of the wonder-full birth announcement by his use of twin tableaus or scenes, a technique that in modern times is called simultaneous action. You've seen it in cartoon strips when, in a series of frames, another theme is introduced by the word "Meanwhile . . ." To set the scene and show John the Baptizer as the precursor of Jesus, Luke opens with the announcement of John's birth. He then

*A precursor is one who goes before another; a forerunner.*

highlights his theme by setting Jesus' story in contrast to John's. Luke identifies John's parents, Elizabeth and Zechariah, both of whom were of priestly families of Judea, faithful to the Law. There was a double obstacle to their having children—sterility and age. While performing his priestly duties, Zechariah received a divine communication announcing that his wife would give birth to a son; Zechariah, however, doubted the angel's words. Six months later, Gabriel was sent to Mary in Nazareth with similarly startling news, but her reaction was very different from Zechariah's.

■ Read the two birth announcements in Luke 1:8–20 and 1:26–39. By what contrasts does Luke show the surpassing superiority of Jesus? How are the two accounts similar?

*Sterility* is the condition of being unable to conceive children. In Israel, it was thought a disgrace—a punishment from God—to be sterile.

The *annunciation* is the mystery in which Mary became the Mother of God.

## Mary in the Annunciation

Mary is the most important person in Luke's infancy narratives. She is the first and best disciple of the kingdom of God. Luke compares Mary to the Ark of the Covenant by using the imagery of the overshadowing cloud that had led the Chosen People in the desert and hovered over the ark. When Mary surrendered to God's mysterious word in the annunciation, she was filled with God's power and presence.

Luke also shows two personal effects of faith—an urgent need to share the Good News, and great joy. Mary and Zechariah became apostles, singing God's praises for all to hear. Their songs are still sung by the Church today. These scenes overflow with joy and wonder. They say that something happened in Israel that made everybody sit up and take notice. And yet the tremendous events are mysterious and hidden, like a newly planted seed.

■ Read Luke 1:21–25 and 39–79. What is the immediate effect of Zechariah's disbelief? Of Mary's faith? What signs of joy do you find?

JESUS

## THEOTOKOS

Pronounced THEE-oh-TOH-kuhs. The *th* is sounded as in *thin*. The main accent is on *toh*.

If a person became the president of the United States, which of the following would be true? His or her mother would be: (1) the mother of the president; (2) the mother of the president's physical self; (3) the mother of the individual person, but not of the presidential personage.

Obviously, such a mother would be the mother of the president. But what if her son is God? Can a human mother be the mother of God?

Jesus experienced himself as "I," a single person. Since that "I" was the Son of God, Mary was the mother of the whole person and truly the Mother of God. It was through Mary, then, that the Incarnation took place. In this mystery, *the Son of God became a human being.*

How did this take place in her? Was there a natural conception that God blessed in a special way? Was Mary sterile and miraculously relieved of her barrenness?

The ordinary age for betrothal was thirteen for women and eighteen for men.

No. Mary was a normal young girl of about fourteen who was betrothed (engaged) to Joseph—that is, legally bound to marry him but not yet living with him. There was no question of barrenness in Mary's case. The faith of the early Christians expressed in the annunciation scenes is that Mary conceived Jesus without human intercourse. She is the virgin mother.

The conception of Jesus was the result of the action of the Holy Spirit as well as of Mary's spiritual receptiveness. Her faith and readiness to accept God's call was so pleasing to God that it attracted God's Son to the world.

We call the mystery of Mary's preservation from original sin her immaculate conception.

We call the mystery of Mary's unique way of giving birth the virgin birth.

All through the centuries, Catholics have pondered Mary's gifts, especially her greatest gift, divine motherhood. All her other gifts flowed from that one. Since it is unthinkable that she should ever have been touched by sin, from the first moment in her mother's womb she was preserved from evil. To honor the mystery of Christ, she remained a virgin before, during, and after giving birth to Jesus. This also points out the uniqueness of her motherhood. As the mother of Christ's body, the Church, she is the channel of every gift God gives because every gift comes through Jesus, and Jesus came through her.

The Greek Church, also known as the Byzantine Catholic Church, is an Eastern version of Catholicism, just as the Roman Catholic Church is a Western version of Catholicism.

An icon is a religious image painted on a small piece of wood. The icon itself is sacred in Eastern churches.

The Greek Church honors Mary under a title from the first centuries of Christianity: *Theotokos,* or "God-bearer." This title is another way of saying that Mary is the Mother of God. In Russian icons of the Theotokos, Mary's body is pictured as a temple in which she shelters the God-man. The background is often gold-leafed to signify the presence of God in the human form of Jesus.

- Study the icon of the Theotokos. What symbols do you recognize? Who are the contemporary God-bearers?
- The conception of Jesus was Mary's greatest privilege. What problems did this privilege bring her? What joys?

# THE BIRTH OF JESUS

## Two Different Stories

Matthew and Luke tell different stories of Jesus' birth. Luke is the source of the Christmas story you are familiar with: the journey from Nazareth, where the angel appeared to Mary, to Bethlehem for the census of Quirinus; the birth of Jesus there—the manger, the swaddling clothes as a sign, the angels; the circumcision; the presentation in the Temple; and Simeon's prophecy of sorrow for Mary.

Matthew passes over the birth in one sentence. But from his pen we have the stories of the wise men, the persecution by Herod, the flight into Egypt, and the return after Herod's death to Nazareth in Galilee for fear of the cruel Archelaus.

*Archelaus, Herod the Great's son and successor, ruled Judea (4 B.C.–A.D. 6).*

How could such different accounts tell the same story? The secret of understanding is to recognize that the evangelists use symbolism. The fact that Joseph had to return to Bethlehem because he was of the House of David was Luke's way of saying that Jesus was of the House of David and fulfilled the prophecy of Micah: "But you, Bethlehem-Ephrathah, too small to be among the clans of Judah, from you shall come forth for me one who is to be ruler in Israel."

Micah 5:1

## Luke and the Shepherds

The heart of Luke's Christmas story is the song of the angels to the shepherds. It is Luke's proclamation that Jesus the Messiah—not Caesar—brings Good News to the world. The first hearers of the joyous message are shepherds, people who were numbered among the outcasts. By this Luke says that none are too poor to find the peace of Christ.

The song of the angels is similar to the one the children sang when Jesus entered Jerusalem: "Blessed is he

Luke 19:38

who comes as king in the name of the Lord! Peace in heaven and glory in the highest!" Both are a version of the song Isaiah heard the angels sing in his vision in the temple. The Jewish people expanded the threefold cry when they prayed: "Holy [in the highest heaven], holy [on earth], and holy [under the earth] is the Lord of Hosts." Through the angelic song, Luke, like Isaiah, proclaimed that God's presence enters the temple of the world—through an infant dressed in baby's clothes.

Isaiah 6:3

The heavenly song had three audiences: the shepherds, "all who heard of it," and Mary.

- Read Luke's account in 2:1–20. How do the shepherds react? What famous shepherd in Jewish Scriptures do they remind you of in their response? What group in the New Testament do they resemble? What is the response of those to whom the shepherds passed on the Good News? Whom does Luke intend these people to represent? How does Mary respond?

See Luke 4:22 and 5:26

- At Christmas, when do you think about the meaning of Christ's coming?
- In your journal, write some thoughts you've had when pondering the mystery in your heart.

## WHAT'S IN A NAME?

Probably the sweetest word you will ever hear is that of your own name. Some people go into elaborate spellings or signatures to show how much they identify with their names.

The Jews did not use surnames, but they placed much meaning in first names, which they believed expressed a person's qualities, vocation, and identity. At his circumcision, Mary's son was given the name announced by the angel—Jesus, which means "Yahweh is my salvation" or, simply, "savior." It was a common name meant to honor the great savior figure, Joshua, who brought the people into the Promised Land.

Luke 2:21

As the firstborn son, Jesus was entitled to a double portion of Joseph's inheritance. Through him he received the Davidic ancestry that put him in line for the messiahship. But as the firstborn of the heavenly Father, he is also the legal heir of divine life. Fully human and the firstborn of the dead, he gives us, his brothers and sisters, a share in his inheritance. Through baptism, God becomes our common Father and we are thus entitled to eternal life.

*Jesus is "firstborn of the dead" because he was the first person to rise.*

"Jesus" is from a Greek translation of the Hebrew name Joshua, but since Jesus spoke Aramaic, he probably answered to the Aramaic version of this name: Jeshua.

*Pronounced yeh-SHOO-ah.*

Gabriel did not address Mary by her Jewish name, Miriam, "most exalted one." He called her "full of grace," or "highly favored." *Grace* or *favor* are other words for *gift.* No one else in the Bible receives so beautiful a salutation. No one else in the world has received so many gifts from God.

■ Name some of Mary's gifts. Try invoking her name as you think about them.

## Matthew and the Magi

Matthew uses the same themes as Luke: Jesus is the Son of God, this Good News is proclaimed by heaven, and certain people come to adore and then return home. But Matthew's stories are different from Luke's.

In Matthew, astrologers, or wise men, from the East observed a star and followed it to the place where the child Jesus was. There, they saw, worshiped, and offered gifts of gold, frankincense, and myrrh.

As in Luke, Matthew's narrative is a reflection on Jewish expectations of a king-messiah, and it is compiled from several Old Testament texts. The star that rises from Jacob (Numbers 24:17) becomes the star followed by the magi. Micah 5:1–3 points to Bethlehem as the origin of Israel's new shepherd. Gifts of gold and frankincense from the nations of the East are foretold in Psalm 72:10 and 15 and Isaiah 60:6.

*The Greek word* magi *refers to those who possess occult knowledge or power.*

*The ancient eastern lands were Babylon, Mesopotamia, and Arabia.*

In the ancient eastern lands from which the magi of Matthew's Gospel came, astrology was taken seriously. As presidents today seek the advice of their cabinets, kings consulted their "wise men," usually non-Jews, who learned their secrets from studying the sky. It was common belief in ancient times that the birth of kings was signaled by unusual signs, such as shooting stars. The gifts of gold, frankincense, and myrrh were customary offerings in the East as signs of homage to kings and other people of great importance.

Yet the kingship of Jesus was so hidden that it took both the resurrection and the Holy Spirit to make people recognize that one greater than Caesar had walked the world.

## REJECTION

The infancy stories proclaim Jesus the Savior and say that the Good News was well received by both Jews and Gentiles. They also had bad news to report.

98

## Herod and the Chief Priests

In arranging to kill all the Israelite sons under the age of two, Herod resembles the pharaoh who tried to destroy all the male children in Egypt. Saint Joseph's escape from Herod into Egypt suggests Moses' escape from the pharaoh to become the great prophet and deliverer of God's people. There are also some overtones of the patriarch Joseph's being sold into Egypt and later becoming the savior of his family. Writing for the Jews, Matthew was careful to put the chief blame for the murder attempt on the half-Jew Herod, whom they disliked. Besides recalling Israel's past, the episode also hints of the future. The plot and the cast of characters has a familiar ring: Herod, the nonreligious leader, and the chief priests plot to kill Jesus.

In this sequence, Matthew presents the entire Gospel message: the Messiah brought salvation to all who believed, but he had to suffer at the hands of those who rejected him. The sufferings of the child foreshadow the sufferings of Jesus as an adult.

■ Read the Flight into Egypt in Matthew 2:16–23. How does Joseph know what to do? How do you know Jesus was born before 2 B.C.? Why did the Holy Family settle in Nazareth? Who are the Herods in today's world?

## Simeon and the Sword

Luke also completes his Gospel-within-a-Gospel on a note of suffering. Simeon sees Jesus as being rejected by Israel but as the Savior of all nations. As the sign of God, Jesus will force people to stand up and be counted—either for or against God. Thus, secret, deep loyalties (thoughts) will be laid open.

Luke deliberately chose Jerusalem as the scene since it is in Jerusalem that Jesus will die. As the Holy Family had obeyed the civil law in going to Bethlehem, they

A woman was considered unfit to worship with the community for forty days after the birth of a son and for eighty after the birth of a daughter. The purification ritual restored her to the community.

now obeyed the Jewish law in observing the two rituals surrounding the birth of a firstborn son.

Although Luke combines the purification of Mary with the presentation of Jesus, he concentrates on the presentation. At the ceremony, the firstborn son was bought back from the priest for an offering. The rite was performed forty days after the boy's birth in thanksgiving for the Lord's protection of the Hebrew's firstborn in Egypt. It also reminded parents that their children are gifts of God, and not their own possessions.

The ancient prophet Simeon and the holy widow Anna stepped forward. Representing all the faithful of the Old Testament, they recognized the Savior in Mary's child. First, Simeon prophesied that Jesus was to be "the glory of Israel," but then he saw that it was not only Israel which would see the Light of the world: Jesus would also be a Light to the Gentiles, the non-Jews. "Now I can die in peace," he said. He had reached the goal of his life—to see the Savior. Jesus was his final comfort. Those who rejected Jesus, however, would find him to be a stumbling block leading to their downfall. Jesus was a sign of contradiction, Simeon said. The comfort he brought the world was purchased by suffering—a sword to pierce the hearts of both Jesus and his Mother.

The meaning of the sword of sorrow that pierced Mary's heart is not entirely clear. Certainly she suffered at the passion of her Son, but perhaps the pain she felt at seeing her Son's love rejected by so many was worse.

Like Matthew, Luke proclaimed the mystery that Jesus is Savior because of what he suffered.

- Read the passage about the presentation in Luke 2:22–40. List each step of the action or record it in a cartoon strip. Write Simeon's canticle in modern English. If you are musical, put it to music and perform it.
- How does this story alone give the entire Gospel message again?

# THE HIDDEN LIFE

Matthew's pre-Gospel stories end with the return from Egypt to Nazareth. Luke, however, inserted a "boyhood" story before the opening of Jesus' public life, and this is what is known as Jesus' "hidden life."

Similar to the boyhood story of Samuel in the Old Testament, the Finding in the Temple stresses three features of Jesus' life prior to his ministry: his obedience to the Law, his wisdom, and his mission.

*Samuel began to prophesy at twelve; see 1 Samuel 3:1–18.*

## Jesus' Obedience to the Law

In the infancy narratives, Mary and Joseph faithfully observed the laws of circumcision, purification, and presentation. As a young adult, Jesus himself kept the Law by worshiping with his parents in Jerusalem. He would be careful of authentic religious obligations to the end of his life. He worshiped and taught in the synagogues, and he told the people to observe the Law as their leaders taught. Like every devout Jew, he celebrated the feast of the Passover in Jerusalem.

*Authentic means genuine—that is, "ordered to true worship." Jesus criticized the observance of rituals that interfered with love of God or neighbor.*

## Jesus' Wisdom

The statements preceding and following the Temple story say that Jesus steadily progressed in wisdom. Like similar statements made of Samuel, they prepare for the divine wisdom Jesus would later exhibit in his preaching. The Doctors of the Law (Jewish scholars who spent their lives studying the Scriptures) reacted just as the crowds would later react—with amazement. As a boy, Jesus was already stunning the elders with his perceptive knowledge of Scripture. During his public life, Jesus would refer to himself as "greater than Solomon."

Luke 2:40, 52

See 1 Samuel 2:21, 26

Matthew 12:42; Luke 11:31

### Jesus' Mission

But perhaps the main lesson of the Temple story is the revelation of Jesus as Son of God. In the annunciation and infancy stories, the angels made the revelation. In the Temple, the proclamation came from Jesus' own lips. When his parents asked why he had stayed behind, he gave the mysterious reply, "Did you not know I had to be in my Father's house?" This reflects the early Christians' post-resurrection faith in Jesus' divinity.

Luke 2:49

Thus the Finding in the Temple on the third day delivers the basic Gospel message once again: Jesus is divine wisdom, the Son of the Father. In the next chapter, at the scene of his baptism, he will be named Son again—this time, the "beloved Son," by the word of the Father himself.

- Do you think Jesus found obedience difficult? Why or why not? What is obedience? How long do children owe their parents obedience?
- Name an instance when obedience to the heavenly Father would come before obedience to your parents. Which word better describes the role of parents to the children: owners or managers? Why?
- What is your attitude toward the laws of the Church? Toward Church worship? Toward supporting the Church? Toward the study of Scripture?

### THE WHOLE STORY

Considered together, what do the Christmas stories say? First, in revealing the mystery of the conception and birth of this child, they proclaim his unique identity as Son of God, the Messiah foretold by the prophets. He himself *is* the Good News.

Second, they tell that although Jesus was conceived by the power of God, God's presence was concealed in

weakness—a swaddled (diapered) baby, hunted by murderers from his first days.

Third, they tell that this "young God" did not force worship like the emperors of Rome; rather, he allowed people to respond freely. Those who accepted him— the humble Jews and the searching Gentiles—broke into song at their discovery. Those who rejected him— Israel, Herod, and the chief priests—were destined for a fall.

Above all, the Christmas story teaches that God's love is greater than human rejection. Jesus was a suffering Savior who, according to his Father's plan, willed to give his life, even for his enemies. The infancy narratives are truly mini-versions of the gospel as a whole.

*"On the third day" reminds the reader that Jesus will be "found" as the Christ at the resurrection on the third day.*

■ Review the Christmas stories. Find two examples of actual history, of references to Old Testament prophecies, of prophecies about Jesus' future, of symbols, and of theology (interpretations of the meaning of events).

## SUMMING UP

1. *Words to know:* Bethlehem, celebrate, nativity, Incarnation, infancy narratives, conception, *Pax Romana,* Herod the Great, birth announcements, barrenness, betrothal, virgin birth, precursor, Ark of the Covenant, new Eve, astrology, magi, Jerusalem, Gentiles, purification, presentation, sword of sorrow, Doctors of the Law
2. How did the Christmas stories come to be written? Why did only two evangelists make them part of their Gospels?
3. What things do the first chapters of Matthew and Luke use to dramatize the infancy stories?
4. Why was Jesus' coming so timely?
5. What was the traditional Old Testament way of calling attention to the fact that a birth was to be important in salvation history?
6. How did the evangelists adapt this form for Jesus?
7. How did each of the two evangelists express the early Christian belief that Jesus was the Son of God from his conception?
8. What was the personal effect of faith in the lives of Zechariah, Elizabeth, Mary, and Joseph? How did each express his or her faith?
9. What similarities do you notice between the stories of Luke's shepherds and Matthew's magi? What does each story teach? What prophecies does Jesus fulfill? How do the three separate audiences to the proclamation of Christ's birth receive their divine messages? Whom do they represent?
10. Why is the massacre of the infants included in the Christmas story?
11. What prophecies does the aged Simeon make?
12. What features of Jesus' later life were stressed during the presentation in the Temple? How does it deliver the entire basic Gospel message in miniature?
13. What do the infancy narratives as a whole teach?


### Think/Talk/Write

1. How are Joseph and Zechariah alike and different? Mary and Elizabeth? Jesus and John?
2. Do you see any connection between Jesus' infancy and his passion?

3. The Christmas story highlights the Christian belief that God gives eternal life to average human beings, even the poorest, if they believe in Jesus. This makes Christians the supreme optimists of the world. When do we celebrate this optimism? What are God's greatest gifts to you? What can you give in return?
4. How is the spirit of poverty shown in the manger connected with peace on earth and peace of mind?

## Activities

1. Using photos, paintings, and Christmas cards of different styles of crib sets, arrange a bulletin-board display or class collage showing how natural it is to visualize the descriptions and symbols of the well-loved infancy narratives.
2. Write a Christmas poem using one of these symbols as a central theme: star, myrrh, light, incense, magi, Bethlehem, gift, Egypt, gold, tree, manger, animals.

## Scripture Search

You may have seen Christmas cards with these words: "The Word was made flesh." That line is from the opening of Saint John's Gospel. In place of infancy narratives, John begins with a prologue that sounds the main themes of his book, but this prologue is just as much a Christmas story as the others. Read it in John 1:1–17 and then answer the following questions.

1. Matthew and Luke proclaim Jesus the divine Savior from the moment of his human conception. What does John say about Jesus' origins in verses 1–3? Which three verses speak of the *entry* of the Word (or Light) of God into the world?
2. Matthew and Luke show characters who accept Jesus and others who reject him. Find one verse in John 1:1–17 that says Jesus was accepted and one that says he was rejected. According to John, what is salvation or Christ's purpose in coming into the world?
3. When John says in 1:13 that those who believe in the Word do so not by their own human power but by God's, what mystery is he revealing about Jesus? (Also see verse 18.)

SIX

What does John the Baptizer preach?

What event officially launched Jesus on his mission?

What is the significance of Jesus' encounter with Satan in the desert?

What was the main thrust of Jesus' preaching?

What kind of people did Jesus call to be his associates?

*To have as little as possible to do*
*with the making of my own career.*
*What God wills, let it be done to me.*
*To be ready, so far as I may, for anything and everything. . . .*
*To do the duty of each day as it comes*
*because it is the gift of God to me,*
*not looking too far into the future.*
*Fidelity in the present spells fidelity in the future.*
*If the duty is done, the fruit will come.*
*To know that God almighty and all-loving*
*is behind all, with his hand on every thread,*
*personally interested in all things, in me,*
*in his own great design,*
*in that portion of it for which he has particularly made me.*

(Archbishop Alban Goodier)

# The Time Is at Hand

I baptize you in water for the sake of reform, but the one who will follow me is more powerful than I. I am not even fit to carry his sandals. He it is who will baptize you in the Holy Spirit.

(MATTHEW 3:11)

## HOW DO YOU DECIDE?

Suddenly Craig faced his sister-in-law. "How did you ever get mixed up in all that?" he asked, pointing to her blue habit. He had never really thought about a vocation to religious life before.

Taken off guard, the nun thought a moment. "How did you ever marry my sister?" she answered. "After all, you came from different parts of the country. You have different religions, and you even talk differently."

Craig nodded slowly. It made sense. Or, rather, it didn't. He saw that every vocation is a mystery.

- Ask three adults how they discovered what they wanted to do in life. Discuss your findings in class.
- What will you do with your life? What are your choices? How are you going about deciding your vocation?

## PREPARING FOR PUBLIC MINISTRY

### Jesus' Early Years

How did Jesus know that he was called to preach the kingdom? We have no detailed account of his years at Nazareth, but we do know that his vocation came about as the result of a gradual, natural evolution.

At an early age he felt drawn to prayer. His decision at thirty to retreat to the desert for forty days had to come from a profound realization of the importance of prayer to his vocation. His habit of going off to pray alone for long periods while he was on the road in later years certainly had roots in his earlier life. Like the crowds drawn to Jesus during his preaching years, his friends must have found encouragement and wisdom when Jesus shared with them what he had gained in prayer.

But he didn't impress others as being unusual during all those years in his father's workshop. Later, when he had begun his mission, his Galilean neighbors were the first to reject him. They had watched him grow up and thought of him as no more than the carpenter's son. Jesus said, "No prophet is without honor except in his native place, among his own kindred, and in his own house."

Mark 6:4

He also loved Scripture from his boyhood. At twelve he became so involved in discussing the Law with the Doctors in the Temple that he let his parents leave for home without him. By the time he reached adulthood, the Scriptures were part of his thinking. With the Pharisees he showed that he understood even the fine points of the Law, which could only have been the result of long years of daily meditation. From Luke's description of the incident in the synagogue in Galilee, we know that, like the other men, Jesus took his turn reading the Scriptures.

Matthew 19:1–2, 22:29–32, 41–46

Luke 4:14–22

The strong impulse he felt during his public life to make known his Father's ways must have had its beginning while he was still in Nazareth. The urgency of this need kept mounting until one day, when he was about thirty, in the fifteenth year of the reign of Emperor Tiberius, Jesus set out for his ministry.

## John the Baptizer

Having prayed over and pondered his Father's will, Jesus was alert and ready to recognize his own mission when John the Baptizer came out of the desert to announce the time of salvation. The first we hear of Jesus in his public role is through the mouth of John: "Make ready the way of the Lord, clear him a straight path. All mankind shall see the salvation of God."

Luke 3:4, 6

John's unusual appearance attracted notice and won him respect. Probably deeply tanned by his stay in the desert, where he had prepared himself for his mission, John wore the rough garments of a prophet—a tunic of harsh camel's hair gathered in with a heavy leather belt. Much as athletes limit themselves for the sake of self-discipline, he had restricted his diet to edible locusts and wild honey.

Mark 1:6

The strength and asceticism of his character brought crowds from all over Palestine to the banks of the Jordan. The Jewish leaders felt threatened by this dynamic prophet who lured the people away from them. John attracted all classes of people, including tax collectors, prostitutes, and soldiers. Among the mobs was Jesus, who—although he went unrecognized and had not begun his own public life—was in full sympathy with the message of John.

*Asceticism* is characterized by renouncing luxury and doing penance.

Luke 3:12–14

John boldly preached that to be Jewish by birth would not automatically guarantee salvation. Don't depend on the fact that you have Abraham for your ancestor, he said, but make known by your deeds that you have turned away from your self-centeredness.

Matthew 3:8–9

When people asked what they could do to prepare for the expected Messiah, John outlined a program to reflect a "changed heart." The people were disappointed. John himself was such a moral giant that they

Luke 3:8–14

*Metanoia* is the Greek word for the changed or converted heart that John asked for in preparation for the Messiah.

believed *he* must be the Messiah they were expecting momentarily. John flatly denied this, predicting that the Messiah would be greater than he. When the Messiah comes, he said, he will baptize with the Spirit and with fire, not merely with water. He, John, was not worthy to untie the Messiah's sandals. The evangelists were making the point that even the greatest prophet of the Old Testament was powerless compared to Jesus, who alone could win salvation and eternal life for humankind.

*Sandals were an important symbol of prestige in Palestine. For instance, unloosening and giving another your sandals was a sign of submission in a contract.*

## Jesus' Baptism

According to the earliest tradition, when Jesus approached to be baptized, John recognized him and asked to be baptized by Jesus. By submitting to John's baptism, Jesus did two things: he identified himself with our sinful human race and he formally accepted his vocation—the mission of being the Messiah, the one who would conquer the power of evil by willingly submitting himself to it for love of his Father and us. In being submerged under water, a sign of death, Jesus showed his willingness to die to bring a new life to the world—a "fire of the Holy Spirit," John called it.

*At first, John thought Jesus was Elijah, the fiery prophet who was to return before the coming of the Messiah. But Jesus referred to John as Elijah—the prophet preparing his way.*

By the symbols of the heavenly voice and the dove, the evangelists express what they had learned after the resurrection: that God at this time anointed Jesus for his role as the Savior.

*Anointed means consecrated, set aside for service to God.*

After the other people present had been baptized, Jesus himself was baptized. While he was praying, "he saw the sky rent in two and the Spirit descending on him like a dove. Then a voice came from the heavens: 'You are my beloved Son. On you my favor rests.'"

*Mark 1:10–11*

In their use of the phrase "the sky rent in two" or "the heavens opened," the writers show that the public appearance of Jesus at the Jordan was the beginning of God's great outpouring of grace and favor in the person of his well-beloved Son. The world's salvation was now under way.

Following the strong lead of the Holy Spirit, Jesus went into the desert after his baptism. A desert is a desolate, lonely place where there is nothing but brown land and blue sky. Scripture uses the desert as a symbol of a "space" in which to meet God—any experience where we directly confront God and ourselves.

One of the greatest mysteries surrounding Jesus' early career was that, after forty days and nights of fasting, he was tempted by the devil on a high mountain. This event recalls the test of the Israelites in the desert after their release from Egypt. Unlike the Chosen People, who had proved to be unfaithful by worshiping idols, Jesus, the New Israel, came through his test strongly faithful to God his Father.

In the brief story of the temptation, the evangelists summarize the entire Gospel: Jesus, the all-holy one, was sent to confront the evil one and, after a struggle, was victorious. He rejected Satan's kingdom in favor

*Forty is a number used in the Bible to mean a special or sacred period of time.*

of his Father's, which he then went out to proclaim with great assurance. Jesus entered his ministry with a clear understanding of his goals. He spoke and acted from a great reservoir of inner strength. The story of Jesus in the desert teaches the following important lessons:

A *reservoir* is a place where something is stored.

1. Jesus gives us an example of the need to "go apart" to consult God's will before the major enterprises of life—to distance ourselves from the clamor of daily pressures in order to hear the tiny voice of God.
2. Jesus' struggle with Satan teaches that the devil is alive and active in the world, a force to be reckoned with.
3. Jesus' experience of temptation makes it possible for us to approach him with confidence, knowing that he understands what we must face to be faithful.

■ Read about John's prophecy and Jesus' baptism in Luke 3:1–22, Matthew 3, and Mark 1:1–10. How does John apply the image of fire? Explain two other images he uses. What kind of preacher do you think he was?

## ANNOUNCING THE KINGDOM

When his forty-day fast was completed, Jesus began his work. Instead of going to the area where John had preached, on the lower Jordan, Jesus made his headquarters in Galilee, in the north. There the things he said and did sent waves of excitement throughout the countryside.

His message was similar to John's—the need for an immediate change of heart: "Reform your lives and believe in the Gospel!" However, to those who listened closely, the key words were not "Prepare the way of the Lord" but, rather, "The kingdom of God has already come to you. It is *now!*"

One Sabbath, Jesus went as usual to the synagogue at Nazareth. But on this occasion the Scriptures he read seemed to take on special significance.

Mark 1:15

*Kingdom of God* is an expression referring to the reign (success, ultimate victory) of God.

Luke 4:18–19; also see Isaiah 4:4, 40:2

The spirit of the Lord is upon me;
    therefore he has anointed me.
He has sent me to bring glad tidings to the poor,
    to proclaim liberty to captives,
Recovery of sight to the blind
    and release to prisoners
To announce a year of favor from the Lord.

Luke 4:20–21

When he had finished reading, "he rolled up the scroll, gave it back to the assistant, and sat down." All the people in the synagogue had their eyes fixed on him. Then Jesus said to them, "Today this passage is fulfilled in your hearing."

Then Jesus traveled the countryside fulfilling what he had read—teaching the Good News of salvation, healing the sick, freeing those suffering from the guilt and oppression of sin.

■ Compare the Gospel accounts of John's program of conversion for the people in Matthew 3:7–10 and Luke 3:7–14 with the signs of salvation Jesus points out in Luke 4:14–21. Whose disciple would you rather have been? Why?

## CALL OF THE DISCIPLES

Like other rabbis, Jesus attracted people by his preaching. His miracles drew the masses, but he personally called a small group to be his close followers. God's work on earth is carried on, even by Christ, with the help of a community.

*The Apostles were sometimes referred to as "the Twelve"; see John 20:24.*

Why did Jesus choose twelve men? Twelve is a biblical number. The Chosen People had sprung from the twelve tribes of Israel, and Jesus was calling together the foundation stones of a New Israel. The fact that there is some vagueness in the different listings of the Apostles, that Paul refers to "the Twelve," and that Luke records the immediate election of Matthias to replace Judas seems to confirm the fact that there actually were twelve Apostles.

JESUS

## Apostles

The *Apostles* constituted the inner circle of his closest friends. The Hebrew word for *apostle* means "someone officially sent"—for example, rabbis outside Palestine were commissioned by Palestinian authorities to carry out official duties for them by laying on of hands. Similarly, Jesus commissioned his associates: "As the Father has sent me, so I send you." Jesus is sent by the Father just as he sends his Apostles. Today, the mission of the Father is carried on by priests and laity who are commissioned by the bishops and who, together with the Holy Father, continue Christ's redemptive work on earth. Like cabinet members in relation to a president, the Apostles were to have a special share in Jesus' saving action, not only by preaching and curing in Jesus' name, but by a priestly role in his greatest gift: the Eucharist. Their intimate friendship cost them dearly. All except John were called to martyrdom for the sake of the kingdom. John 20:21

The wide variety of men whom Jesus chose demonstrates that he was not looking for any particular kind of personality, job, or political leaning among his helpers. He wanted all kinds of men, from well-to-do to poor, including the tax collector who preyed on his own people as well as the liberal zealot who worked for the overthrow of Rome.

Within this group, three men seem to have been special to Jesus: Peter, James, and John. He allowed them (and sometimes Andrew) privileged information and experiences. Jesus knew that one of these, Peter, would deny him. Jesus even told Peter that he had prayed especially for him, so that Peter's faith would not fail. Peter's relationship with Jesus was secure. Even after his triple denial, he could pick himself up and give himself completely to the spread of the kingdom, asking to be crucified upside down in deference to the Master. Luke 22:32

One of the Apostles, however, proved to be a complete failure. After his betrayal of Jesus, Judas Iscariot despaired instead of repenting. It is important to rec-

John 13:27

ognize that even though Jesus knew of Judas' disposition ahead of time ("Be quick about what you are to do," he had said), he left him free. Jesus called Judas "friend" even to the last moment when Judas betrayed him with a kiss.

## Disciples

Luke 10:1–12, 17–20

The seventy-two disciples were closer to Jesus than the crowds, but not as close as the Apostles. Disciple means "learner." The disciples listened closely to Jesus and helped spread his teachings; but when they returned, excited about their missionary activities, Jesus soberly reminded them to rejoice only because their names were written in heaven.

Luke 8:38–39

Although the seventy-two were not invited to join Jesus in his priesthood at the table fellowship of the Last Supper, they too were specially chosen. Some men were refused discipleship. After Jesus had exorcised the possessed man of the Gerasenes, the man wanted to follow Jesus, but Jesus told him to be a missionary in his own neighborhood.

## People of Faith

Among the crowds at large, there were people of deep faith, such as the wealthy and educated Nicodemus and the pagan centurion. There were the women who followed Jesus and provided for his personal and material needs. There were also large numbers who turned away when they realized the cost of following Jesus.

It is the miracle of miracles: such an assortment of people drew from a carpenter's son the greatest love the world has ever known.

- ■ To which of the four groups would you like to have belonged? Why? To which do you now belong?

## THE GALLERY OF APOSTLES

1. Simon bar (son of) Jonah from Bethsaida, renamed Peter (Cephas, Petros), which means "rock." Clearly the leader of the Twelve, Peter confessed Jesus as the "Son of the living God" and Jesus gave him "the keys to the kingdom of God." A colorful personality, Peter was the Apostle who walked on the water to Jesus but then sank. When he protested Jesus' suffering, Jesus called him Satan. Peter denied Jesus three times, but repented and spent the rest of his life telling others about Jesus. He died about A.D. 64–67, and possibly was crucified upside down.

2. James (the Greater), a son of Zebedee the Fisherman, nicknamed by Jesus a "Son of Thunder." James was one of the privileged three Apostles (Peter, James, and John) who exclusively shared certain episodes with Jesus. He was present with Peter and John when Jesus raised Jairus' daughter, at the transfiguration, and at the agony in the Garden. He was beheaded by Herod Agrippa in A.D. 42, in Jerusalem.

3. John, "the beloved disciple," a son of Zebedee, the Fisherman, younger brother of James the Greater. John was nicknamed a "Son of Thunder" by Jesus and was one of the privileged three who alone shared certain moments of Jesus' life. He complained about someone casting out demons in Jesus' name without authorization and asked Jesus to call down fire from heaven to kill the inhospitable Samaritans. John rested his head on Jesus' breast at the Last Supper; he was present at the foot of the cross when Jesus told him to take care of Mary; and he witnessed the empty tomb. John is the source of the fourth Gospel and the book of Revelation. He is the only Apostle not to be martyred. He died in exile on the island of Patmos.

4. Andrew, Peter's brother, a fisherman from Bethsaida, sometimes included with Peter, James, and John

in private moments with Jesus. Andrew called attention to the boy with the loaves and fishes and acted as a go-between for the Greeks who wanted to meet Jesus. He was a comfortable person to be with, the type who "fits in." (See John 1:41, 6:8, 12:22.)

5. Philip, the conversationalist who asks Jesus at the Last Supper to reveal the Father. His question triggered an important explanation by Jesus (John 14:8). He was probably closely associated with Jesus because some Greeks asked him to introduce Jesus to them (John 12:21). His Greek name means "lover of horses." (See John 1:43.)

6. Nathaniel (or Bartholomew), the son of Tolmai. Jesus called Nathaniel an "Israelite without deceit" when he honestly expressed his doubt about Jesus: "Can anything good come out of Nazareth?" Jesus saw that Nathaniel's heart was good, despite his skepticism. (See John 1:45, 21:2.)

7. Matthew (or Levi), the son of Alphaeus. He left a lucrative business to follow Jesus. He was a rich tax collector who was hated by his fellow Jews. He held a big banquet after his conversion to honor Jesus at which other tax collectors and sinners were guests. (See Mark 2:14; Matthew 9:9.)

8. Thomas, "the twin," known as "doubting Thomas." He is prominent in John's Gospel. He urged the Apostles to accompany Jesus to Judea to die with him (11:16), he asked a key question at the Last Supper (14:5), and he was one of the group who met the risen Jesus on a fishing trip (21:2). Thomas is most remembered for doubting Jesus' resurrection; then, however, Jesus appeared and had Thomas place his hand in the wounds of crucifixion. His repentant reply was, "My Lord and my God."

9. James (the Less), son of Alphaeus. James is mentioned in Matthew 10:3, Mark 3:18, Luke 6:15, and Acts 1:13. Traditionally, the letter of James is credited to him. He died in A.D. 62.

10. Jude (or Thaddeus), possibly the brother of James the Less. Jude is referred to as "the brother of the Lord" in Matthew 13:55. He is traditionally thought to be the

author of the letter to Jude. (Also see Luke 6:16 and Acts 1:13.)

11. Simon the Zealot, called "the Canaanite." Simon was once a member of the radical zealot party that advocated a Jewish revolution against Rome. He may have been uncomfortable with Matthew the tax collector. (See Matthew 10:4 and Luke 6:15.)

12. Judas Iscariot, son of Simon, known as "the Betrayer." Judas carried the common purse of the Twelve, expressed disapproval of Mary's extravagant display of love for Jesus, and finally betrayed Jesus after the Last Supper "for thirty pieces of silver." Jesus said "it would have been better for that man if he had never been born." A complex and tragic figure, when he saw that Jesus was going to be crucified, he despaired and committed suicide.

- Which Apostle do you like most? Why? If the Apostles were so full of human frailties, why do you think they were so successful in spreading the Gospel?
- Whom does Christ choose today to build his Church on?

## SUMMING UP

1. *Words to know:* public ministry, John the Baptizer, asceticism, metanoia, anointed, temptation, synagogue, kingdom of God, Apostle, disciple, the Twelve
2. Why is everyone's vocation a mystery?
3. How did Jesus know he was to be a preacher?
4. What kind of person was John? What was his role? What was his message?
5. What were the differences between John and Jesus?
6. Why did Jesus ask to be baptized? What was the meaning of the voice from heaven and the appearance of the dove at his baptism?
7. Why did Jesus go into the desert after his baptism?
8. What does Jesus' handling of the temptations show about him? What lessons do the temptations hold for us?
9. Who were the Apostles? Why were there twelve? Name them.
10. What is the difference between an apostle and a disciple?
11. What kinds of persons are needed to build God's kingdom on earth?
12. How many disciples were there? What did they do?

### Think/Talk/Write

1. John the Baptizer did not succumb to fear or desire for popularity. He spoke out against evil when it meant prison and death. What does his kind of courage have to do with temptation? What temptations lead teenagers away from God? How can a young person today practice John's virtues of self-denial, self-control, mortification, and penance and still live a normal life?
2. Recent books and magazines about the devil have revealed a revival of interest in the occult. What is the Church's teaching about belief in the devil? Is it superstitious or not? How powerful is the devil? What can he do? What are his limitations?
3. Robert Frost's poem "Fire and Ice" predicts the end of the world by fire (love), although he admits that ice (hate) is also great and can do the job of destroying the world as well. What is your opinion? Which will win—the forces of love or those of hate? Why do you think as you do?

## Activities

1. Interview three persons who have dedicated themselves to spreading God's kingdom on earth to find out how and why they took up their life style. Include priests, sisters, brothers, deacons, or other ministers of the Church. Sample questions you might use are:
   a. How did you come to realize that you were called?
   b. Why are you doing what you are doing?
   c. What are the rewards of your life work?
   d. What are some of its difficulties?
2. Who are Jesus' disciples today? How does any call to discipleship come? What "signs" are given? Describe any vocation you know about or read the life of one of the following persons and report on how the vocation came to be known.

   Saint Elizabeth Ann Seton    Charles de Foucauld
   Jesse Jackson    Billy Graham
   Mother Teresa of Calcutta    Saint Terese of the Child Jesus

## Scripture Search

1. Certain passages in the New Testament show Jesus as one before whom evil is powerless. Read Luke 4:16–22. The perfect tense of the Greek verbs carries the sense of accomplishment, as though the action is already complete—present in the person speaking. In the light of this information, what is the passage saying?
2. Jesus has high expectations for those who would follow him. Read Luke 9:57–62. What excuses do the people make for not following Jesus promptly? What excuses might people give today? What does Jesus answer?
3. In Luke 14:25–27 Jesus makes some strong demands. The word "hate" in Greek translates as "love less." What does Jesus mean by his two statements? Do they apply only to religious or to all Christians?
4. What is so hard about following Jesus? Read Matthew 10:5–33 and Luke 10:1–11, 17–20, where Jesus sends his followers out to preach. What are the rules? What are the difficulties? What is the reward?
5. Read the following passages and decide what they tell you about Peter: Matthew 16:18; 17:4, 25; 18:21; Acts 3:1–15, 9:32–41; Luke 9:55; Mark 8:23.

# SEVEN

Did Jesus go through normal stages of development from infancy to adulthood?

Why can Jesus be called a "people person"?

Did Jesus have emotions and sexual feelings?

Was Jesus ever aggressive?

Did Jesus value the friendship of everyone, even outcasts and sinners?

What did Jesus reveal about himself when he used the title "Son of Man"?

*Jesus, you are my truest friend.*
*You accept me as I am,*
*You love me as I am.*
*You will never betray me.*
*Teach me to know you better*
*So that I may understand your friendship better,*
*Be a better friend to you.*
*Show me what it means to believe in you*
*That I may believe in myself and in others.*
*Help me to spread*
*The warmth of your friendship*
*Wherever I go.*
*Live more fully in me*
*And through me*
*That your love*
*May grow in the world.*

# Jesus the Person

Tempted in every way that we are, yet never sinned.
(HEBREWS 4:15)

## IMAGES OF GOD

For many people, *God* is a frightening word. It stands for majesty, unapproachableness, and power. The Old Testament often presents God as awesome. Moses is asked to remove his sandals before approaching the burning bush. Uzzah is stricken dead when he merely touches the ark. In a vision, Isaiah sees the Lord seated on a high and exalted throne.

2 Samuel 6:7

Isaiah 6:1

If the Gospels do anything, they turn the notion that God is fearful inside out. Through Jesus, God shows us that he not only wants people to come to him, but that he reaches out to them. The New Testament shows clearly that the early Christians believed Jesus to be truly and fully human as well as truly and fully God. Yet Jesus is spoken of as *one* person, a single embodiment of the Son of God and a real man. He was able to do the "mighty deeds of God" and at the same time he underwent the experiences common to the human race.

- What is your image of God? Describe it in a short essay, a poem, or a story, or illustrate it in a drawing.
- Ask five persons to describe their idea of God. Record your findings and report them to the class.

## Physical Development

Although Jesus was conceived by divine power, from the moment of his conception until his death he followed the normal laws of development. Like all human beings, he was born hungry and naked. He had his mother's Jewish features.

When Mary took him to the Temple after forty days, as was required by the Law, the infant Jesus didn't speak to Simeon or understand what was going on. During his boyhood, his parents taught him what he needed to know to fit into his Jewish culture: speech, Scripture, good manners, a trade, and Jewish customs.

Although Jesus' discussion with the Doctors of the Law at age twelve reveals that he was well trained and bright, the evangelist does not portray him as godlike. Like any other young person, he returned home with his parents "and was obedient to them." Luke 2:51

Saint Luke says that, like everyone else, Jesus grew Luke 2:52 and developed in body and spirit. He went through the normal stages of growth—infancy, childhood, adolescence, and young manhood—gradually acquiring all that was needed for human maturity. When he was Luke 3:23 between the ages of thirty and thirty-five, he entered public life.

## The Appearance of Jesus

We can be sure that Jesus was like other people, but we have no idea what Jesus looked like. Since he commanded respect in every situation, he may have been a tall man. Yet, unlike most tall persons, he had a way of slipping into the crowd and disappearing.

All through the centuries there has been discussion about Jesus' appearance. Some early Fathers of the Church said that he was short, not pleasant in appearance, and not striking in any way. This description may have been drawn from the psalms and prophecies that allude to a suffering savior. In these, the mysterious sufferer is described harshly:

*Early Fathers of the Church were bishops, teachers, and writers who lived in the second and third centuries.*

Isaiah 53:2–3

> There was in him no stately bearing to make us look at him, nor appearance that would attract us to him. He was spurned and avoided by men, a man of suffering, accustomed to infirmity; one of those from whom men hide their faces, spurned, and we held him in no esteem.

Another group of early Fathers stressed Jesus' handsomeness as portrayed in Psalm 45:3: "Fairer in beauty are you than the sons of men." The Gospels are silent on this matter.

From the Gospels we can surmise that Jesus was healthy and able-bodied. The daily travels of an itinerant preacher in rough and dusty Palestine were taxing, and Jesus was constantly on the go. His long years of work with lumber no doubt developed his arm and shoulder muscles. He did not die during the brutal scourging, and had strength left to speak while on the cross. His compassion for others must have been written in his eyes, but his inner strength must also have been visible. We can only guess.

- Why does each race picture Christ as a member of its own people?
- There seems to be some scientific evidence for the authenticity of the Shroud of Turin, the burial cloth that is believed to have wrapped Jesus' dead body. Almost certainly not an artificial reproduction, it must date back at least to before A.D. 300, when Roman crucifixion was outlawed. You may want to investigate the dimensions and features of this relic.

# THE PERSONALITY OF JESUS

If the appearance of Jesus has never been pinned down, Jesus as a person has been almost as difficult to capture. Thousands of books have explored the depths of his mysterious and challenging personality. Although different traits have surfaced in different ages, the beauty, sublimity, and goodness of his character have inspired millions of believers. Even nonbelievers see him as someone to be admired.

A prominent modern rabbi writes, "To Jews, Jesus appears as an extraordinarily beautiful and noble spirit, aglow with love and pity for men, especially the unfortunate and lost, deep in piety, capable of keen insight into human nature, endowed with a brilliant gift of parable and epigram, and an ardent Jew, moreover, a firm believer in the faith of his people."

Of the many sides of his rich personality, we can only briefly look at some—his love of people, his understanding of human nature, his love of sincerity, his human feelings and emotions, his compassion, and his friendship. As we glance at these traits, we might remember that even as Jesus is a model for us, he also reveals the God we cannot see.

*In the fourth century, thinking centered around the divinity of Christ to counteract the Arian heresy, which denied that divinity. The human Christ was emphasized during the Renaissance. The Eastern Church has always dwelt on the glory of Christ.*

Milton Steinberg, *Basic Judaism* (New York: Harcourt Brace Jovanovich, 1975), pp. 106–7.

## Jesus: A "People" Person

Which of these three questions would you be most likely to ask when you sign up for a new class?

1. How much homework will there be?
2. What does the course cover?
3. What's the teacher like?

If you answered number 1, you are a "things" person, interested in the way things work. Number 2 would indicate that you are an "idea" person, someone who concentrates on the why and wherefore. And number 3 would indicate that you are a "people" person, concerned mainly with relationships.

The Gospels show conclusively that Jesus was a "people" person. He genuinely liked people, and, sensing the genuineness of his concern for them, they flocked to him.

Matthew 11:19

Comparing himself with John the Baptizer, who fasted and drank no wine, Jesus said of himself, "The Son of Man appeared eating and drinking." He deliberately chose to engage in activities that brought him into close union with others. His public ministry opened with a wedding feast at which he supplied an enormous amount of wine. He spent his last hours on earth at a Passover meal that he had been longing to share with his closest friends.

All during his ministry, Jesus accepted invitations to eat with others. There are accounts of meals taken at the homes of a Pharisee, Levi the tax collector, and Simon the leper where he enjoyed the company of his good friends Lazarus, Martha, and Mary. He invited himself to the house of Zacchaeus, another publican, and at least once he provided the food himself. After his resurrection, he ate a piece of fish on the beach with his Apostles, broiling the catch himself.

A *publican* was a tax collector.

■ Why do you think he participated in these social gatherings?

He had deep convictions about the worth of people regardless of their social, economic, or religious position. Even though he knew he would be criticized, he did not exclude the hated tax gatherers from his company; Matthew and Zacchaeus are two members of this class who recognized Jesus as a friend. Sinners, lepers, and Samaritans completed the range of Jesus' social circle. When the Doctors of the Law questioned him about his friends, Jesus answered firmly, "People who are healthy do not need a doctor; sick people do. I have come to call sinners, not the self-righteous."

Mark 2:17

Although Jesus often went off to be alone, he wasn't a hermit. He recognized and accepted the fact that he was a social being who needed others. He was basically a person who knew the value of working with others.

Times when Jesus was alone: Mark 7:24; Luke 6:12, 9:28, 11:1.

One of his first public actions was to invite twelve local men to share his mission. As time went on, he gathered more disciples around him, and after his death it was through the community of his followers that he continued to live. Even today the Christian community celebrates God's goodness by gathering at a meal in memory of Jesus. This celebration is known as the Eucharist.

■ What does Jesus' gathering people around him tell you about him? About those who believe in him?

## Jesus and Sincerity

One of Jesus' main personality traits is great truth. "I am the truth," he said. Jesus is outstanding for hating hypocrisy. He recognized the silliness of vanity. He implies that being real—that is, sincere before God—automatically prevents us from making fools of ourselves before others.

John 14:6

Jesus was his own man. He who was entirely sincere, the holiest of all, hid his holiness carefully and bade his followers do the same. Your best friend shouldn't know when you have done something good, Jesus said. It's enough that God knows, because he "who sees in secret will repay you."

Sincerity *comes from two words:* sine *("without") and* ceres *("decay" or "break").*

Matthew 6:4

■ Why do people so often pretend to be something they are not?
■ What do you think helps people be who they really are?

## Jesus' Feelings

Jesus had feelings just as we do. Although he reached heights of nobility in his forgiveness of his enemies and in his acceptance of his fate, Jesus felt the pain and struggle of the human situation.

The Gospels tell us that Jesus looked steadily and with love at the rich young man who came seeking eternal life. He was *disappointed* when the man couldn't give up his wealth for the sake of the kingdom. And Jesus was *tired and thirsty* when he spoke to the Samaritan women at the well. Saint Mark gives a touching picture of Jesus *sleeping* with his head on a pillow during a storm at sea. Jesus sometimes *overflowed with joy,* and he showed *amazement* when a Roman officer, a non-Jew, showed faith in him. He *changed his mind* after refusing to cure the possessed daughter of a foreign woman from Phoenicia. He was *greatly surprised and frustrated* by the lack of faith in his hometown in Galilee.

He *felt hurt* when only one leper returned to thank him for a cure, and *complained* that his own people didn't recognize him. Just after multiplying the loaves he *grew impatient* with the slowness of his followers to understand and believe. And, of course, Jesus *suffered and died* in perhaps the cruelest manner known to history.

You have a Redeemer who understands what it means to be human. Because he himself was personally involved in the trivia as well as the great moments of life, he can now be personally interested in your ups and downs.

- Is it appropriate to pray for a football or basketball victory? Why or why not?

## Jesus' Sexuality

Jesus was not afraid to communicate his feelings through his body. There was no stereotyping of his masculinity. He wept openly before others. He outwardly expressed his anger. He touched and had no fear of being touched by women as well as men. He felt no embarrassment in touching and holding children in public. In a culture where contact with blood was believed to defile a person, he cured a hemorrhaging

*Hemorrhage* is uncontrollable internal bleeding.

JESUS

woman. His relationship with men was balanced. He was not afraid to show a preference for some of his Apostles and a special affection for the teenager, John, who leaned on his breast at the Last Supper. His touches always communicated clearly what was in his heart, and if he thought anything he did might not be understood, he explained it, as he did at the washing of the feet.

Women followed and supported Jesus throughout his ministry. Jesus must have been emotionally drawn to women and occasionally tempted to compromise his mission by giving in to this human drive, but there is no hint of it in Scripture. Yet the Letter to the Hebrews says that he was tempted in every way that we are. This means that Jesus can truly sympathize with you in everything, including your struggles to integrate all the aspects of your personality in these years of dizzying growth.

Hebrews 4:15

## Jesus and Assertiveness

Many modern pictures of Jesus show him with a kindly, almost saccharine-sweet facial expression. It's true that he was kind and compassionate toward the poor, the sick, and the crowds, but he could also be courageously assertive when it came to defending his principles. He did not hesitate to verbally attack one of his dearest followers, Peter, even calling him Satan, for suggesting that Jesus should not suffer. Although he respected individual Pharisees who, like Nicodemus, were sincere and praised one of them as "not far from the reign of God," he frequently got into heated verbal battles with the scribes and Pharisees, whom he criticized as hypocritical distorters of the law of Moses. He was not afraid to face them with direct statements ("You are badly misled"), to call them names ("Vipers' nest. Brood of serpents!"), or to ask tricky questions that silenced them. The act that brought him into confrontation with the Temple leaders, and that was perhaps

Mark 12:34

*Scribes* were Doctors of the Law.

Matthew 21:12–16

*Avery Dulles, the son of former Secretary of State John Foster Dulles, is a Catholic convert who is a Jesuit priest and professor.*

Avery Dulles, *A Testimonial to Grace* (New York: Sheed & Ward, 1946), pp. 69–70.

*Authenticity* means truth.

Matthew 7:29

the main reason for his death, was chasing the money changers away from the Temple.

When Avery Dulles was studying the life of Christ, he noticed that two of the greatest ancient philosophers—Socrates and Plotinus—had come to only shaky conclusions about the existence of God and the purpose of life even after much reasoning and discussion. But Jesus, he noted, "spoke with finality about these matters. He could use keen logic, and often did, but his knowledge of God was direct and immediate." Jesus had no need to "think through" the existence and nature of God. He knew what he stood for, and he spoke with absolute conviction. This gave his words force— a ring of authenticity—that is the keynote of a natural leader. The people commented that "he taught with authority and not like their scribes."

Jesus' great integrity comes through strongly in these confrontations. He had a dynamic personality and deep convictions—and the tremendous courage needed to stand by them.

- How would you answer someone who says that it is not Christlike to get angry?
- Where do Christians today need to possess the courage of their convictions, possibly even to the point of death?


## Jesus and Compassion

At the tomb of Lazarus, at the Last Supper, and in the Garden, Jesus shows deep human emotions—profound grief, tremendous love of his people, and terrible fear. Yet one of his most appealing human qualities was his compassion.

The word *compassion* comes from *passio* ("to suffer") and *com* ("together with"). Jesus did not look down on those who suffered. Rather, he *shared* their suffering and took it on himself as if it were his own. This deep concern for others was not a passing thing

See Matthew 9:36, 15:32, 20:34; Mark 1:41

or something tacked onto his personality. The Gospels tell us he was *moved* to compassion. From deep inside him, this emotion flooded over and surfaced in his outward expression.

Frequently he reached out to touch the sufferers or lay his hand on them as a sign of his union with them in their pain. Unlike a brusque doctor who hurries through an examination and casually prescribes a formula for a cure, Jesus *healed by his very presence,* by the love that continually flowed from his person. Luke 8:54–55

On one occasion, a woman suffering from hemorrhage stretched out her hand to touch his cloak. Jesus immediately felt the power of healing go out from him. The woman came forward, trembling at what she had secretly done. Jesus was not content to heal her physical malady. "Go in peace," he said, reassuring her after her cure. Mark 5:34

In those three words, "Go in peace," are hidden a secret of Jesus' uniqueness. He was interested in establishing peace in the hearts of those who came to him. We experience this peace by knowing God's love. We lose it only by sin.

Jesus' compassion was not the kind of pity that looks down on others. He made demands of those he cured. Jesus regarded people with great respect for their potential. "Have faith," he said before a cure, and "sin no more," he advised afterward. He knew how strong people might be if they had faith in him and trust in his Father, and if they avoided sin. He called them to much more than wholeness of body. He called them to total wholeness, which is holiness. See Mark 2:3, 7:29–30, 9:23–24, 52; Luke 7:9, 9:30

■ Divide the class into four groups, each of which represents an evangelist. Let each group read the following passages, either by dividing the Gospel among the members of the group or letting every member read the entire selection: Matthew 8:1 to 25:30; Mark 1:21 to 12:44; Luke 4:14 to 21:4; John 1:43 to 11:43. Note any incidents that show Jesus' compassion, understanding, individual treatment, mercy, or other "people-conscious" qualities.

## MISSIONARY TO THE OUTCASTS

Officially, Father Damien was appointed to be the pastor of the Catholics on the leper colony of Molokai in the Hawaiian Islands in the mid-eighteenth century. His real mission was to love—deeply, passionately, and unto death.

When he arrived on the island where no priest had ever been before, he found that the physical aspects of their disease were not the lepers' greatest problem, although the ugly and painful disease caused suffering enough. The lepers, who had been isolated for their entire lives and were forced to live in the most squalid conditions with only death to look forward to, were depressed and lacked hope and ambition. Because there were neither police nor courts, crime and immorality were rampant. The children received no education and often contracted the dread disease.

Working without assistance for ten years, the Belgian missionary wore many hats: he was physician, counselor, housebuilder, sheriff, undertaker, and gravedigger. Only his strong missionary determination to build a decent life for his eight hundred parishioners kept him going in the face of poor communication with the mainland, lack of supplies, and the ingratitude and even malice of some of the islanders, who would have preferred to keep things the old way.

One day Father Damien's simple words from the pulpit, "*we* lepers," announced the inevitable. Rather than leave the island for a cure, Damien chose to remain with his own to the end. He died five years later at the age of forty-nine. His example has inspired many men and women of both the Catholic and Protestant faiths to give hope to sufferers from Hansen's disease, the formal name for leprosy.

## Jesus and Friendship

Friendship is a matter of life and death to everyone, as being a friend is one of the most human of qualities. Modern psychology tells us that alienation is a form of hell. Saint Teresa said, "Hell is not to love anyone." But just what is friendship?

*Alienation* is a state of isolation.

- Describe your idea of friendship in a few sentences and share it with the class.

When a class was asked what they understood friendship to be, the most frequent definition was "having someone there when you need them." But is friendship a matter of just "being there," or is it a *special way* of "being there," a particular quality of presence? People can work side by side and even work closely together for years and not be true friends, while other people can meet for only a few hours and experience a deep bond that is never forgotten.

Consider the call of the Apostles. Jesus approached Simon and Andrew while they were deeply involved in their fishing business. He looked at them, somehow putting his whole personality and his respect for what these two men were into his look. They recognized the relationship they were being called to—they *experienced* Jesus' love. Jesus communicated his need for them. They dropped everything and never deserted Jesus after that. Whatever constitutes the capacity for friendship, Jesus had it.

Mark 1:16–20

Jesus tried to share his innermost self with *all* people, but during his life he was successful only with his friends—the Apostles and several others like Mary and Martha, Lazarus, and Nicodemus. He revealed his Father's love by both explaining it and giving his friends a personal experience of his own love. Part of that experience was listening to them, answering their questions, sharing his feelings with them, forgiving them, serving them.

Cicero, a Roman scholar who lived during the first century B.C., said that friendship is a love of benevolence—*bene* ("well") and *volere* ("to will")—that which wants a good, or a better, life for another. Jesus' love goes beyond Cicero's definition. Jesus' friendship extends beyond the people of his own time.

■ What do these Scripture passages show about how Jesus related to his friends?

> John 3 (Nicodemus)
> John 6:25–71 (the crowds)
> John 11:13–44 (Mary and Martha)
> Mark 9:2–13 (Peter, James, and John)
> Mark 10:32–34 (the Twelve)
> John 14:5–10 (Thomas and Philip)
> John 13:21–30 (the Twelve)
> John 21:15–17 (Peter)
> John 13:1–9 (the Twelve)

■ What insights into Jesus' friendship do you gain from the statements in these passages: John 10:10; 15:4, 9, 13, 15; 19:34; Luke 23:42–43; Mark 15:29–32.

■ Jesus explores friendship on many levels in John 13–17. Slowly read any one of these chapters, or all of them. Write a paragraph on what you learned about friendship through your reading.

### SON OF MAN

It is by the mysterious title "Son of Man" that Jesus most often designates himself in the Gospels—eighty-three times, to be exact. It is his very own name for himself because he is the only one who uses it. Without doubt, Jesus used it to tell us something about himself.

The title "Son of Man" is drawn from the Book of Daniel, in which—almost a hundred times—God addresses the prophet Daniel as *Ben Adam,* Son of Man, in the sense of "mortal man." Not the same as "man" or "mankind," the Aramaic *bar Neśā* ("the Man") means "the individual person," but it also suggests the "new" or "different kind" of man—not so much the mortal man as a better or fuller human being. We know that

*Mortal* means subject to death.

Romans 8:29

Jesus was the firstborn of a whole new race of people who possess the immortal life of God.

Colossians 1:15

Jesus used this title for himself in two ways. In the first, he connects it with his *greater than human power,* as in forgiving sin (Mark 2:10), in his exercise of authority over the Sabbath (Mark 2:28), in reference to his resurrection (Mark 9:9), his coming in glory (Mark 8:38) on the clouds of heaven (Mark 13:26), his sitting at the right hand of God (Mark 14:62), and in other signs of the second coming (Matthew 24:27, 37, 39). These uses correspond to Daniel's apocalyptic vision of a powerful royal personage—the Son of Man—who would come surrounded by clouds and possess God-given authority, knowledge, and power that would inspire all nations to serve him.

*Apocalyptic* means "pertaining to a revelation or prophecy of the End Time."

The second way he applies this title is when he speaks of the *suffering* by which this royal power will be achieved. Some instances of this usage are in his predictions of the passion, his future sufferings, and the description of his role as servant.

See Mark 9:31, 10:33; Matthew 8:20; Mark 8:31; Matthew 11:19; Mark 10:45

Altogether, Jesus seems to be saying that although he is quite fully a man, he nevertheless has the power and authority of God.

To the Jews, the title Son of Man definitely did not mean "the expected Messiah," and yet it did refer to the royal personage of the Book of Daniel. Thus by a divine stroke of genius, Jesus both conceals and reveals his messiahship, showing it to be spiritual rather than political, achieved through suffering and service.

The Gospels are jammed with evidence of Jesus' humanness. He developed normally, experienced basic human needs, and valued social relationships. He encountered everyday frustrations, freely showed his emotions, correctly valued and made use of his masculinity, and was courageous and strong in standing up for what was right. He was perhaps most attractive as a person of sensitivity, compassion, and friendship. In his own title for himself, Son of Man, he suggests that he is both divine and human.

- ■ What other examples of Jesus' humanness are to be found in the Gospels?

## SUMMING UP

1. *Words to know:* Shroud of Turin, "people" person, assertiveness, compassion, Son of Man
2. What do we know about the physical appearance of Jesus? About his development as a person?
3. How do the Gospels show Jesus as a "people" person?
4. Give several Gospel instances in which Jesus shows his emotions and his sexuality.
5. How was Jesus a man of courage? Give several instances in which Jesus asserted himself.
6. What are some ways in which Jesus shows compassion for the physical and spiritual needs of the people?
7. How did Jesus show himself to be a true friend?
8. What does the title Son of Man tell us about Jesus?

### Think/Talk/Write

1. Why do you think phoniness was so repulsive to Jesus? What causes phoniness? How can phonies be helped?
2. What is the difference between sinful and righteous anger? Give an example of each.
3. What is friendship? Is it possible to have a true friendship that does not include Jesus?
4. If Jesus lived in your community today, what do you think he would be like? What do you think he would do?

### Activities

1. Develop a class presentation of the ways Jesus has been depicted by artists through the centuries.
2. Identify the "outcasts" of today's society. What are some of their problems? How can you help draw them into the circle of the "acceptables"? What groups or organizations are dedicated to helping them?

3. Write and perform a skit that brings out your ideas on outreach for outcasts.
4. Assemble a booklet or chart or give a report in which you show how Jesus is still curing people physically and spiritually through the members of his Church.
5. Write a poem on Jesus our healer, Christ-courage, or another topic based on qualities discussed in this chapter.
6. Interview five adults who believe in Jesus, asking which of Jesus' personality traits are most appealing and which are least appealing. Report your findings to the class.
7. If you draw, work with ceramics, or like to write, create a Christ that expresses your image of him. What qualities does your creation reveal?

**Scripture Search**

Read the Gospel accounts of the incidents listed below. What do these incidents reveal about Jesus' personality?

The wedding feast of Cana (John 2:1–12)
The feeding of the multitudes (John 6:1–15, 25–70)
The dinner at Simon's house (Matthew 26:6)
The dinner at the Pharisee's house (Luke 7:36–50)
The Last Supper (John 13:1–38)

# EIGHT

What kind of teacher was Jesus?

How did Jesus get his message across so well?

What were the main subjects of Jesus' teaching?

What new commandments did Jesus propose for the New Age he preached?

What does Jesus expect of his "students"?

*Jesus, you call me*
*to be real—*
*to really pray,*
*even when no one is looking;*
*to really love others,*
*even when they don't*
*give back love in return;*
*to really rely on God*
*and not only on my own talents, wisdom, connections, or possessions.*
*To be only who you want me to be,*
*to do only what you want me to do,*
*Here I am, Lord,*
*I come to do your will.*

# Jesus the Teacher

Blest are they who hear the Word of God and keep it.

(LUKE 11:28)

## JESUS' QUALITIES AS A TEACHER

Take a moment to think of the best teacher you ever had. What was it about his or her personality that impressed you? Why was he or she interesting? Did this teacher change your life in any way?

### Rabbinic Skill

*Rabbi* is the title given to Jewish religious teachers. Its literal meaning is "my master."

Unlike priests or ministers, rabbis did not conduct worship; their role was to reflect upon and teach the law of Moses. They were taught and examined by another rabbi, and—when they were judged qualified to pass on Israel's heritage—they became scribes, or Doctors of the Law.

A rabbi instructed groups of followers in the Temple courts and explained Scripture in the synagogues. He settled questions of the Law in specific cases of daily life. Rabbis, who were the models of honesty, goodness, and prayerfulness, had a tremendous influence on the people.

Similarly, Jesus taught in both the synagogues and the Temple of Jerusalem. He also addressed people wherever they might gather—on a hill, on a plain, at a banquet, or from a boat—and answered questions concerning the interpretation of the Law. The people flocked to hear him. Why? What drew them?

*Saint Paul's teacher, Gamalial, was one of these influential rabbis (see Acts 12:2).*

## Authority

From the start of his ministry, Jesus was recognized as an outstanding teacher. He was different. He never quoted other rabbis to prove his interpretation, and when he cited Scripture, he used it to illustrate his meaning rather than to support his point. He didn't merely pass on the Jewish heritage he had learned from some other rabbi; he enriched it and made it clear through the power of his own experience of God. As Matthew comments, "He taught with authority, and not like their scribes."

Matthew 7:29

Jesus had a unique way of showing that what he said sprang from conviction. By placing a double *amen* at the beginning of his sentences, instead of at the end as others did, he gave his statements a ring of great solemnity and authority.

Picture Jesus sitting on a tree stump with a noisy crowd of colorfully dressed people clustered on the ground around him. Every eye is upon him. "Amen, amen, I say to you," he begins, probably nodding his head slightly to emphasize the words. Like a president making a declaration of great importance before Congress, he makes his points with clarity and strength.

The Hebrew word *amen,* even today, means "truly" or "certainly." As Jesus used it, *amen* can be translated "I tell you with greatest certainty." This unique use of *amen* is a hallmark of Jesus' teachings. No one else has ever used it. There is the same tone of authority when Jesus contrasts his teaching with the Judaic tradition

*Modern Bibles translate the phrase as "I warn you," "I solemnly assure you," or in similar words.*

See, for instance, Matthew 5:38–39

Even though Jesus was speaking as a rabbi to rabbis, who often criticized one another, his accusations still took courage.

in the Sermon on the Mount: "You have heard it said . . . but I say to you."

Jesus' commanding power flowed from his deep experience of God. Doing his Father's will was his "meat"—the substance of his life. That will was to reveal God as our Father.

■ Find five examples of Jesus' use of *amen* ("I assure you") or "You have heard it said . . . but I say to you" in the Sermon on the Mount in Matthew, Chapters 5–7.

## Forcefulness

Jesus hated even the shadow of hypocrisy, and his passion for truth made him a fearless and forceful teacher. He publicly corrected the honored rabbis, criticizing them for adding hundreds of laws to the Law of Moses and for not lifting a finger to help anyone. He pointed out that instead of using their authority in the service of the people—that is, to help the people know and love God—they used it to lord their "superiority" over others. While preaching humility, they themselves demanded respect. Jesus, on the other hand, practiced what he preached. He freely associated with and sought out the poor, the outcast, and the sinners, and often shared meals with them. He tried to avoid adoring crowds, kept his reputation for healing as quiet as possible, and would not accept flattery. For him, true freedom was in living the truth.

See Matthew 19:17

Jesus also had strong words for those who refused the Good News. Hearing God's Word wasn't enough. It was to be *heeded*—that is, actually followed. To reject his teaching was to reject salvation. He condemned whole cities (for example, Bethsaida and Chorazin in Galilee) for failing to reform. He rebuked the Apostles for their lack of faith during a storm at sea, and he even called Peter "Satan" when Peter protested at the thought of Jesus' suffering.

See Matthew 11:21

- Read Jesus' strong sermon against the religious leaders in Matthew 23. What faults does Jesus find with them? Why was this passage included in Scripture when the Jewish leaders no longer figured in the Christian communities?
- Look through any one of the Gospels for examples of Jesus' severity toward those who didn't accept him in faith. What is your reaction to Jesus' forceful teaching? What things might Jesus strongly disapprove of today?

*By the time the evangelists wrote the Gospels, the Christians had developed a hostility toward the Jewish leaders that Jesus himself may not have felt.*

## Gentleness and Openness

Jesus was the kind of person whom people instantly trust, which helped him be an effective teacher. A penetrating look and a few words were enough to inspire his Apostles to leave behind family, occupation, and home for an entirely new and risk-filled mission. All but one of these men remained loyal, even through persecution and martyrdom.

See Matthew 4:18–28 and 9:9

Jesus never spoke to faceless crowds, but rather dealt personally with people. He let children crawl up on his lap, touched people to console and heal them, and did not draw back from lepers. He never healed people automatically and impersonally, but asked for trust. Once, even though he was worn out, he took time to speak to a woman about her personal life; she was so impressed with his kindness that she changed from a sinner to his follower. At the Last Supper, he said, "I call you friends," and he washed the feet of the Apostles to show that friendship is a two-way street, and that as Lord and Master he was willing to do more than his part.

See John 4:4–26

John 15:15

Jesus always gave people another chance. When speaking to the woman caught in adultery and about to be stoned, for example, he said compassionately, "I do not condemn you. You may go. But from now on, avoid this sin." And he never got so wrapped up in himself or his message that he forgot the people. Some-

John 8:11

See John 6:10–11

times he personally provided food for the crowds who had come a long way to hear him.

- What other situations can you recall where Jesus showed the qualities of friendship, pity, gentleness, or mercy? Locate and read them in the Bible.
- Which of Jesus' qualities as a teacher appeal most to you? Why? Do you think he would be approachable? Why or why not? What questions would you ask him if he were to walk into your classroom today?

## HOW JESUS TAUGHT

Perhaps you've known a teacher or a speaker who went on and on, talking over your head. This was not Jesus' style. His profoundest teachings were laced with simple comparisons and examples that everyone could understand.

*Images* are picture words.

He touched the minds and hearts of his hearers with images from everyday life: food, drink, the weather, animals, plants, work, leisure. Jesus saw ordinary things as windows to the mystery of God's kingdom.

JESUS

- Make a list of any images you find in Chapters 5–7 of Matthew. Which appeal most to you? Why? Which might need an explanation for today's audience?

*These chapters, called the Sermon on the Mount, sum up many of Jesus' teachings.*

## Parables

Jesus gathered these images into teaching stories called parables, from the Greek word *parabole*—"placing things side by side for the sake of comparison." Although parables are not factual, they are simple, true-to-life stories that teach religious truth through comparison. There are more than thirty-five parables in the Gospel; if the simpler comparisons are included, there are nearly seventy.

- Read Matthew 13:1–17 and Mark 4:10–13, in which Jesus gives reasons for speaking in parables. What does he mean? Do you agree with his reasons? Why or why not?

If Jesus wanted so urgently to proclaim the kingdom and have his listeners accept it, why would he use parables that partly hid or disguised his teaching and made his message harder to understand? He did this for three reasons.

1. *To get his message across without antagonizing his audience.* The Jewish nation expected a worldly messiah who would lead them against their political oppressors. In order to correct this false notion gradually, and confront his listeners directly with the fact that they were expecting the wrong kind of messiah, Jesus used parables.

2. *To preserve the mystery of the kingdom.* Trying to explain the kingdom of God was like trying to describe what the world is like to someone from another galaxy. It is a mystery that human words can only hint at. Through the parable, the listener is drawn into the mystery and invited to experience

*"Many teachers of the world have tried to explain everything—they have changed little or nothing. Jesus explained little and changed everything"* (E. Stanley Jones).

it directly, even though the kingdom is greater than their minds can comprehend.

3. *To involve his audience.* Jesus so aroused the curiosity of his listeners that they couldn't resist listening to the whole story. At a certain point, they suddenly realized that the story demanded a personal response from them. They were involved before they knew it.

The parables have two levels of understanding. One is the actual story situation that Jesus describes. It is called the *literal* level. Usually there is little trouble grasping this level. But there is also a *meaning* level, which requires thinking on the part of the hearer. Jesus does not state the meaning, but leaves it open—a riddle to be figured out. When the listeners understand, they realize they will have to change their lives.

■ Read the parable of the Sower (Mark 4:3–20). In this passage, not only is the story told, but the meaning of the story is given as well. Can you spot any problems in the explanation? What other meanings not mentioned in the explanation can you see in this parable?

■ Try your parable power. What is the meaning level in each of the three parables in Matthew 13:24–35? What effect do these parables have on you? What have you learned about the kingdom from them? What question about the kingdom do they leave with you? How would you describe the kingdom to a small child or to a person unfamiliar with Christianity?

## WHAT JESUS TAUGHT

As a Christian, you are familiar with the teachings of Jesus. How well would you be able to summarize these teachings for someone who had never heard of Christ? To help you, the following sections review some of the major areas covered by his teachings.

## The Age of the Messiah

Two thousand years before the launching of the Space Age, Jesus appeared on the Galilean scene to launch a far more significant age. Matthew reports that when Jesus heard John had been arrested, he left Nazareth and went to live in Capernaum. "From that time on Jesus began to proclaim this theme: 'Reform your lives! The kingdom of heaven is at hand.'" It was the opening of the Messianic Age.

Matthew 4:17

The theme of Jesus' teaching was the "kingdom of God." The idea was not original with him, for the idea of God's kingship has a long history. Since the days of Moses, Israel had never allowed any king but Yahweh. However, when the twelve tribes of Israel were threatened by warring neighbors, they asked their religious leader, Samuel, for a king to lead them to victory. Reluctantly, Samuel consented. Most of the kings turned out to be power-hungry and corrupt, but as the Jewish people looked back on their history, they saw that David, the king who never tried to put himself above God's law, was the best representative of Israel's true king, Yahweh.

To reward David's faithfulness, God made a promise to him of a mysterious "eternal" kingdom. It was to be brought about through a Messiah who would be David's descendant. The prophets reinforced this promise. The Messianic Age would come, they said, when power-seeking was over and there was justice for the poor, the widowed, and the orphaned. In that day, the blind would see, the deaf would hear, and the lame would leap like deer.

See 2 Samuel 7:16

See Jeremiah 7:5–7

See Isaiah 35:5–6

The Pharisaic rabbis of Our Lord's day taught that the people could hasten the reign of Yahweh by being very careful about keeping the many laws that they had added to the law of Moses. The difference between the teaching of the Pharisees and that of Jesus was that Jesus announced that the kingdom of God was already here and that he himself was bringing it. At the beginning of his ministry, he stood up in the synagogue to read one of Isaiah's prophecies, which listed the signs

Luke 4:21

by which the Israelites would recognize that the time of the Messiah had arrived. Then, sitting down, and with all eyes upon him, he said, "Today this Scripture passage is fulfilled in your hearing." It was indeed the launching of a New Age.

## The Kingdom of God

It took his followers a long time to understand what Jesus meant by the kingdom. The problem was that the people wanted a Messiah to free them from Roman occupation. Jesus had to warn against making too much of his miracles lest the people think he was going to lead an uprising against Rome. Even after his resurrection, the Apostles were still asking if he was now going to restore the kingdom of Israel.

See Acts 1:6

But the kingdom of God in Jesus' teaching is neither a nation nor a state. Jesus said to Pilate, "My kingdom does not belong to this world. . . . My kingdom is not here." *Kingdom,* as Jesus used it, means something close to the "kingship" or "reign" of God. It is God's goodness, justice, and truth winning out over the kingdom of Satan and evil. This victory brings peace to the world.

John 18:36

*Saint Augustine says that peace is the result of order.*

Luke 17:20–21

The kingdom is invisible and mysterious. "You cannot tell by careful watching when the reign of God will come," Jesus replied to some Pharisees who asked him when the kingdom would arrive. "Neither is it a matter of reporting that it is 'here' or 'there.' The reign of God is already in your midst." Yet, at other times, Jesus spoke of the kingdom as something in the future—like a seed, still growing.

- ■ Read the short parables of the Pearl of Great Price and the Treasure in the Field in Matthew 13:44–46. What do they tell you about the response the kingdom requires? Name three practical ways to carry out the lesson of these parables.

## THE PRAYER OF THE KINGDOM

Jesus' prayer about the kingdom is the Our Father. In just three main sections and a few more than fifty words, it summarizes Jesus' teaching on the kingdom of God.

*Section 1*
> Our Father, who are in heaven,
> hallowed be thy name.

Two words tell of God's closeness. What are they? What two words tell of God's "otherness"—his distance from us and his holiness? Which attitude best summarizes this section: praise, sorrow, or petition?

*Section 2*
> Thy kingdom come
> thy will be done
> on earth as it is in heaven.

What attitudes toward the kingdom does Jesus express in this section of the prayer?

*Section 3*
> Give us this day our daily bread;
> and forgive us our trespasses
> as we forgive those who trespass against us;
> and lead us not into temptation,
> but deliver us from evil.

In this final section, the Christian response to the kingdom is outlined. Summarize it in a word or two. Which of the themes do you also find in the Beatitudes?

## A Deepened Understanding of God

The second commandment is "Thou shalt not take the name of the Lord thy God in vain."

Jesus changed people's idea of God for all time by calling him a new name. The Chosen People had always had a deep respect for God's name, which they identified with God himself. Over the years that reverence grew to an almost superstitious fear. By the third century before Christ, the Jewish people never pronounced the name Yahweh, but always substituted "the Lord" or some other expression instead. God was very awesome to them.

Around the time that Jesus was teaching, some of the Pharisees referred to God as a Father, but they never addressed him as such directly. Jesus not only refused to use roundabout, overly reverent ways of addressing God, but he actually called God by the familiar or intimate name *Abba,* which Jewish children call their fathers. It was like the word *daddy*—a loving name.

See Matthew 7:11

Matthew 10:30

Besides hinting at his own indescribably close relationship with his Father, Jesus also taught that, far from being a high-and-mighty monarch with little concern for his creatures, God is a loving parent who never abandons his children as human parents sometimes do. He is utterly dependable. He more than provides for all creation, right down to the smallest sparrows. Why then would he neglect his favored children? "Every hair of your head has been counted," Jesus said. He meant that the Father can be trusted, for he is more than generous. He pays more wages than his workers deserve and he invites all to share the food of his table.

*Jesus often compared the kingdom to a joyous banquet.*

- What word does Jesus use in his personal prayer during his agony in the Garden (Mark 14:36)? What do Jesus' last words on the cross (Luke 23:46) tell us about Jesus' relationship with the Father?

## The Father's Mercy

Mercy is compassion shown to an offender.

Of all God's qualities, Jesus places mercy highest. God, he says, is not a hard taskmaster counting up in his black book everyone's failures to observe the Law, as some of the religious leaders of the day seemed to imply. Jesus lived out God's love for sinners, but he also told parables to make the message more vivid.

Three parables of God's mercy are found in Chapter 15 of Luke's Gospel. The people listening to these parables include the outcasts of Israel and the religious leaders. Read the "twin parables" of the Lost Sheep and the Lost Coin in Luke 15:1–10 and discuss these questions.

- What is the point of each parable? How are the two similar? Why has the Good Shepherd been so popular a story through the ages, even in industrial societies? What do the parables say to you personally about God?

Following these parables comes one of the most loved stories in the world: the parable of the Prodigal Son. Prodigal means "extravagant," and actually it is the father who is prodigal with his mercy more than the son with his money.

*Some Scripture scholars today prefer to call this either the story of the Lost Son or the Father's Love.*

- Read the parable in Luke 15:11–32. How does this parable relate to the teaching of the first two parables you read? What do you learn about God's kingdom from the first part (verses 11–14)? Why was the second part of the parable (verses 15–32) added? What part of the teachings about the kingdom does the elder son have trouble with? In what way is everyone a little like the elder son?

## New Commandments for a New Age

Jesus did more than heal physical illnesses; he offered a prescription for curing the ills that destroy people from within themselves. His commandments were "doctor's orders" for the New Age.

*"The healthy do not need a doctor; sick people do" (Luke 5:31).*

When most people hear the word *commandments,* they think of rules. Jesus identified the keeping of the commandments with loyalty to himself: "If you love

*John 14:15 (Good News)*

Mark 12:30–31

John 15:12

*me,* keep my commandments." His greatest new commandment was to be built on a personal relationship with himself. He sums up the Old Law as the love of God and of neighbor as of one's self. But Christian love was to go a step farther. "Love one another as I have loved you." This generous love can take people beyond the loneliness of crushing self-confinement. Jesus' New Commandment challenges everyone to heroic greatness.

Although Matthew presents a summary of Jesus' moral teachings in the Sermon on the Mount, Jesus' commandments cannot be put into ten or twenty neat statements. As human love affects every detail of life, so his commandments are woven into the very fabric of all four Gospels.

*The Sermon on the Mount is found in Matthew 5–7. In Luke 6:17–49 it is called the Sermon on the Plain.*

## The Meaning of Riches

Jesus' commandments frequently turn a "common-sense" approach to things upside down. For instance, people commonly believe that money can buy a good life. Yet the first Beatitude says, "How blest are the poor in spirit." Jesus doesn't teach that the rich can't enter the kingdom, but he never says, "How blest are the rich." Why?

*The Beatitudes are statements of the happiness of those who follow Jesus. They are found in Matthew 5:3–12, and introduce the Sermon on the Mount.*

- Read the parable of the Rich Young Man in Matthew 19:16–26. What does Jesus ask of the youth? What is the youth's reaction as he goes away? Do you see any connection between his sadness and his riches? Who is the rich young man today? How does Jesus respond to the Apostles' surprise in the remainder of the incident in Matthew 16:27–30?
- Read the parable of Lazarus and the Rich Man in Luke 16:19–31. What keeps the rich man out of heaven? What is the meaning of Abraham's last response to the rich man? Do you think anybody, even someone who is poor, could be like the rich man? Why? What is the point of the parable?

## THE SANDALED SAINT

As a young man he was popular. He could well afford to be generous with his friends because his father was a wealthy textile merchant. He was also an adventurer, dreaming of a knight's career. Captured in a battle and imprisoned for a year, he began a conversion to Christ that led him to renounce all his possessions, even the very clothes he wore. After much prayer and a call from God in a dream, he gathered together a community of friars—brothers—who shared everything in common and lived in absolute poverty, owning nothing. Before his death in 1226, more than 27,000 men had joined him, dramatically offsetting the worldliness of some of the clergy of the day.

Francis of Assisi was probably the most Christlike man ever to have lived. The freedom and happiness

that characterize the Franciscan spirit even today are signs of the lightheartedness that accompanies detachment from material things.

■ Catherine de Hueck, founder of Madonna Houses in the United States and Canada, said she acquired a great love for Francis when she was nine. After she heard his story, she always prayed a Hail Mary for every poor person she met. Research her life to find out what practical measures she added to her prayers. What is your reaction to Saint Francis? If you know a Franciscan, hold an interview on what "giving up all" for love of Christ is like.

The Little Poor Man of Assisi composed this prayer that poetically sums up the message of Jesus:

*Prayer of Saint Francis*

O Lord, make me an instrument of your peace.
Where there is hatred, let me sow love;
Where there is injury, pardon;
Where there is doubt, faith;
Where there is despair, hope;
Where there is darkness, light;
And where there is sadness, joy.

O Divine Master, grant that I may not so much
Seek to be consoled as to console;
To be understood as to understand;
To be loved as to love.
For it is in giving that we receive;
It is in pardoning that we are pardoned;
And it is in dying that we are born to eternal
     life.

■ Have small groups think of practical ways to carry out some of the petitions of this prayer. Present these ideas to the class.

## Compassion

Jesus' revelation of the Father's love makes us all brothers and sisters. The parable of the Good Samaritan teaches you who your neighbors are. Some things to notice are that the man the Samaritan stopped to help was his enemy, not a child or a woman. The Samaritan probably used his own headcloth to bind the wounds of the victim. Presumably a merchant who carried his wares on a second donkey, he poured his own oil and wine on the wounds and loaded the victim onto the donkey he rode. Going out of his way, he took the wounded man to an inn and paid the man's board.

The fact that people put themselves out for others is always news, but the greatest blow to Jesus' audience was the comparison of this hated Samaritan's unselfish actions with the uncaring response of the two priestly characters who were the official representatives of God's love.

■ Read the parable in Luke 10:25–37 and write what your personal feelings are on this question: "Who is my neighbor?"

*See Luke 10:25–27*

*Samaritans, a people of mixed Jewish and Gentile blood, lived in what was formerly the Northern Kingdom of Israel. They were looked down upon as traitors to the faith of Israel because they refused to worship in the Temple in Jerusalem.*

## Nonviolence and Forgiveness

If you feel inclined to strike back, you are normal. But Jesus challenges you to something more heroic. "Offer no resistance to injury," he said. "Love your enemies, pray for your persecutors."

*Matthew 5:39, 44*

Brother Stanley Kolowski of New Jersey learned this difficult lesson the hard way. He didn't need to see the TV film *Holocaust*; he has only to look at his left arm to remember it. There, midway between his elbow and wrist, is the number 12988, tattooed on him by the Nazis at their concentration camp in Auschwitz.

Brother Stanley, a native of Poland, survived only because there was no more room in the gas chamber on his appointed day. When he was liberated by American troops just two hours before he was to be executed at

Matthew 5:8

*"Humanity is never so beautiful as when praying for forgiveness or else forgiving one another" (Jean Paul Richter).*

a second camp, he weighed eighty pounds. Today, he is a burly Franciscan friar who preaches forgiveness.

Brother Stanley said he came to understand one of the most liberating lessons of his life in Auschwitz—that others can't destroy you unless you let them. In teaching nonviolence, Jesus makes available the only weapon that can stop the destruction of hate: love.

- Read Matthew 5:39–41. What nonviolent actions does Jesus prescribe? Is Jesus speaking literally? How would you follow this advice today?
- In the parable of the Unmerciful Servant (Matthew 18:23–25), Jesus reveals the motive for the high ideal of forgiveness. What connection can you see between this parable and Jesus' teachings on nonviolence?

## Sincerity

People who are firmly convinced of their own worth have no need to put on airs or to do underhanded things to enhance their self-image. Their actions spring from their true self, and that keeps them consistent.

Jesus taught that his followers must be authentic—real. Because God is pure truth, hypocrisy or phoniness of any kind makes people unlike God and less true to themselves. Blessed are the single-hearted, Jesus said. They shall see God, and others will see God in them.

By advocating honesty, Jesus did not mean "telling it like it is" when the harsh truth may hurt others. He himself was careful not to anger or hurt others unless he saw that he would have to compromise the truth of his own life style.

He taught that because sin starts in the mind and heart, those who wish to keep his commandments have to begin by thinking right thoughts.

- Read these texts from Matthew and write a sentence telling what Jesus taught in each: 5:13–16, 21–26, 27–30, 33–37; 6:1–4, 5–8, 16–18; 7:1–5.

## KINGDOM COME

This, then, is the kingdom as Jesus taught it: The mercy of God, the great worth of each individual, total confidence in God the Father, loving concern for one another in imitation of God's own love, and utter sincerity and authenticity of life style. The kingdom begins secretly in each heart, as noiselessly as a mustard seed dropping into the ground. It grows mysteriously, takes root, and develops into a great tree where many birds make their nests.

This kingdom of love does not come all at once, but in stages. Jesus launched it by his presence and through his preaching, but its power was not to become noticeable until Jesus had passed through his hour of darkness. Jesus abided by his own teachings on the commandment of love. In complete submission to his Father's will, he gave his life because he loved all people. With his ascension to the Father's right hand, the kingdom took root in the world. Christ has already won the victory over sin and death, and he has left his teachings with us so that we might follow.

The kingdom calls on you today to change your heart and to hear and keep the Word of God. Only you, in the secret of your own mind, can respond to Christ and the Father in love and trust.

- Divide the class and have each group read one of the parables listed below. First give its literal level and then state its meaning level.

> The Thief in the Night (Matthew 24:42–44)
> The Coming of the Bridgegroom (Matthew 25:1–13)
> The Great Feast (Luke 14:15–24)
> The Two Sons (Matthew 21:28–32)
> The Two Builders (Matthew 7:24–27)
> The Three Servants (Matthew 25:14–30)

- The parables of the Thief, the Two Builders, and the Three Servants are called "crisis parables." Why?

*Crisis parables* are parables that demonstrate the urgency of repentance.

## SUMMING UP

1. *Words to know:* rabbi, Pharisees, amen, images, parables, literal level, meaning level, Messianic Age, kingdom of God, *Abba,* mercy, prodigal, conversion, New Commandment, Sermon on the Mount, Beatitudes, Samaritan, crisis parables
2. How was Jesus different from the rabbis of his day? What was unique about his manner of speaking?
3. How did Jesus show his strong convictions?
4. How was Jesus' gentleness apparent in his teaching?
5. What means did Jesus use to get his message across to the people? What is a parable? Why did Jesus use parables so extensively? Name at least three of Jesus' parables.
6. The kingdom of God is a main theme of Jesus' teaching. How did it become part of Israel's heritage? What did Jesus mean by the kingdom of God?
7. What new name did Jesus give God and what is its significance for us?
8. What qualities of the Father did Jesus reveal?
9. What is meant by the conversion required by the Gospel?
10. What are the New Commandments Jesus preached? Which is the greatest?

### Think/Talk/Write

1. If someone said to you, "In the Beatitudes, Jesus says we should patiently accept unfair wages, deprivation of human rights, and other forms of oppression," would you agree? Why or why not?
2. In Matthew 6:26, Jesus speaks of Divine Providence—the way in which God cares for and nourishes all his creatures. What evidence of Divine Providence do you find in nature? In history? In your own life?
3. What is the cause of evil? If Jesus established the kingdom, why is there still evil in the world?
4. Close your eyes and concentrate on forgiveness—especially your personal experiences with it. When you feel ready, choose an occasion of forgiveness that stands out in your mind. Who was it that

you forgave? What happened that needed forgiveness? How did the moment of forgiveness come about? How did you feel before, during, and after forgiving? Write out the incident in your journal and discuss the results of forgiving with the class.

**Activities**

1. Be a journalist: Compose a newspaper of one or more pages in which all the news is about people who live according to the message of Jesus.
2. Be an adman: Compose an advertisement giving the advantages of being a member of the kingdom. Be sure to include the price.
3. Be a playwright: Adapt one of the Gospel parables to modern times. For instance, put the Good Samaritan on the football team of a rival school. Or rewrite the explanation of the parable of the Sower using modern temptations in place of thorny bushes, rocky ground, and so on. Act out the parables if you like.

**Scripture Search**

Jesus was constantly searching for new ways to explain the mystery of the reign, or kingdom, of God—the New Age which he was bringing about. Look up the Gospel passages below and write down the figures of speech Jesus used to describe the kingdom. Then explain what each of the images means to you. A Bible commentary will help you clarify the meaning of these terms.

| | |
|---|---|
| Matthew 13:33 | Mark 13:28 |
| Matthew 13:44–49 | Luke 8:16–17 |
| Mark 2:21–22 | Luke 12:54–56 |
| Mark 4:26 | John 4:35 |

How important are the miracles of Jesus?

Were biblical miracles understood in the same way as ours?

What did the miracles of Jesus signify?

What did Jesus' miracles reveal about the Father?

What did the miracles of Jesus reveal about the kingdom?

What difference do the miracles make to you?

*Here is my servant whom I uphold,*
*my chosen one with whom I am pleased,*
*Upon whom I have put my spirit;*
*he shall bring forth justice to the nations,*
*Not crying out, not shouting,*
*not making his voice heard in the street.*
*A bruised reed he shall not break,*
*and a smoldering wick he shall not quench,*
*Until he establishes justice on the earth;*
*the coastlands will wait for his teaching. . . .*
*I, the Lord, have called you for the victory of justice,*
*I have grasped you by the hand;*
*I formed you, and set you as a covenant of the people,*
*a light for the nations.*

(Isaiah 42:1–4, 6)

# Jesus the Healer

What are we to do with this man performing all sorts of signs? The whole world will believe in him.

(JOHN 11:47–48)

See Matthew 8 and 9

## A BURST OF MIRACLES

Everyone knows people who are big on talk but short on deeds. Jesus was definitely not that kind of person. The Gospel portrays him reaching out to ease the burdens of the people as he taught. He worked miracles of all kinds, including exorcism, healing, mastery of nature, and power over death.

■ Make four columns on a sheet of paper and label each column with one of the four types of miracles. List all the miracles you can remember that fit each of the categories. Why do you think Jesus worked miracles?

All four evangelists present Jesus as an extraordinary person with extraordinary powers. In Mark, Jesus opens his ministry in the lake region of Capharnaum with a great shower of miracles. Even Gentiles received the benefits of his compassion. Matthew neatly clusters ten miracles into two later chapters of his carefully designed Gospel, but he reports that there were many more. In an earlier chapter, he notes that from the outset of Jesus' ministry the people of Galilee and all the surrounding areas "carried to him all those affected with various diseases and racked with pain. He cured them all." Matthew 4:24

In his Gospel, Luke introduces the public ministry with Jesus reading Isaiah's description of the Messiah as one who would perform works of mercy. He then weaves the accounts of Jesus' miracles throughout his pages to show Jesus fulfilling that prophecy. John's Gospel contains only seven great "signs," but each is carefully chosen to illustrate a different part of Jesus' mission. The Acts of the Apostles also describes Jesus as a miracle worker. Luke 4:18–19; Isaiah 6:1 Acts 2:22

- Use the miracle accounts in the first ten chapters of Mark to complete the chart you began. What impression did Jesus make by working miracles?
- Read Mark 1:35–37, 45; 3:10–12, 20–21; and 5:31. What was Jesus' life on the road like? What impression of Jesus do you get from the miracle accounts?

## The Modern Meaning of Miracles

All four Gospels place heavy emphasis on Jesus' miracles. But today, miracles are few and far between.

A group of students were returning to Cleveland by Greyhound from a convention in Detroit. It was an express bus, with no stops until they reached the terminal in downtown Cleveland. Since Gail lived thirty miles west of the city, she was in a predicament: if she went to the terminal, there was no way she could get back to her town.

She finally persuaded the driver to drop her off at the exit to her city. As she made her way alone in the dark along the off-ramp, she gradually realized the danger she was in. There was absolutely no one around, and she was half a mile from the toll gate.

Suddenly a car slowed next to her. Her heart skipped a beat. The car stopped. She was terror-stricken. "Gail!" her mother shouted out the car window. "What are you doing here?" The relieved girl couldn't believe it! Her parents, returning from a weekend out of town, happened along at the exact time her bus had left her off.

■ How would you explain this incident? Why? What is your definition of a miracle? Do you believe in miracles? Why or why not?

Many people today have difficulty believing in miracles. We know much more about the causes of disease, mental problems, storms, and earthquakes than the people of the Bible did. We are convinced that everything has a cause, even if for the moment it seems beyond explanation. There is no such thing as a footprint in the snow unless someone walked there. In a modern miracle, something takes place that is caused by something or someone outside our familiar, physical world. Its cause lies beyond the laws of nature. A miracle today, then, is any observable *exception* to a natural cause-effect relationship.

### Biblical Miracles

The English *miracle,* from Latin *miraculum* ("something to be marveled at"), is not correct for the words in the New Testament: *dynamis* ("an act of power"), *semeion* ("a sign"), or *ergon* ("a work"). To the early Christians, miracles were works, or signs, of God's power, not a suspension of the laws of nature.

To the biblical mind, a miracle was something that showed more clearly God's control over this world, which is his creation. A miracle was a wonderful sign of the power that God exercises in less obvious ways all the time.

The "miracle" of an earthquake or of a plague of locusts at just the right moment made people reverent, even fearful, but they were not surprised by it. The

JESUS

Gospels often note that the crowds were "amazed" at Jesus, but they weren't amazed at what he did. Their wonder sprang from what his actions said about him—that God was working in an especially powerful way through him. Matthew notes, "At the sight [of Jesus' miracle], a feeling of awe came over the crowd, and they praised God for giving such authority to human beings." Their attention was more on the miracle-worker than on his deed. This comes through in the shout of the people as Jesus entered Jerusalem: "Blessed is he who comes in the name of the Lord!" The miracles had convinced them that God was working through Jesus as he had once worked through the prophets.

See Matthew 9:33, 12:23, 13:54, 14:33, and 15:31 for the reaction of the crowds to Jesus' miracles.

Matthew 9:8

Matthew 21:9

## WHAT GOD'S PRESENCE MEANT

Except for John the Baptizer, it had been at least four centuries since God had sent Israel a prophet to speak in God's name. What promise from God did the signs signify? Political power? Freedom from hunger and disease?

To answer these questions you need to understand how the ancient Jews viewed their world.

### Israel's World View

Before studying some of the beliefs of Israel, you may wish to examine your own world view. Which statements below reflect your own beliefs?

Sickness or handicaps are always the effect of personal or parental sin.

Sickness and death are the results of the sins of the world.

Evil is willed by God.

People who commit evil deeds are always punished in this life.

There really is a devil.

*Evil* is anything that causes distress or harm.

The Jewish people had developed a keen sense of the sinfulness of humanity, but they did not believe that human sin was the only source of evil. To them, the mystery of sin originated in a force beyond the human race—Satan, an evil being who exerted a powerful hold over the world. They associated all forms of disease, illness, and natural calamities with his power. Genesis told them that when Adam gave in to the temptation of Satan, all human beings lost God's friendship and were made more susceptible to sin. Other effects of sin included all kinds of suffering and death. Even nature was somehow pitted against them as they tried to work out their existence.

## What Their Experience Told Them

When the people of the first century looked around, they saw a picture of the universal effects of sin. Hospitals of any kind, much less for the mentally ill, were unknown. The blind and the lame lined the roads begging for alms, while lepers, the insane, and other outcasts were condemned to the outskirts of town. Feared and avoided, the afflicted were repulsive reminders of the mysterious forces that make victims of us all.

In Jesus' day there was still a strong feeling that sickness or handicaps were the effects of personal sins or of the sins of one's parents. Even so, some thinkers faced the fact that disaster sometimes falls on good people as well. To them, it seemed obvious that something had gone wrong with the original plan of God. The universal power of evil was immense and mystifying.

## The Sign Value

As every calamity was a sign of Satan's power, every miracle showed God's power over the Evil One. Like

*Leprosy* is a term that refers to a number of semitropical skin diseases.

small battles in a war, the miracles of Jesus were the beginning of the great rescue that would be complete only when all evil—in individuals, in society, and in nature—was wiped out forever.

To all with faith, Jesus working miracles in Galilee was a sign that their God willed to save them; he was not someone to fear. He had sent someone stronger than the devil to fight the one war that was beyond their strength.

Most of the people, however, misinterpreted the sign, hoping that they could use Jesus to lead them in revolution against Rome or to make their life easier in material ways. It wasn't until after the resurrection that even the Apostles began to grasp the real meaning of Jesus' "sign language."

■ The theme of a well-known scientist's talk to a group of distinguished fellow scientists was that the human race can eventually eliminate all suffering simply by applying itself to experimentation in science. What would an ancient Hebrew have said to him? How would you answer him?

## WHY MIRACLES?

Why did Jesus work miracles at all? What does it all mean for us today?

### For Imitation

They say that actions speak louder than words. In Japan, children learn to play musical instruments without ever reading a book or studying a note. They simply watch their teacher. The Suzuki method is based on the fact that people learn very quickly when they imitate what they see.

Jesus used the ideal method of "show and tell." He became a living sign of everything he preached. From him the disciples learned compassion and sensitivity to others. By not brushing aside the children and the pressing crowds, Jesus taught that, in a loving heart, there is always room for one more. As they watched him sympathize with parents and slavemasters and those who mourned their dead, they entered more deeply into the sufferings of others. Observing Jesus' tenderness, the Apostles became more tender. Jesus' personal service to the poor and miserable has been imitated by millions ever since.

## Signs of the Father's Compassion

On a deeper level, Jesus' miracles were the natural out-flow of his close relationship with God. In his personal prayer and meditation on Scripture, he had profoundly experienced his Father as a God of mercy and compassion. Jesus lavished his Father's love on others. Not only would it have been unfeeling and inhuman to refuse to help those in need, but it would also have been contrary to what he knew of his Father's ways.

As he preached God's mercy by word, his deeds showed clearly that God's love extends to the most needy people in society. The fact that it reached far beyond justice and fairness showed that it was a pure gift, generous beyond our imagination.

JESUS

- Name in one word what you consider to be the main motive of Jesus in these passages: Mark 1:40–41, 8:1–3; Matthew 9:12–13, 9:36–10:1; Luke 7:12–15.

## Signs of the Kingdom

Jesus is not just a social worker or a physician. The Gospel describes Jesus' miracles not as *kindness* but as *signs* and *power.* Jesus' miracles are presented as signs of the power of God versus the power of Satan. And so the key to understanding why the early Church made the miracles of Jesus so prominent in the Gospels is the kingdom. As Jesus' teachings were centered on this basic theme, so his miracles were signs that God's kingdom was to put down the evil of the world. The four types of miracles that Jesus performed light up different aspects of the mystery of that kingdom.

*Exorcism of demons.* With renewed emphasis on the occult in America, there has been a revival of interest in the devil. As you know, the Israelites believed that evil enters the world with the sins of the individual, but finds its original source in Satan, who as a "roaring lion" goes about looking for someone he can devour. Jesus directly confronts Satan in bodily form only once, in the mysterious scene of the temptation in the desert. Normally, his combat is waged against the effects of evil that are seen in human suffering.

There is a reason why Mark and Luke listed an exorcism as Jesus' first miracle—the possessed are the most obvious sign of human helplessness before Satan's power.

- Read Mark's account in 1:23–28 and the reaction of the Pharisees in 3:22–27. Why do the spirits leave screaming? What logic does Jesus use to answer the Pharisees? Who is the "strong man" Jesus refers to and how has he been put under restraint?
- What claim does Jesus make about himself in Luke 11:20?

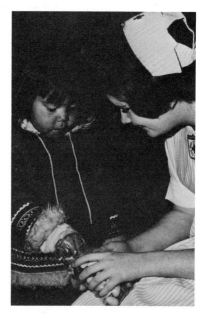

*Exorcism* is the casting out of evil spirits.

1 Peter 5:8

The *possessed* are those whom Satan has entered into and firmly controls.

## JESUS: ONLY AHEAD OF HIS TIMES?

*Faith-healing* is a process of curing brought about by the faith of the victim. The cured in the Gospels had faith, but it was the power of God that cured them.

A *demoniac* is someone possessed by demons.

Matthew 4:24

*The passage over the Sea of Reeds may have been the result of natural tides or marshes that the Egyptian chariots could not get through. The manna may have been a sweet resin that dripped naturally from the desert shrubs.*

Some scholars have tried to explain away Jesus' cures by claiming that he used ordinary methods such as hypnosis or faith-healing far ahead of his time. They feel the people cured were not really possessed, but merely epileptics or neurotics. They say that Jesus recognized some of the "dead" as victims of coma and that he merely saved them from being buried alive.

It is probable that some of the victims were epileptics, but the Gospel adds demoniacs to the list. From the description of the self-destructive actions of some of the Gospel epileptics, it seems likely that they were possessed by the devil. The demons cursing or pleading with Jesus showed that they recognized him as the Messiah.

Other scholars think that because the ancient peoples didn't understand the causes of disease and mental illness, they had only a superstitious awe of Jesus' power. But not only are the miracles in the Bible more than the superstitious beliefs of a primitive people, they are also more than faith healing in the modern sense. They do not take place gradually, over a period of weeks, as would be necessary if Jesus were only using natural means to cure. They are usually instantaneous and occur solely by force of Jesus' words or touch. Sometimes, as in the case of the Roman officer's servant, they take place a good distance away from Jesus.

Jesus' healing actions are unique in the Bible. In the Old Testament, the great miracle of the Exodus and the manna might possibly have natural explanations, and only two prophets—Elijah and Elisha—work a few miracles. There is nothing like the burst of miracles of every kind that the Gospels report of Jesus.

Neither have the miracles been invented by the faith of the early Church to convert a pagan world that believed in wonderworkers. Jesus had performed his miracles publicly. The evangelists could not have succeeded in passing off such stories as fact if there had not been many eyewitnesses to confirm their accounts. There are also too many of them—thirty-five or forty individual miracles are recorded in the Gospels, in addition to those referred to in several summary paragraphs. Half, or 200, of the 425 verses of Mark 1–10 deal with the miracles. The Gospels would be greatly weakened if they were removed. It would take a very inventive mind to have thought up the very particular details and the many varieties of the miracles.

Miracle chapters: Matthew 8, 9; Mark 1–10; Luke 4–9; John 2, 4, 5, 6, 9, 11.

For summary paragraphs, see Mark 1:32–34, 3:10–12; 6:54–56.

The miracles of Jesus can neither be explained away nor brushed aside. They are a phenomenon of Jesus' life that must be reckoned with in order to understand him correctly.

A *phenomenon* is a fact that can be observed.

- Cite five details of action or description surrounding some of the miracles. For instance, one man yells out from the side of the road. Who, besides Jews, are cured?
- What would you say to a friend who says he or she believes in Jesus, but not in his miracles?

See John 9:1–3 and Luke 13:1–5

*Rebuked* means sharply reprimanded. Jesus speaks to the fever as if it were a person.

Luke 5:20

*The nature miracles include the multiplication of the loaves, the walking on the waters, the calming of the storm at sea, and the miraculous catch of fish.*

*Chaos* is the confused, unorganized state existing before the creation of definite things. By keeping everything in existence, Yahweh is constantly conquering chaos.

*Physical cures.* Those who suffered severe forms of disease were considered "unclean" and were not allowed to worship until their cure was confirmed by the priest. Jesus insisted that the sick or the victims of calamity were not necessarily any more sinful than others in good health, but he did see sickness in general as an effect of sin.

When Jesus cured Peter's mother-in-law, the Gospel says that he "rebuked" her fever as if it were the devil. He cleansed lepers, who were considered walking symbols of sin. Before curing the paralytic, he said, "Your sins are forgiven you." The cures of Jesus are clearly meant to be signs of God's love for sinners and of his ready forgiveness of their sins. Each person's repentance was the first step toward restoring the lost order of the universe.

■ Read Jesus' own words on the connection between sickness, disaster, and sin in these short incidents: the man born blind (John 9:1–3); natural disasters (Luke 13:1–5); Peter's mother-in-law (Luke 4:38–39); and the paralytic (Luke 5:17–24). In your judgment, which most clearly connects illness or disaster with sin? What do you learn about Jesus as a person from all these incidents?

*Power over nature.* It is easy to see how healing miracles and exorcism are signs of the kingdom, but how do acts of power over the forces of creation—the nature miracles—fit in with the kingdom theme?

In the Jewish Scriptures, Yahweh is pictured as the master of nature. He brings rain and storm and sends wind to dry the flood.

In Psalm 89:9, immediately following the statement that the Lord God Almighty "rules over the surging of the sea" and "stills the swelling of its waves," there follows this line: "You have crushed Rahab with a mortal blow." Rahab was a legendary sea monster that represented the forces of chaos and evil. So when Jesus calms the storm or, like Yahweh, "treads upon the crests of the sea," he is exhibiting the power of Yahweh himself in controlling nature, which, Genesis says, became hostile to humanity due to the sin of Adam. Jesus is the restorer of the original order of the universe.

Jesus was not the first person in Israel's history to exhibit divine power. The feeding of the multitude is an echo of the miraculous manna in the desert and of the prophet Elisha feeding a hundred men with twenty barley loaves. The early Jewish Christians, who were very familiar with the Old Testament, saw a continuation and fulfillment of God's action in Jesus.

See Genesis 8:1; Exodus 16:4–5, 14:21; 1 Kings 17:1–6; 2 Kings 4:2–44; and Deuteronomy 11:14–15 for exhibitions of divine power in the Jewish Scriptures.

■ Read the story of the Storm at Sea in Matthew 8:23–27, and of the Walking on the Waters in Mark 6:45–52. What impression of Jesus did the evangelists try to convey?

*Power over death.* The strongest sign of Satan's reign is death, which no one can avoid. Some prophets had shown that God's power could postpone death; Elijah brings back the dead son of the widow of Zarephath, for example, and Elisha revives the son of the Shunammites. By raising the daughter of Jairus, the son of the widow of Naim and Lazarus, Jesus demonstrates the same power. Although none of these miracles permanently defeated death, they pointed to the greatest

*"By the sweat of your face shall you get bread to eat, until you return from which you were taken"* (Genesis 3:19).

miracle—his resurrection. By freely accepting death, Jesus crushed Satan forever and God's eternal life became available to all.

■ Compare the resurrection stories in 1 Kings 17:17–24; 2 Kings 4:18–37; Mark 5:35–43; and Luke 7:11–17. Which imply greater power? Why? What name would you give to the God who works these miracles?

Jesus' miracles show that he was so close to God that God's creative life flowed out to heal and liberate those who came in contact with him. His success in mastering not only sickness and possession but also nature and death reveals his vocation to destroy Satan's hold over humanity and re-establish God's life.

## FURTHER THOUGHTS ON MIRACLES

There still remain certain questions concerning Jesus' miracles that require examination. Why did Jesus try to keep his miracles secret and even refuse to work miracles at times? Why was he unable to work miracles in certain places? What practical meaning does faith in Jesus' miracles have today?

### Jesus Keeps His Miracles Quiet

Somewhere in your experience you've watched a magic show that probably mystified or amused you. Jesus was not a magician. He doesn't entertain. He saves. When you consider that if Jesus had been more popular he could have spread the kingdom even farther, it seems logical that he should have used his gifts to impress people.

But Jesus always surprises us and takes the unexpected course of action. Just as he partially concealed his teaching in parables, he often warned the people that he healed not to tell others what he had done. "He would not permit [even] the demons to speak," Mark notes, "because they knew him."

Mark 1:34

It is not certain why Jesus tried to keep his miracles quiet. Some writers say that Mark added these warnings to explain why more people didn't realize who Jesus was during his ministry. But in his complete honesty, Jesus may not have wanted people to give him a false glory, which would honor him for the material benefits his miracles brought. At the multiplication of the loaves he dashed the peoples' false hopes that his power might make their lives easier. On several occasions he actually refused to work miracles just for the sake of working miracles, for example when Satan dared him, when Herod wanted to see him work a "trick," or when the Pharisees or others asked for a "sign." In a parable, one of his characters tells why. He says that people who will not follow the ordinary path of belief in the Scriptures "will not be convinced even if one should rise from the dead."

See Mark 1:44

See Matthew 4:9, 12:38–42; Mark 8:11–13; Luke 23:6–12

Luke 16:31

Jesus understood that the ability to work miracles is of itself meaningless. Once he said, "Keep praying. . . . False messiahs and false prophets will appear performing signs and wonders to mislead . . . even the chosen. So be constantly on guard!"

Mark 13:18, 22–23

■ Read Luke 10:17–20. What should be the prime source of a Christian's joy? Does this mean that you can't be happy in this life? Explain.

## Signs of Contradiction

Jesus may have kept his miracles quiet because they often stirred up resentment, jealousy, and even hatred among those who witnessed them. It was just after the raising of Lazarus, where Jesus' divine identity shone forth most brilliantly, that he was seriously rejected and some of the Pharisees began to plot his death. The Jewish leaders understood very well what Jesus' miracles meant—that they were "parables in action." These parables taught that Jesus was the one sent to inaugurate the kingdom and to break Satan's hold. To accept Jesus was to accept salvation. Those who accepted him in faith became the nucleus of the Church. Those who said no were to share with Satan a last brief hour of seeming triumph before God would have his way.

- What responses do Jesus' miracles bring out in these passages? Matthew 8:16–17; 9:33–34; 11:20; 12:14, 24; 13:54–57.
- Name some persons who were disapproved of for trying to be good to others. Have you ever experienced opposition in doing what you felt was right? How did you react? How did Jesus react to the misunderstanding his actions aroused?

## Obstacles to Jesus' Miracles

Sometimes people made it impossible for Jesus to work miracles. He helped anyone who came to him in genuine need. But at times people were missing the one thing necessary to complete the circuit—faith.

- Look up the following passages. How does each one show that Jesus required or rewarded faith? Mark 1:40–41, 6:5–6, 9:19–23; Matthew 9:27–30; Luke 7:1–10; John 4:46–51.

## MIRACLES—A SUMMONS TO FAITH

Jesus' miracles symbolize the very meaning of his life: he is the great forgiver. In calling forth faith, they open the way for God to heal all creation through Christ.

Jesus' main intention in working cures was not to do away with suffering. After all, the people he helped would possibly get sick again, and all would die, even those he had raised from the dead. The miracles were ultimately meant to stir up faith. A miracle, then, might be defined as a visible sign of God's power that brings about the invisible sign of God's power, the miracle of faith in Jesus as the One sent by God.

People responded to the miracles with varying degrees of faith. Some, like Caiaphas, refused to believe. Some followed Jesus for the sake of material benefits but, like the multitudes at the multiplication of the loaves, many turned from him when their faith was tested. Some, like the Apostles, wavered in their faith but then gave Jesus their unflinching fidelity. The miracles they saw with their own eyes helped their faith; at the end of the last Gospel, however, Jesus praises those who do not see and yet believe.

*Caiaphas was the high priest who was perhaps the first to suggest that Jesus be killed to avoid trouble. See John 11:49ff.*

- Why should you believe without seeing?
- If you have ever experienced an unusual benefit from God, what inner transformation were you aware of? How was your life changed?
- Is Jesus still releasing the captives of Satan, opening the ears of the deaf, and giving the blind their sight? Give examples.

Jesus continues to work through the Spirit. Just as he shared the life of his Father with the people of his day, he now makes it mysteriously possible for you to experience his miracles and to work the same miracles. He opens your ears to hear the living Word of God in Scripture and gives you the eyes to see him in the sacraments. He uses you to bring consolation and healing to others. To believe that he is present in ordinary events is to accept Jesus as the Son of God, the One who still does the works of God. To say yes to this mystery is to live the petition of the Lord's Prayer— "thy kingdom come on earth as it is in heaven."

Miracles remain mysterious even after two thousand years. Evil still seems very much a part of our world. But just as Jesus' deeds in his own time were a promise of God's final victory, each "miracle" in our day brings that victory closer. "This is how we win the victory," says Saint John, "with our faith." Jesus' miracles are a call to you to believe, to be healed, and to be Christ's instrument for the healing of others.

*1 John 5:4*

## SUMMING UP

1. *Words to know*: miracle accounts, miracle (modern), miracle (biblical), evil, leprosy, living sign, exorcism, Messianic Secret, parables in action, faith healing, demoniac
2. How large a part do miracles play in the Gospel accounts?
3. What is the modern understanding of a miracle? Why do people today find it difficult to believe in miracles?
4. What was the Hebrew notion of a miracle?
5. What did Jesus' miracles call attention to? What did the evangelists call them?
6. How did the Jewish people of Jesus' time think of sickness, disaster, and death? Where did they get their idea?
7. What did the miracles of Jesus signify to the people of Israel who had faith?
8. Why wasn't Jesus satisfied with only preaching about the kingdom?
9. What did the miracles reveal about the Father?
10. How do each of the four types of miracles Jesus worked throw light on the mystery of the kingdom Jesus was establishing?
11. Why did Jesus try to keep his miracles quiet?
12. What messages did Jesus' "parables in action" send to the religious authorities of Israel?
13. How can Jesus' power be hindered? What was the ultimate purpose of his miracles?
14. How do Jesus' miracles symbolize the meaning of his life?
15. What do Jesus' miracles ask of you today?

### Think/Talk/Write

1. What do you think about the belief in faith-healing, which affirms that faith can triumph over any illness? What do you think about those who believe it is wrong to permit blood transfusions, to perform surgery, or to take medicine?
2. If it could be proved that all demoniacs in Galilee were merely victims of nerve disease, would that fact lessen the sign value of Jesus' cures? Why or why not? What is the sign value of Jesus' miracles?

## Activities

1. Mother Teresa of Calcutta tells the story of her kitchen for the poor running out of food one Friday. For the first time in twenty-five years, the seven thousand people who came daily would not be fed. Mother Teresa prayed. By a previous arrangement with the government, any schools with a surplus of bread regularly sent it to her kitchens. That Friday, thousands of loaves poured in, more than enough for the weekend.
   a. Was this incident a miracle? Why or why not?
   b. Ask several people if they've ever experienced a "private miracle." Share your experiences with the class.
2. Make a chart of all the miracles in any one Gospel, dividing them according to the four types. Next to each type, write the deeper significance of all the miracles in that category.

## Scripture Search

Like the parables, Jesus' miracles could be read on two levels—the literal level of what actually happened and the meaning level, which taught some lesson. All the evangelists capture both levels in their reports. Research the following passages to learn the full significance of Jesus' miracles.

1. Read the following passages and then tell how the cures are accomplished, what the diseases symbolize, and what Jesus' action symbolizes in each case: Mark 7:31–36; Luke 7:11–16; John 5:1–15.
2. After unsuccessfully treating a man with severe stomach cramps for two years, the doctor called the man's minister. "I can't do anything for my patient," he said, "unless he returns the inheritance he cheated his sister out of. Maybe you can help him." How does the miracle in Luke 5:17–25 relate to this story?
3. In the first three quarters of the Book of Signs in John's Gospel (1:19–12:50), Jesus' actions are more symbolic than in the synoptics. They are called signs because they point out who Jesus is. Read the account of the multiplication of the loaves in all four evangelists (Mark 6:33–44, 8:14–21; Matthew 14:13–21; Luke 9:10–17; John 6:1–14, 22–59) and tell which accounts obviously explain the meaning of Jesus' actions and which only suggest it. What is the symbolic meaning? How can you "multiply bread" in our day?

**TEN**

Are you saved?

What are you saved from and for?

How are you saved?

What do you believe about heaven and hell?

Why is the Paschal Mystery central to Christian life?

How does the knowledge that you are saved affect your life?

*Blessed be the Lord, the God of Israel;*
*he has come to his people and set them free.*
*He has raised up for us a mighty savior,*
*born of the house of his servant David.*
*Through his holy prophets he promised of old*
*that he would save us from our enemies,*
*from the hands of all who hate us.*
*He promised to show mercy to our fathers*
*and to remember his holy covenant.*
*This was the oath he swore to our father Abraham:*
*to set us free from the hands of our enemies. . . .*
*In the tender compassion of our God*
*the dawn from on high shall break upon us*
*to shine on those who dwell in darkness and the shadow of death,*
*and to guide our feet into the way of peace.*

(Canticle of Zechariah)

# The Paschal Mystery

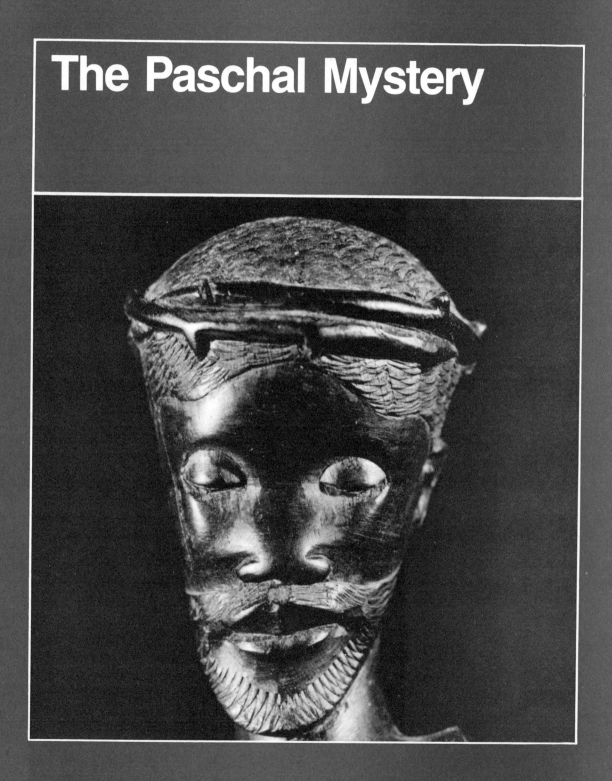

God so loved the world that he gave his only Son, that whoever believes in him may not die but may have eternal life.

(JOHN 3:16)

## ARE YOU SAVED?

For the Jews of the Old Testament, the word *salvation* signified God's power to free them from oppression and liberate them from their enemies. Salvation was dependent on their willingness to repent and to be obedient to God's commandments.

For Christians, Jesus is the source of salvation. Except for the Christmas stories, the Gospels directly refer to Jesus as "Savior" only once, but the Epistles and Acts use the title twenty-one times. Later Christian writers use it even more extensively.

You learned that the "saving deeds" of Jesus—his cures—were a sign of spiritual healing. They showed God's power and required a response of faith. In Luke's Gospel, Jesus is not just the Savior, he is the embodiment of salvation. On entering Zaccheus' house, he says, "Today salvation has come to this house." Jesus' greatest healing action, however, was accomplished on the cross. "It is through his blood that we have been redeemed," writes Saint Paul. But salvation through

Luke 19:9

Ephesians 1:7

184 JESUS

Jesus is not dependent on anything you do. It is a pure gift, something humanly impossible that is made possible by God.

See Matthew 19:26

- At one time or another, everyone has experienced a feeling of being saved from a disaster. What tragedies have you been rescued from? How did you feel?
- What were you taught about redemption—that is, about being saved? What are you saved from? What are you saved for?

## What Are You Saved From?

While many people pray to be saved from sickness, unemployment, personal catastrophes, losses, or evil, Jesus came primarily to save us from sin. By overcom-

ing what is contrary to God within us—evil—he brings all things back into harmony with God's plan and heals the deepest sources of human unhappiness.

Genesis 3:1–7

The Genesis story tells what sin is. The serpent in the Garden of Eden presents the temptation to Adam and Eve (man and woman) to follow their own ideas rather than God's. Their disobedience is known as the Fall. The imagery of the tree representing the knowledge of good and evil symbolizes each individual's desire to be independent of God rather than to do his will. But human ideas are not so important as God's. In fact, they tend to backfire and lead people to greed and selfishness. These ideas bring about their own self-destruction in war, crime, violence, fraud, deceit, distrust, and the neglect of others. Each person coming into the world is influenced and limited by these evils, and so personal sin leads us away from union with God and others, and destroys our personal peace.

All this adds to the tangled web of evil and suffering already present in the world. The evils of corruption cannot be cured by mere human effort. Redemption must come from a greater-than-human healing source.

In winning salvation, Jesus, the God-man, made it possible for everyone to be reunited with God, to move out of selfish isolation, and to contribute to the salvation of others. All that is required is faith in Jesus as your Savior.

- What fears, pressures, weaknesses, or needs have the power to draw you away from Christ?
- What practical effects does knowing you are saved have on your life? How can you tell when people are "saved"?
- Pause for a moment to speak to Christ about your great desire to follow him. Place the person deep within you in contact with him. Use your own words or these words of the Communion of the Mass: Lord Jesus Christ, Son of the Living God, free me from all my sins and from every evil. Keep me faithful to your teaching and never let me be parted from you.

## WHAT ABOUT THE AFTERLIFE?

What do you believe about the afterlife? State whether you agree or disagree with the following positions.

1. Heaven is an eternal state but we don't know what it is like.
2. There is a hell and there are people in it.
3. There is a hell, but we don't know if anyone is in it.
4. Life will continue forever after death for those who believe in Jesus and follow his commandments.
5. Hell is annihilation—the total discontinuance of life and existence.
6. Hell is a possibility for everyone, but Christ has rescued everyone from it.
7. Heaven is a possibility for everyone.
8. Heaven and hell are here, not in the afterlife.
9. Heaven and hell begin here and continue into the afterlife.
10. Not everyone will receive eternal life.

## Hell

We do not know very much about the afterlife. Some of Jesus' words in Saint John imply that those who cut themselves off from God will just be deprived of life after death, but we can't take these words too literally because, in the synoptics, Jesus uses many images to show that loss of eternal life is something more painful than merely not living on.

Jesus describes the permanent loss of God quite vividly. He says it is a continual death, like burning forever in an unquenchable fire or in the huge blast furnaces such as Israel used for smelting iron. At least a dozen times he calls hell the flaming valley of Gehenna. This valley was the garbage dump of Jerusalem in Jesus' day, but it had in years gone by been a pagan place of human sacrifice—a place utterly repulsive to every Jew. To describe the loss of salvation, Jesus also uses images of a prison with a torture chamber and chains, and he pictures the misery in the kingdom of the dead by sounds of endless weeping and gnashing of teeth. Those who refuse to live the life of the Spirit, he says, enter into a process of unending corruption. He borrows Isaiah's image when he warns that the worms which feed on the corpses in the afterlife will never die. Sometimes he depicts the dwelling of the damned as a deep pit which, despite its flames, is a place of utter darkness where the wicked are destroyed body and soul.

You see the contradictions—eternal death and darkness on the one hand, and eternal fire on the other. The evangelists could not find the words to convey the hell of losing God's friendship forever. By using these negative images, Jesus highlights the urgency of remaining friends with God. A healthy fear of hell is a step toward loving God.

## Heaven

Jesus' revelation of what it means to be saved doesn't end with the torments of hell or promises of a better life here. There's more. The Gospels are full of vivid descriptions of what life in his Father's kingdom is like.

John 10:10

For Jesus, life and salvation are synonymous. "I have come that you may have life," he said. Salvation is not just mere survival, as the Jews had so long believed, and it is not just not dying. Jesus revealed that God's plan includes a life we cannot imagine.

*The Jews believed that the dead lived on in a numb state of nonactivity in the land of the dead, called Sheol.*

In a moment of deep personal prayer, Saint Paul once caught a glimpse of heaven and wrote to the Church in Corinth, "Eye has not seen, ear has not heard, nor has it so much as dawned on anyone what God has prepared for those who love him."

1 Corinthians 2:9

Jesus did much more than catch a glimpse of the Father. He was in the Father and the Father was in him. "No one knows the Father except the Son," Saint Luke

Luke 10:22

wrote. Jesus revealed the indescribable life of heaven with the Father in images we can identify with. They all revolve around love and friendship. He said his Father's kingdom is like a banquet where friends gather to have fun and laugh as they eat and drink the finest bread and the best wine. He himself often enjoyed taking his meals with others.

Probably nothing celebrates ongoing life so well as a marriage. Jesus said the kingdom is like a bridegroom going on to meet his bride. He also compared heaven to an eternal wedding reception. The happiness of the bride and groom and all their relatives and friends is only a dim shadow of the joy of living in his Father's kingdom.

The most astounding revelation, however, is that Jesus claims to be able to give us this life despite Satan's great power. "I am the life," he said. He assures us that we possess this life the instant we are joined to him. And we are saved every moment that we stay close to him and try to avoid sin.

Jesus has saved us for a life of eternal love in the company of his Father. Or, as Saint Paul so beautifully puts it, "You can think of yourselves as dead so far as sin is concerned, but living in fellowship with God through Christ Jesus."

John 14:6

Romans 6:11 (Good News)

- Do you believe that heaven really begins here on earth for the just? Do they have it better than people who deliberately choose to sin?
- Return to the questions about redemption that appear near the beginning of this section. How would you answer them now?
- What are some ways to recognize the personal weaknesses that might separate you from Christ? What things can you do to strengthen yourself against these weaknesses?
- When were you united with Christ's death and resurrection?

# THE MYSTERY OF DEATH AND RESURRECTION

If Jesus has saved the world, why is there still so much evil? Even baptism and faith do not, as if by magic, clean up the world.

As you have seen, one reason for the continuance of evil is that God cannot restrict people's freedom if he is to be genuinely loved. They have the tremendous power to accept or reject their creator. The other answer is locked in the mystery of how things are now that sin has entered the world. It is that mystery which you will now explore.

## The Sign of Total Weakness

On the spire of every Catholic church, in a prominent place in every sanctuary, at the head of every procession, on the chest of every bishop you find the crucifix. The cross of Jesus is the central symbol of Christianity. Why?

*A crucifix is a cross with the crucified body of Jesus (the corpus) affixed to it.*

- Every religion has its identifying symbol. The Muslims have the star and the crescent, Buddhists the eight-spoked wheel, and Jews the six-pointed star. What does the central symbol of Christianity say about Christianity?

Any Christian will instantly answer that it was by his death on the cross that Jesus took away the sins of the world. You have heard it hundreds of times, but have you ever seriously asked the meaning of this action?

*To take away the sins of the world means to reunite the human race with God.*

To say that Jesus is God and redeemed the world by his divine power is not enough. It is true that Jesus could have crushed Satan forever by a single, powerful word. Or, as he himself said at his capture, he could have asked his Father "to provide at a moment's notice more than twelve legions of angels." But one hard look at the crucifix will show that the words Jesus utters on the cross are not words of power. They are an admission of complete and total weakness. The crucifixion is the

Matthew 26:53

story of total failure and the cruelest of human deaths. The challenge is to try to grasp what was going on at the crucifixion. What *was* the Father's plan to redeem the world?

A quick look at the cycle of death and resurrection as it occurs in the natural world may help give you additional insight into the mystery of why Jesus died to save us.

## Parallels in Nature

The mysterious contradiction of life arising from death has been part of human understanding for a long time. In an ancient Egyptian myth, the phoenix, a bird resembling an eagle, burns itself to death every five hundred years to make possible the birth of a new phoenix out of its ashes. The way the Egyptians saw it, dust and ashes—the product of death—were the raw materials of new life. The account of creation in Genesis likewise uses the symbolism of dust and earth as primary sources of human life.

For centuries the Chinese have held their festivals of life not in summer, but in the dead of winter. They know that the lifelessness of the cold earth is only an illusion. In the deep winter stillness, life gathers momentum to "spring" into activity. When do they honor their dead? In the middle of summer when everyone feels most alive. That's the way it is, they say: life in death and death in life—but only the wise can see it.

Many things suggest that life mysteriously grows out of death. Take, for instance, the birth of each day. Every morning, light and life win out over night and death. Seeds, caterpillars, and flowers must "die" to go on living. Even the atom must be smashed to release its tremendous store of energy.

■ What other examples of life arising from death does nature produce?

### Parallels in Human Life

Human life itself parallels nature in its death-to-life pattern. From its first breath, a child must "die" to the dark, warm security of its mother's body in order to experience the fresh air and risk-filled freedom of a new world. Teenagers shed the limited horizons of childhood for the wide open but sometimes frightening spaces of adult possibilities. Everyone requires a certain amount of deathlike sleep in order to be productive.

In fact, growing into the stimulating life of any new experience requires a lot of dying. Consider the painful stiffness and sore muscles of the high school football player as he trains for the season. A doctor, teacher, pianist, ballerina, sister, brother, or priest puts in years of hard study and apprenticeship before acquiring the freedom to live his or her chosen life. The gift of life often arrives in a box marked "Sorrow," "Pain," or "Hard Work."

And, odd as it may seem, it often takes obstacles to spur people to excellence. Some injured Olympic skiers have achieved better downhill speeds than people with

two perfectly healthy legs. It is well known that De-
mosthenes, the famous Greek orator who was born with
a lisp, improved his faulty enunciation by increasing
his disability: he practiced speaking with pebbles in
his mouth. Although the famous Babe Ruth hit 714
home runs, he struck out 330 times in the effort. Ernest
Hemingway, the American novelist who won the 1954
Nobel Prize in literature, had to rewrite the last chapter
of one of his best books, *A Farewell to Arms,* thirty-
nine times. In our world, suffering seems to be a mysteriously necessary ingredient of glory.

- What successes have you heard of or experienced
  yourself as a direct result of a drawback?
- What "deaths" do some people you know willingly endure for the rewards of vocation, career,
  hobby, or sports?

## THE PASCHAL MYSTERY

Like all of us, Jesus experienced many lesser deaths
and resurrections, but the last event of his life plunged
him most deeply into the mystery. This event, known

as the Paschal Mystery, was the climax of his life and mission. His suffering, death, and resurrection, as well as his ascension to glory and sending of the Spirit, were a single action—a journey from the Land of the Dead to eternal life. By this "passover" Jesus saved the world.

## The Mystery

We call the death and resurrection of Jesus the Paschal Mystery for two reasons. First, it is a mystery. *Mystery,* from the Greek word *mysterion,* means "secret thing." The "secret" was God's plan to save the world. God had always willed our salvation, even before the first sin, but as a teacher cannot present the mysteries of algebra or geometry to first-graders, so God could only reveal his plan to the human race on a gradual basis. He had to wait until his people were ready to encounter the living God.

*The Israelites were ready to pass from a seminomadic life to a more stable form of agricultural life when God called Abraham.*

After perhaps fifty thousand years or more, God chose to entrust the knowledge of his plan to Israel. He gave them prophets who passed along the hope of a savior. The mystery was then gradually unfolded over a period of nearly two thousand years. Finally, when the time was right, God revealed his entire plan, which was to save the world through Jesus' death and resurrection.

Mark 4:11

One day Jesus said to his disciples, "To you the mystery [secret] of the reign of God has been confided. To the others outside, it is all presented in parables"—that is, in ways they couldn't easily understand.

*The outsiders do not have faith.*

- Why do you think it was so hard to figure out the meaning of the crucifixion and the resurrection?

## The Passover

The second reason why Jesus' death and resurrection is called the Paschal Mystery is that Jesus' final acts bear a mysterious resemblance to the Jewish Passover, or Pasch, which in Hebrew is known as *Pesah.* This word originally meant "a limp or kind of hopping jump" and described an action that reminded the Israelites of the night the Angel of Death had "jumped" or "passed" over the Hebrew houses whose doorposts had been smeared with the blood of a lamb sacrificed in obedience to Yahweh's command.

Because of his fear of the growing numbers of Hebrews, the pharaoh had ordered the massacre of all newborn Hebrew sons. This would have led to the extinction of the Israelites as a people. On the historic evening of the Passover, the plague that killed the first-born sons of Egypt forced the pharaoh to release the Israelites from slavery. The Chosen People were saved to carry out the plan of God. It was a new creation.

So, too, in the Paschal Mystery. By the blood of Jesus smeared on the cross, the Angel of Death "passed over" every person in the human race. The sacrifice of the Lamb of God forced Satan to release the death grip he had held so long. Now we are no longer confined to a life bound by death but are free to live the eternal life of the Spirit. It, too, is like a new creation. No longer are we only the sons and daughters of Adam and Eve, the servants of the devil, but a new people, the children

The plan of God is to bring every person into his kingdom.

of God, fit to carry out the plan of God until the end of time.

By leading the Israelites through the Red Sea, God opened their way to the Promised Land. In a covenant made through Moses and sealed in the blood of animals, God promised to be their God and to give them every help to reach that land.

Jesus, too, opened the way back to the Father. Through the waters of baptism Jesus leads his people into the kingdom of peace and love lost in paradise. Jesus makes a new and eternal covenant between God and the Chosen People he has formed, sealing it in his own blood. The animal sacrifices of the Old Testament could hardly have accomplished the salvation of the world, but Jesus' free and personal sacrifice was more than sufficient to crush Satan's power forever and take away the sin of the world.

The first Passover had cost God nothing. In the second, God's love is revealed as never before. He gave his only Son for love of the human race. What did he ask of Jesus? Suffering? No, he asked only for his obedience. Jesus' work was to reverse the disobedience of Adam and Eve.

In accepting the death that came to him because others were free to reject God's love, Jesus willingly fit himself into the death-life pattern of the world his Father had created. He had to close his eyes to this life to win eternal life. He had to break all ties with earth to establish a new relationship with heaven. "Son though he was, he learned obedience by what he suffered," the Letter to the Hebrews says.

Only from the cross—the lowest position on earth—could Jesus reach even the lowest sinners to gather them into his Father's saving love. Thus he became the second, or new, Adam in two ways: as the head of a new race who would be obedient to the Father instead of rebellious as Adam was, and as a source rather than a destroyer of eternal life for us all. It is all this that makes the Paschal Mystery the central event of the Christian life. By death, Jesus brought the world to resurrection.

*In pride, Adam had eaten from the forbidden tree. In humility, Jesus accepted the tree on which he died.*

JESUS

## Why Death?

It may still not be clear to you why Jesus had to die to do this. Couldn't there have been some other way? Evidently not, in this world.

Just as a caterpillar casts off its furry cloak and temporarily rests in the darkness of a cocoon in order to be released into the new and free life of a butterfly, so too was Jesus wound around with a shroud and plunged into the dark and still tomb for three days. He broke open the gates of the Land of the Dead and passed over into life. In the creed, Christians affirm that Jesus "descended into hell" before rising on the third day.

A *shroud* is the cloth in which ancient people wrapped their dead to prepare them for burial.

These are symbolic ways of expressing what took place in the Paschal Mystery. Actually, it is inexpressible: power in weakness, life in death. We don't have the words for it. Death was the only way Jesus could save us because it was the only way he could show that God was the absolute center of his life. On the cross he had no other source of hope but his Father. The moment Jesus died, God's powerful Spirit-life, which had always filled him but which had been hidden by his humanity, was released and flooded the world. Only by laying down his life could Jesus show how much the Father loved us—completely. There was nothing more he could have done to show his love for us. "There is no greater love than this: to lay down one's life for one's friends."

John 15:13

By the total gift of himself, Jesus was able to breathe God's Spirit and life back into every person who accepts that gift. At the instant of Jesus' death, we were empowered to pass over with him from death to life. "If we have died with Christ," says the letter to the Romans, "we believe that we are also to live with him." For the unsurpassable gift of the Paschal lamb slain for us, the Church on Easter sings out, "Alleluia!"

Romans 6:8

- How importantly do Lent and Easter figure in your life? What practical effects do they have?
- Think of five loving things you have done for someone recently. In your journal or in a small

group, discuss what effect your actions had on the other persons. How did your action affect you? What price did you have to pay? Was it worth it? Why or why not? How much do you think you might be personally willing to suffer for a friend?

## MAKING CHRIST'S STORY YOUR OWN

*It has been said that suffering makes one either bitter or better.*

In the way he faces his crisis, Jesus teaches that even if suffering can't always be understood, it can be turned to good. Accepting hardship in union with Jesus—which means accepting it with the same humility, love, and forgiveness that he did—you can become more human and more like Christ. Suffering can draw you closer to God and put great peace into your life, even though the pain may not be lessened by your acceptance of it. People with a deep understanding and appreciation of the role of suffering in life are generally considered to be wise.

*To think and act in Jesus' spirit is to become more human, because Jesus was the most human person ever to live.*

It was by his death that Jesus made it possible for any action you do to become a pleasing gift to God. In the Eucharistic Prayer III, the priest asks the Father to make the gifts of bread and wine holy so that our lives may become the very body and blood of Christ, our Paschal sacrifice. The more you make Jesus' story your own, and the more closely you are linked with the Father as his son or daughter, the more you can share in the Paschal Mystery and help heal the world. This is what being a Christian is all about.

*Mary and the Apostles are honored above the other saints because they had a privileged role in the Paschal Mystery.*

### A Source of Christian Joy

*Acts 5:41 (the Name is a reference to Jesus).*

*2 Corinthians 11:24–27*

The Apostles understood this mystery so well that they were full of joy when they left the Sanhedrin after being flogged "for the sake of the Name." They felt that by their sufferings they were drawn into the events of the crucifixion and the resurrection. Saint Paul boasts of

JESUS

suffering lashings, shipwreck, stoning, hunger, and thirst for Christ.

And so, through the eyes of faith, the early Church discovered in the death of Jesus something much more than a horribly humiliating end. It was more than that, we know, by the fact that the evangelists do not dwell on Jesus' sufferings, but merely state them as objectively as possible. Rather, they saw Calvary and Easter in their deeper, mystical meaning, as one glorious, redeeming action—the Paschal Mystery. Through this human-divine event, the salvation of the world according to the secret plan of God was finally fulfilled in Jesus and continued in a mysterious way in their own lives.

Many of the early Christians freely and joyfully offered themselves, as Jesus had, when called to martyrdom during the persecutions. And through the centuries, the new people of God have understood and entered into the meaning of suffering with and in Jesus.

*Martyrs* are people who voluntarily suffer death as the penalty for refusing to renounce their religious beliefs.

John 11:25

## Your Daily Cross

Hardship of the daily kind is not unique to Christians. But through Jesus you have been shown a way to use it. Every "cross" (or crisis), large or small, is a call to make the Paschal journey to conversion. It has three stages. In *setting out,* you recognize that something must be left behind. In the *descent* (or transition) into hell, you experience the turmoil and pain of renunciation. Finally, with *submission,* or a "yes" to God, you rise to freedom and new life.

It is true that in the Paschal Mystery you bring Christ's sufferings to completion. However, Jesus said "I am the resurrection," not "I am the death." The crucifixion was not the end for Jesus; it was the beginning of new freedom and a new and better life. The same goes for the followers of Jesus who suffer in his name— they grow in their spiritual friendship with the only source of eternal life.

## SUMMING UP

1. *Words to know:* salvation, redemption, the Fall, crucifix, phoenix, Paschal Mystery, mystery, Passover, Lamb of God, descent into hell, martyrdom, cross, Gehenna, fellowship
2. What does salvation mean to Christians? What are we saved from?
3. What is the Fall of Adam and Eve? What effects did it have?
4. Why do we need salvation?
5. Why is the cross the central symbol of Christianity?
6. What parallels between the Paschal Mystery can be found in nature and in human life?
7. Make a chart of some parallels between the Paschal Mystery and the original Jewish Passover. Why is Jesus' passage from death a mystery?
8. What was the central event of Christ's mission? Why was it so important?
9. What does the term Paschal Mystery mean to you?
10. Why did Jesus have to die to save the world?
11. How can Christians share in the Paschal Mystery?
12. What are the stages of conversion?
13. What symbolism do you find in the cross?
14. What images does the New Testament use for heaven and hell? Why did the evangelists include them?

### Think/Talk/Write

1. Do you agree that the Paschal Mystery is the central mystery in a Christian's life? Why or why not? If not, what mystery would you substitute?
2. The help God gave the Israelites on their journey to the Promised Land was his presence, the commandments, manna, and assistance in fighting their enemies. What help does God give his new Chosen People on their journey?
3. Sometimes we bring on our own suffering. A group of students who vandalized a school building were put into a correctional school, where they were deprived of normal family life. Their reputations and records were ruined, and their parents shared the humiliation.

Can the students unite their deserved sufferings with Christ in the Paschal Mystery, or can only innocent suffering be used? Is it fair for parents to suffer for their children's actions? What does Christ's attitude toward his cross say to those who suffer through no fault of their own? Do you believe that accidents, diseases, birth defects, or other misfortunes are true evils? Why or why not?

4. What would you say or do to be of help to someone who either directly or indirectly conveys to you the feeling that "no one really cares a hoot about me"?

5. If you've read books, seen movies, or read articles about people confined to prison, sickbeds, or mental institutions, relate some of the sufferings they endure. What can you as a young person do to help them benefit from their suffering?

## Activities

1. From newspapers, magazines, TV, or films, make a collection of incidents that represent the mystery of life from death. Explain each briefly.

2. Write an original prayer or poem about the Paschal Mystery that might be used as a meditation after Communion during a class Mass.

## Scripture Search

1. Most people keep a list of "Things to Do" to make sure they accomplish their plans. God's plans to save the world were recorded in the Old Testament. Isaiah and the Psalmist were particularly fond of jotting down descriptions of the coming Redeemer. Of course, their vision of this "Suffering Servant of the Lord" was quite vague, but you may be able to pick out the features of the crucified and risen Jesus between the lines. Read the following passages and note which details of the prophecy Jesus fulfilled: Isaiah 50:4–11 (the speaker is the Servant); Isaiah 52:13–15 (the speaker is Yahweh); Isaiah 53:1–12 (the speakers are unidentified persons); Psalm 22; Psalm 88.

2. Saint Paul had brilliant insights into the Paschal Mystery. Read Ephesians 1 and 2, and find five references to it.

## ELEVEN

Why would a person like Jesus be put to death?

How much did Jesus realize what would happen to him?

What was the point of the transfiguration?

What events turned the tense situation in Jerusalem into a crisis?

What did Jesus do on his last night on earth?

*Teach me, my Lord, to be gentle*
*In all the events of life—*
   *in disappointments,*
   *in the thoughtlessness of others,*
   *in the insincerity of those I trusted,*
   *in the unfaithfulness of those on whom I relied.*
*Let me put myself aside,*
   *to think of the happiness of others,*
   *to hide my little pains and heartaches,*
   *so that I may be the only one to suffer from them.*
*Teach me to profit by the suffering that comes across my path.*
*May no one be less good for having come within my influence,*
*no one less pure, less true, less kind, less noble*
*for having been a fellow traveler*
*in our journey toward eternal life.*

# Rejection and Covenant Love

O Lord, how many are my adversaries! Many rise up against me!
. . . But you, O Lord, are my shield. . . . Upon your people be your
blessing!

(PSALM 3:1, 4, 9)

## THE MYSTERY OF REJECTION

Why would someone like Jesus have been put to death?
The Gospels portray him as a person of complete honesty, deep sincerity, and compassionate concern to
whom the rich, the poor, and even outcasts turned for
help. But the Gospels also agree that he was executed
as a criminal and abandoned by practically all his
friends, and that he died apparently rejected by God.
How did such a thing come about? And how did Jesus
react to his failure?

- If you've ever seen an innocent person who was
  made to suffer in some way, describe how you felt
  about it.

## Signs of Trouble

Long before these final events, the Apostles should have suspected the approaching storm.

From the very first days of Jesus' public life, there had been opposition. Luke says that although many marveled when Jesus taught at Nazareth, the whole congregation "rose up and expelled him from the town." And, witnessing his miracles, the visiting scribes from Jerusalem asserted that he was "possessed by Beelzebub." He was accused of being the devil.

Luke 4:29

Mark 3:22

Jesus was a sign of contradiction for the Jews. He showed great reverence for the Law, but criticized the people's legalistic interpretation of it. If a person suffered on the Sabbath, Jesus put charity before the rule that forbade work on the Sabbath and made the cure. He pointed out that making an offering to the Temple did not excuse children from caring for parents in their old age, no matter what the scribes taught. He also ranked fulfillment of a human need like hunger as more important than the ritual of hand washing, and he freely touched the sick to help them, despite the "unlawfulness" of such actions.

*Legalism* is an excessive concern with law for its own sake.

*Ritual laws were ceremonies—like washing three times—that were given a religious meaning and had become traditions.*

Besides setting aside the ceremonial laws in favor of charity, Jesus actually corrected the law of Moses. In matters such as divorce and vengeance, he pointed out that immorality consists of evil within one's heart. He called for sincere love of God, not mere mechanical fulfillment of rules. In addition, his personal association with sinners dramatized his teaching of God's universal Fatherhood and love, and at the same time was a criticism of the religious leaders who rejected people because of their poverty, disease, occupation, or alleged sinfulness.

But the crux of the matter was that Jesus set himself up as someone authorized to forgive sin. Since this power belonged to God alone, Jesus was claiming divine power! To the Jews, this was blasphemy.

In relation to Jesus, *blasphemy* is the claiming for oneself of the attributes and rights of God.

Thus Jesus posed a threat to the religious leaders. If what he claimed was true (and his miracles seemed to indicate God's approval), they should have listened to him and encouraged the people to follow him. But a Messiah who taught a "new way" would threaten their authority with the people. Also, the last thing they wanted was a messianic rebellion; allowing "the whole world to believe in him" would probably result in the destruction of the Temple by Rome and the exile of all the Jewish leaders. Thus they set out to relieve themselves of this danger by catching Jesus in his words. The mystery of the Chosen People's rejection of their Messiah began to unfold.

John 11:48

## THEY WATCHED HIM CLOSELY

Mark 3:2; Luke 6:7

All three synoptics report that the religious leaders "watched" Jesus. People who are persistent usually find what they are looking for. The scribes and Pharisees were persistent, but they were not successful.

In the synagogues and on the road, they challenged Jesus on many topics. Even such an apparently harmless question as "Which is the greatest commandment?" was a test. They wanted to see if Jesus could summarize hundreds of pages of Jewish Scripture in a phrase. To their surprise, they were unable to outwit him. And, while showing a brilliant mastery of the Law, he often revealed the superficiality of his opponents' knowledge.

*See, for instance, how Jesus handles the interpretation of Psalm 110 in Matthew 22:45.*

When Jesus outshone his opponents in these debates, he must have done so with a heavy heart. One of his last parables—the parable of the Vineyard—revealed that he had a clear grasp of what these confrontations were leading to. It was a devastating condemnation of his own people, but it was also a last call to Israel to recognize him as God's Son.

- To find out the topics used to test Jesus, read Matthew 19:1–12 and 22:15–46 and Luke 6:1–5.
- Read Jesus' harshest condemnation of the Pharisees in Matthew 23:1–36, and list the things Jesus criticizes in them.

## Parable of the Vineyard

In the parable of the Vineyard, Jesus made the point that God would reject Israel because of its rejection of him. Because of the shortage of water in the Near East and the importance of grapes for wine, Jewish Scriptures often referred to Israel as a vineyard.

Matthew 21:33–45

Isaiah 5:1–7; Psalm 80:9–16

The Pharisees understood the parable and regarded it as blasphemous. Their reaction was to step up plans for getting rid of Jesus. They tried to arrest him, Mark wrote, because they felt he had told this parable to turn people against them. However, they were afraid of the crowd.

- Read the parable in Matthew 21:33–45. Who are the absentee landlord, the slaves, the tenant farmers, and the others who produce a rich harvest? What was Jesus saying?
- If you had been a Jewish leader, how do you think you would have felt about Jesus?

## PREPARATION FOR THE ORDEAL

### The Predictions

The turning point of Jesus' ministry came at Caesarea Philippi when Peter, the spokesman for the Apostles, openly acknowledged that Jesus was the Messiah. It was a high point in Jesus' teaching because his disciples recognized him as the Messiah, but it was also the beginning of the end. Matthew wrote, "From then on Jesus started to indicate to his disciples that he must go to Jerusalem and . . . be put to death." Immediately after, Jesus privately began to prepare his disciples for the ordeal ahead.

Matthew 16:21

The evangelists condensed what must have been several warnings of his coming passion into three "predictions," each of which consisted of a prediction, a misunderstanding, and an instruction. After one of

Matthew 16:23

these predictions, Peter took Jesus aside to protest. Jesus reprimanded him: "Get out of my sight, you satan! . . . You are not judging by God's standards but by man's."

Matthew 16:24–25

Jesus then instructed his disciples in the doctrine of the cross: "If a man wishes to come after me, he must deny his very self, take up his cross, and begin to follow in my footsteps. Whoever would save his life will lose it, but whoever loses his life for my sake will find it." Jesus well understood his own teaching—that the grain of wheat must die before it can bear fruit.

■ What does Jesus mean by "God's standards" and "man's"? How likely is it that good Christians would judge by "man's standards"? What do you understand by the "doctrine of the cross"?

## The Transfiguration

*Transfiguration* is a marked change of appearance.

In the transfiguration, Jesus strengthened the faith of his Apostles for the test it would soon be put to. About a week after Peter's confession that Jesus was the Messiah, Jesus took his three closest disciples—Peter, James, and John—up to a mountain. There, while praying, he was transfigured before them.

*Although Mount Tabor is referred to as the mount of the transfiguration, at that time the Apostles were in Caesaria, so the place was probably Mount Hermon.*

A comparison with an incident that occurred in France in 1912 may help you to understand the event. A wealthy couple—Felix and Elizabeth Leseur—visited Lourdes in that year. Felix Leseur, a non-Catholic, watched from a distance as his wife, a religious woman, prayed at the grotto. Kneeling there, quite motionless and completely absorbed in her contemplation, she seemed to glow with a radiance that her husband could not explain. Although he initially dismissed the incident, he never really forgot it, and the memory of it brought about his conversion a few years after Elizabeth's death.

If such transformations occur when saintly people touch God in prayer, how much greater must the glory of God have shone in Jesus, his Son, as he prayed. Luke wrote that "while [Jesus] was praying, his face changed in appearance and his clothes became dazzlingly white." White clothing is a frequent image in Scripture for otherworldly glory.

Luke 9:29

What the actual experience of this occasion was like, however, we cannot tell. After the resurrection, the Apostles understood that it had been an important revelation of Jesus as the Messiah and the Son of God.

The Apostles later compared their experience to the deeply religious experiences of Moses and Elijah when they spoke with God on the Mounts of Sinai and Horeb. The Apostles also went up onto a mountain, a kind of New Sinai, and were overshadowed by the cloud of God's glory. They saw Moses and Elijah, who represented the Law and the prophets. The cloud, which symbolized God's presence, told them, "This is my Son, my Chosen One. Listen to him." Jesus was revealed not only as the Messiah, but as the prophet promised in Deuteronomy: "A prophet like me will the Lord, your God, raise up for you from among your own kinsmen; to him you shall listen."

*In Scripture, mountains are the usual meeting places with God. See Exodus 24:15–18 and 1 Kings 19:9–13.*

Luke 9:35

Deuteronomy 18:15

The Apostles later understood that this revelation of the Old Testament referred to Jesus. It is significant that the law of Moses and the coming of Elijah are mentioned together in the last verses of the Old Testament. It shows that Jesus fulfills the Old Testament as he opens the New.

Malachi 3:21–24

At the actual time of the transfiguration, the Apostles Peter, James, and John fell sound asleep, just as they did later during Jesus' agony in the Garden. There is a definite connection between the glory they witness here and the weakness they see in Jesus when he anguishes over his death.

Luke recorded that when the Apostles awoke, they saw two men. Jesus spoke to the heavenly visitors about how he would fulfill God's purpose by his death in Jerusalem and by his resurrection. This religious experience filled Peter with such happiness that he asked to build three tents and to stay there on the mountain with Jesus. He wanted to keep Jesus in his glorified

See Luke 9:28–36

*The Tent of Meeting was the place where the Israelites experienced God's presence in a special way.*

state permanently. But Jesus knew that before the final day of glory he would have to suffer.

The transfiguration, then, was a focal point in the revelation of the kingdom of God. It placed Jesus at the center of history, for it looked back to show how Christ fulfilled the Old Testament and it looked ahead to the great revealing events of the cross, the resurrection, the ascension, and the Second Coming.

- Read about the transfiguration in Luke 9:28–36 and Mark 9:2–8. What differences do you notice?
- Do you react to the revelation in this event with strong belief, wonder, disbelief, indifference, gratitude, or some other emotion? Why? What attitudes can the drowsiness of the Apostles represent?

## The Eve of the Storm

As Jesus journeyed to Jerusalem for the Passover, three events brought the opposition movement to a head: the raising of Lazarus, the triumphal entry into Jerusalem, and the cleansing of the Temple.

Jesus was summoned to Bethany, where he raised his friend, Lazarus, who had been dead three days. When the chief priests heard of it, they called a meeting of the Sanhedrin. "If we let him go on like this," they said, "the whole world will believe in him. Then the Romans will come in and sweep away our sanctuary and our nation." From that day onward, their plan to kill him slowly began to take shape.

*John 11:47–53; also see John 12:9–11*

With the hostility of these leaders at its height, as the Passover approached there was much speculation about whether Jesus would dare show his face in the city. Excitement mounted as the news spread like wildfire that he and his disciples were leaving Bethany for Jerusalem. Then, when the crowds caught sight of Jesus riding on a donkey's colt, they carpeted the road with their cloaks and enthusiastically waved branches as they escorted him into the city shouting, "Hosanna! Blessed is he who comes in the name of the Lord! Blessed is the King of Israel!"

*John 12:13*

The Apostles later realized that Jesus was fulfilling the prophecy of Zechariah: "Shout for joy, O daughter Jerusalem! See, your king shall come to you; a just savior is he, meek, and riding on an ass, on a colt, the foal of an ass."

*Zechariah 9:9*

"As [Jesus] entered Jerusalem," Matthew concluded, "the whole city was stirred to its depths, demanding, 'Who is this?' And the crowd kept answering, 'This is the prophet Jesus from Nazareth.'"

*Matthew 21:10–11*

Surrounded by the noisy throng, Jesus made his way through the city and entered the Temple precincts. When he saw that his Father's house had been turned into a marketplace, his anger incited him to bold action. Making a whip out of cords, he drove out the animals of sacrifice and overturned the tables of the money-changers who charged a fee to change foreign money into the Jewish shekels needed for the temple tax. In calling the Temple his Father's house, Jesus claimed to be the Son of Yahweh. When asked by what authority he did these things, Jesus said to the priests, "Destroy this temple, and in three days I will raise it up."

*John 2:19*

Thinking he was speaking of the building, which was already forty-six years under construction, they mocked him. Jesus, however, was referring to the temple of his body, which would die and be raised on the third day.

Thus, Jesus made a last call to his people to accept him as the true shrine of God's presence. He showed great respect for his Father's house, calling it "the House of God," and wept because he knew it would be destroyed. But when it became a cover for the spiritual hollowness of Israel, Jesus showed that another temple would replace it. That temple was to be himself and all the faithful who would unite with him to build a dwelling place for the Spirit of God throughout the world.

Matthew 12:4; Luke 19:41

■ Read two of the three incidents—the Raising of Lazarus (John 11:1–54), the Triumphal Entry into Jerusalem (John 12:12–19), and the Cleansing of the Temple (John 2:13–25). Find the line in each that (1) shows the danger Jesus was in and (2) appeals most to you. Explain why.

## THE MYSTERY OF COVENANT LOVE

### Final Instructions

As Jesus gathered his friends around him to celebrate a last meal together, the impending danger could not dampen his tremendous love for them. The presence of Judas, who betrayed him, makes this last gathering all the more stirring.

Although there is no mention of the paschal lamb or bitter herbs during the meal itself, the Last Supper is linked by all four evangelists with the week-long Passover rituals being celebrated in Jerusalem. Early in the evening, Jesus had made special provisions for the meal by sending two of the disciples ahead and giving them mysterious directions about getting the room where they were to eat.

The Law required every family in Israel to eat this most solemn meal at the same time, after sunset, to celebrate their unity. Jesus, acting as the head of his "family," opened the meal with an unusual display of emotion. "I have greatly desired to eat this Passover with you before I suffer," he said. Saint John added, "He had loved his own in this world, and would show his love for them to the end."

Luke 22:15

John 13:1

The Apostles were just settling into the celebration after the introductory prayers and ceremonies when Jesus did a surprising thing, which threatened to cause some hard feelings. He removed his outer cloak, tied a towel around his waist, and washed his Apostles' feet, including Judas'. He then replaced his cloak and returned to the table, saying, "If I washed your feet— I who am Teacher and Lord—then you must wash each other's feet."

John 13:14

Fully conscious of his dignity and power, Jesus made his action a symbol of his New Commandment of Love. He would express this completely generous love most fully when he laid down his life the next day. But at the Last Supper, he demonstrated that his love was no sentimental impulse, no good feeling, no fine theory. *His love is something you do.* "Blest will you be if you put [these things] into practice," he said.

John 13:17

■ Read the account of the Farewell Supper in Luke 22:7–13 and John 13:1–17. What was mysterious about Jesus' orders to find a room? What sacrament is foreshadowed in the pre-supper scene? How? Who in the group is humble? Who is loving? How important are humility and love to each other?

## The Memorial

After these preparations, the group then probably ate the main course of lamb, a reminder of the Lord's command to mark the doorposts of each Israelite house with blood, the sign for the Angel of Death to pass over and spare their firstborn sons. Then with the warm feeling

Luke 22:19

that came after a good meal with the men he loved most, Jesus took the unleavened bread that had previously been set aside. He blessed it, gave thanks, and broke it. He distributed it around the table, saying, "This is my body to be given for you."

Not only did Jesus give his very self as his last and greatest gift to his Apostles, but he made the gift a means of renewing his final sacrifice of love. Only afterward did the Apostles remember the miraculous multiplication of the loaves. The words he had said then were mysterious: "The bread I will give is my flesh, for the life of the world." Jesus was about to fulfill the words of the prophet Isaiah, who said that a servant would suffer to give life to his people.

John 6:51
*In the Jewish way of thinking, "flesh" was the same as "person." A person's body was one's very self.*

Then, taking the third cup, the "cup of blessing," Jesus gave thanks, drank, and passed it around to signify the Apostles' closeness to him and to one another. "They all drank from it," Mark reports, while Jesus said, "This is my blood, the blood of the covenant, to be poured out on behalf of many."

Mark 14:23–24
*Jesus' blood is (1) the fulfilled covenant of Moses, (2) his blood to be poured out on the cross, and (3) himself given in the Eucharist.*

With these momentous words, Jesus declared that his coming sacrifice was to be the sign of a new relationship between God and "many"—the entire human race. It is a closer relationship than that of the Old Covenant instituted by Moses on Sinai because it was made in person by the Son of God and it was sealed in his own blood, not by the blood of animals. It is the New Covenant foretold by Jeremiah: "The days are coming, says the Lord, when I will make a new covenant with the house of Israel . . . and write it upon their hearts."

Jeremiah 31:31, 33

Jesus ended the first Eucharist with these words: "I tell you, I will not drink this fruit of the vine from now until the day when I drink it new with you in my Father's reign." There was a note of sadness in these words, expressing Jesus' need to leave the Apostles, but they also held a mysterious ring of hope in his promise to return. In the interim, he commands his followers to "do this as a remembrance of me." This is possible because his sacrifice connects all points in time. By this memorial meal, his one great act of love was made

Matthew 26:29

Luke 22:19

available to all generations and continues to be shared to this day. Even though civilizations and cultures have risen and fallen, the Eucharist continues to be celebrated everywhere in the world as a memorial of the great event of redemption.

As his men drained the cup, Jesus grew deeply troubled and spoke of his betrayer. He did not directly identify him, but privately he told Judas to do quickly what he was to do. The others thought that Judas, who kept the purse, had left to buy some forgotten item or to give a donation to the poor, as was the custom at this festival.

## The Last Discourse

*A discourse is a long talk.*

When Judas left, Jesus turned his full attention to the remaining eleven. Between the final hymns, he probably looked lovingly at each of these men he had come to know and love so well. He opened his heart freely and gave them his "New Commandment," which fulfilled and replaced the Ten Commandments: "Love one another. Such as my love has been for you, so must your love be for each other." This New Commandment would gain its full meaning only after the crucifixion, when the Apostles would understand the extent of his love. "This is how all will know you for my disciples: your love for one another," he added.

John 13:34

John 13:35

He then spoke of his coming glory and said that he would soon be leaving the world. Puzzled, the Apostles were full of questions. Jesus reassured them: "Do not let your hearts be troubled. . . . In my Father's house there are many places; otherwise, how could I have told you that I was going to prepare a place for you?" Jesus could offer the world his supreme gift of peace because by his sacrifice all would be welcome in his Father's house.

John 14:1–2

Jesus' words seemed to tumble over each other as he poured out his incredible love and longing for friendship.

## THE PASSOVER AND THE LAST SUPPER

The *Pesah,* or Passover, took a standard form in every Jewish family.

1. The opening prayer—the blessing of the cup (the first of four cups of wine passed around during the ceremony).

Matthew 26:23

2. The dipping of herbs in salt water.
3. The breaking and laying aside of some unleavened bread by the head of the household.

Luke 22:17

4. The recounting of the story of the first Passover in response to a question from the youngest member of the family, the singing of Psalms 113 and 114, and the drinking of the second cup.

John 13:4–12
*Jesus substituted the washing of feet.*

5. The washing of hands in preparation for the meal, the saying of grace, and the eating of bitter herbs dipped in sauce.
6. The festive meal of roast lamb. [Jesus probably instituted the Eucharist after this, breaking the unleavened bread set aside earlier and passing around the third cup of wine—the "cup of blessing."]

Matthew 26:30

7. The singing of the Hallel (or Halleluia), Psalms 115–118, and the "Great Hallel," Psalm 136.
8. The drinking of the last cup of wine.

The setting of the Last Supper during the Passover celebration suggested to the early Church that Jesus thought of himself as the Passover lamb, sacrificed for the deliverance of his people. The wine-become-blood signified not only his death but the ratification of a New Covenant that would reconcile God with the human race.

Until Jesus appears again at the Second Coming, we follow his Eucharistic command as a memorial of what he did for us.

## The True Vine and the Promise of the Spirit

Jesus explained that his followers were not just "members" of a religion, but his very dear friends. "I am the vine, you are the branches." The Apostles shared his very life, which was also the life of the Father.

John 15:5

Jesus said, "If I fail to go, the Paraclete will never come to you" and "I will not leave you orphaned." He promised that his Father would send another Comforter besides himself—one who would make them understand everything he had come to reveal. This new Teacher would remain with his followers forever, guiding them in the truth. Jesus warned that his disciples would have to suffer, but the time of grief would be like that of a woman in labor: at the birth of her child she forgets the suffering and is filled with joy.

John 16:7, 14:8. The Holy Spirit is also called *Paraclete*, which means "helper" or "comforter."

Jesus ended the discourse with a long prayer to the Father. In it he prayed for Peter, whose role would be to strengthen the faith of the others, but he also prayed for all the future generations who would believe in him through the word of the Apostles. His one petition was that all humanity be united in love as he and the Father are one in the Spirit.

*This prayer is often called Jesus' High Priestly Prayer because, as our great Priest, Jesus intercedes for us before the Father.*

As the last cup of wine was passed around, Jesus finally revealed that the feeling against him was reaching a climax, and he would soon be counted among criminals in order to fulfill the Scriptures. The Apostles were outraged at the thought. Simple, practical men, they offered Jesus their swords to defend himself, but he rejected the use of violence. His Father's plan would be carried out in the mystery of weakness, suffering, and death. Only through his sacrifice could the new and eternal covenant be established—the promise God had made to save his people.

Luke 22:37

Luke 22:38

- Slowly read one of these chapters in John: 13, 14, 15, 16, or 17. Then choose a thought from it to expand into a written meditation.
- In your journal, write out your personal covenant with Jesus. State the terms on both sides of the agreement.

# SUMMING UP

1. *Words to know:* legalism, ritual laws, blasphemy, transfiguration, triumphal entry into Jerusalem, Temple, Last Supper, last discourse, Paraclete, Old Covenant, New Covenant, psalms
2. What was the "new way of salvation" that Jesus taught?
3. Why was Jesus a threat to the established religious leaders?
4. Briefly recount the parable of the Vineyard. What does it reveal about Israel and about Jesus? How did the Pharisees react to it?
5. How did Jesus prepare his Apostles for the final trial?
6. Tell what happened at the transfiguration and describe the significance of the following: white clothing and radiant face, mountain, cloud, Moses, Elijah, the voice from the cloud, the sleepiness of the Apostles, the conversation of Jesus with the heavenly visitors. Why couldn't Peter stay on the mountain?
7. What were the three events surrounding Jesus' coming to Jerusalem for the Passover? What did each reveal about Jesus?
8. What were Jesus' sentiments as he prepared to celebrate the Last Supper?
9. What is the meaning of the washing of the Apostles' feet? What connection does it have with the New Commandment?
10. What final thoughts did Jesus impart to his disciples at the last discourse? You may wish to cluster your ideas around these words: vine and branches, the Spirit, a time of grief, High Priestly Prayer.
11. Why was the Eucharist Jesus' greatest act of love? What connection do you see between the Eucharist and the Passover?
12. What serious lack of understanding was displayed by the Apostles when they handed Jesus their swords at the end of the Passover feast?

## Think/Talk/Write

1. Do you think Jesus' strong convictions lessened the bitterness of being "watched"? Why or why not?
2. Do you think the transfiguration was a pure vision, a real occurrence, or a symbolic dream? Why?

3. The three chosen Apostles were allowed to experience both the agony and the ecstasy of true devotion to the Father. Name the "agony" and the "ecstasy" of any work of service you, or someone you know of, have done in Jesus' name.
4. To you, is the Eucharist more a sacrifice or a meal? Why?
5. The corporal works of mercy are practical ways of carrying out Christ's New Commandment. They can be summarized by these key words: hunger, thirst, nakedness, homelessness, sickness, imprisonment, death. Jesus said they would be the standard by which you will be judged. Name one practical work a teenager can do for each. For example, *hunger:* Doing the shopping for an elderly person who lives alone.
6. *Covenant* is a word no longer in common use. What modern words could be substituted for it?

## Activities

1. Have a group dramatize the parable of the Tenants in the Vineyard (Matthew 21:33–45).
2. Plan and carry out a New Commandment project in your school or neighborhood. Make it a program of practical service—for instance, helping out in a nearby nursing home or giving to the poor.
3. Interview five persons about the following things, and then write or orally share with the class the findings of your investigation.
   a. The relation of the Eucharist to the suffering, death, and resurrection of Jesus.
   b. The role of the Holy Spirit in their prayers and life.

## Scripture Search

1. Tell what Jewish leaders were "watching" for in these passages: Mark 3:2; Luke 6:7, 14:1, 20:20.
2. Describe the stand Jesus took in any two debates in Matthew 15:1–9, 16:1–4 or Luke 14:1–6.

# TWELVE

How did Jesus face the prospect of his death?

Why did Jesus have to suffer so cruelly?

How did Jesus react to his captors?

How did the witnesses of the crucifixion respond to it?

What does the crucifixion mean to you?

*To God, my defender, I say,*
 *"Why have you forgotten me?*
*Why must I go on suffering*
 *from the cruelty of my enemies?"*
*I am crushed by their insults,*
 *as they keep on asking me,*
 *"Where is your God?"*
*Why am I so sad?*
 *Why am I so troubled?*
*I will put my hope in God,*
 *and once again I will praise him,*
 *my savior and my God.*

 (Psalm 42:9–11, *Good News*)

# All Is Fulfilled

He had loved his own in this world, and would show his love for them to the end.

(JOHN 13:1)

## THE SCANDAL OF THE CROSS

Your best friend, Greg Jordan, involves you in his father's political campaign. To work at the campaign headquarters, you quit your job, cancel two classes, and even decide not to go home for spring break. The opponents run a smear campaign, but the polls indicate that your candidate will sweep the election.

Then, one night the police raid the Jordan home and march Mr. Jordan off to jail. The morning headlines blast the news that he is implicated in a narcotics operation. The opposing candidate is credited with the discovery.

■ How would you feel? What would you do?

In America no one would be legally charged, tried, and executed in one day. But within thirteen or fourteen hours, Jesus was captured, tried, condemned, mocked, beaten, stripped, nailed to a cross, and left to die.

The whole affair left his followers reeling, but the suddenness of Jesus' death wasn't the only thing that stunned the Apostles. Roman crucifixion was one of the most humiliating executions ever devised. The fact that Jesus died by this method was so scandalous that, from the beginning, his followers couldn't even mention it without also referring to the resurrection.

A wall-drawing from the second century shows a cross on which hangs a man with the head of a donkey. Beside it stands a second man. The inscription reads, "Alexamenos worships [his] God." It reveals the ridicule Christians were still subjected to because of their faith, a hundred years after Christ. Yet the crucifixion of Jesus became the greatest sign of love the world has ever known.

The passion account probably originated to silence denials of the resurrection based on rumors that Jesus had not really died. Then as the significance of Jesus' death dawned, it was read at every Eucharist, the memorial of his sacrifice. The passion narratives are the oldest part of the Gospel, and are in greater agreement than any other part of the Gospel.

A close examination of the passion story reveals that the evangelists quickly pass over the physical torments of Jesus, but spend a great deal of time explaining the meaning of his suffering. You may remember growing restless when the passion was read in church. Although

it covers less than twenty-four hours of Jesus' life, it forms a third of the Gospel. The writers lace the tragic and humiliating event with symbols, scriptural quotations, and allusions to messianic prophecies to express their faith in the suffering Jesus as Messiah, king, and Holy One of God.

■ Why do you think the evangelists don't spell out Jesus' sufferings? How would you have reacted to the crucifixion?

## JESUS IN GETHSEMANE

The agony in the Garden centers around one theme: our need for God. Just before Jesus and the Apostles walked out to Gethsemane (probably an olive grove, because the name means "oil-press"), Peter boasted that he would never leave Jesus, even if the others did. Yet Jesus knew Peter's weakness. Without rejecting him, Jesus foretold Peter's denial. He even noted the time—before cock crow of the next day.

In the Garden, Jesus' three closest friends—Peter, James, and John—fell asleep while Jesus prayed for strength to face the suffering ahead. The three felt no particular need to pray: everything would be all right. Jesus warned them of their powerlessness against temptation.

*Jesus lets the three whom he had strengthened at the transfiguration witness his suffering in the Garden.*

The temptation Jesus referred to is not just the attraction of the devil; it is the inner evil inclination to prefer to have things go one's own way instead of God's. This tendency cannot be overcome without divine help. Jesus himself appeared to experience reluctance in submitting to God's will. Terrified and in agony, he fell to the ground and asked his Father over and over again to remove his cup. Unlike the Apostles, he was well aware of his need of God.

*Throughout the Bible, the cup is a symbol of either blessing or disaster.*

Finally, after what must have been several hours, Jesus rose from his draining experience with an almost joyful vigor and went to meet his betrayer. "Get up! Let us be on our way! See, my betrayer is here." He was relieved that his "hour" had come.

Matthew 26:46

- Read the account in Matthew 26:36–46. What lesson does it hold for you? Do you think anyone can be saved (withstand temptation) without prayer? Why or why not?
- Some people say that Jesus could not really have suffered deeply because he knew that he would rise to be glorified. What do you think? What did Jesus shrink from? Who can receive comfort from this scene?
- What does it mean "to watch and pray"? What did Jesus mean when he said that the spirit is willing but the flesh is weak? Give an example.

## FREE TO LOVE

If Jesus had been forced to die on the cross, or if he had wanted to die, his action wouldn't have been worth much.

That's why his willingness to die was such a mystery. To do something willingly does not mean that you have to like what you are doing. Jesus definitely did not like the idea of death. In fear and sorrow, he begged his Father to spare him. Yet he accepted his death and had predicted his passion several times. To the Pharisees he said, "On the third day my purpose is accomplished."

Luke 13:32

But how do we know Jesus was willing? When he took bread, saying, "This is my body to be given for you," and when over the cup of wine he said, "This is my blood, the blood of the covenant, to be poured out in behalf of many for the forgiveness of sins," he mysteriously offered the crucifixion for them. Even as "his hour" began, Jesus was in control of the situation. As he had said, "I lay down my life to take it up again. No one takes it from me; I lay it down freely."

Luke 22:19; Matthew 26:28

John 10:17–18

But wasn't Jesus responsible for his death? Didn't he deliberately agitate the religious leaders by criticizing them and claiming to be a higher authority than they or their laws were? Jesus had to be who he was: God's Son. He could not change his Father's message to please those in power.

Why did Jesus die? He says of himself: "For these sheep I will give my life. . . . This command I received from my Father."

John 10:15, 18

- How do you feel when you realize that Christ willingly gave his life for you?

## THE ARREST

Three things stand out in Jesus' arrest: his tremendous strength of character, his refusal to use violence, and his loving forgiveness of those who deserted him.

Just moments after the agony, Jesus, who knew what was going to happen, went to greet the hostile crowd that had come to meet him. The bystanders shrank back, unconsciously recognizing Jesus' strength. Repeating "I am he" when his captors hesitated, Jesus fearlessly demanded that the Apostles be left free.

See John 18:4, 8; Matthew 26:45

Jesus' strength is spiritual. He controls by love, not violence. He addressed Judas gently, as a friend, not in anger: "Judas, would you betray the Son of Man with a kiss?" When Peter pulled his sword to attack a servant of the high priest, Jesus rebuked him by asking, "Do you not suppose I can call on my Father to provide at a moment's notice more than twelve legions of angels?"

Luke 22:48

Matthew 26:53

But Jesus' meekness did not make him indifferent or passive. He appealed to any shred of decency and reasonableness in his captors: "Am I a criminal that you come out after me armed with swords and clubs? When I was with you in the temple you never raised a hand against me."

Luke 22:52–53

The scene closes with Jesus' meaningful words as he, the liberator, is taken captive: "But this is your hour— the triumph of darkness." Jesus had longed for this "hour" even as he dreaded it. It was actually nighttime, but it was also symbolically night, the time when evil would close in on and apparently snuff out the Light of the World.

Luke 22:53

*Hour* refers to the time ordained by God for the fulfillment of his plan of salvation.

Even in captivity Jesus continued to love and to save. All the Apostles fled except Peter and John, who followed to the high priest's residence. While John went in, Peter was seated near a fire, waiting to see how it would end. During the long night, he tried to remain inconspicuous, but as different people asked him his connection with Jesus, he grew fearful. Finally, the third time, Peter cursed and swore that he didn't even know "the man." By this action, the Gospel writers hint at the complete loss of nerve of all the Apostles at the crucifixion.

See Matthew 26:69–75

At the second cock crow, just as Jesus passed by, he directed a piercing look of sadness at his first Apostle. Peter then remembered. Unlike Judas, who according to one tradition hanged himself, Peter went out and wept bitterly. To the risen Jesus he would openly declare his love three times, and in the end he gave his life for his Lord. With his faintheartedness swallowed up in Christ's mercy, Peter's boast of loyalty became a reality after all. So it is with all who come to Jesus after a fall.

- Compare the accounts of Mark 14:66–72 and Luke 22:54–62. What details are different?
- What does it take to be strong in hard times? How would you prepare for your "hour of temptation"?
- Describe someone you know who has exercised leadership after some fall.
- In your journal, describe any weakness that you inwardly "weep over" and wish you could master for Christ. What means will you use to improve?

## THE TRIALS

The trials of Jesus were a mockery of justice. The court scenes are sketchy and confused. There seem to have been two trials before the priests, one near midnight at the house of the former high priest, Annas, the other the next morning before the full court presided over by Caiaphas, the present high priest. This was followed by a session with Herod and at least two appearances before Pilate. The two scenes of mockery highlight the two charges brought against Jesus.

### The High Priests and Jesus' Messiahship

Since it was illegal to hold court at night, the first session was only a preliminary hearing. The chief priests wanted witnesses to prove that Jesus had made himself a prophet. In Jewish law, the agreement of two or three witnesses constituted evidence. The testimony about Jesus' threat to destroy the Temple and rebuild it in three days was inconsistent. Lacking the solemnity of a formal gathering, Jesus was treated roughly by an official who struck him for speaking to the high priest as an equal.

The morning session before the Sanhedrin was more orderly. According to Deuteronomy 17:21, this ruling body had the power to sentence Jesus to death as a false teacher. Two issues were raised. If Jesus were proved a false messiah/prophet, he could be executed by Jewish law. If he were proved a false messiah/king, he could be prosecuted as a revolutionary against Caesar. When questioned by the high priest about his teachings, "Jesus remained silent; he made no reply." In refusing to submit his teachings to the high Jewish court, he showed clearly that he regarded his authority to be from God. This claim was his crime. But it wasn't enough; Jesus must be made to discredit himself. The high priest asked Jesus outright if he were the Messiah. Jesus said, "I am," and quoted a prophecy of Daniel about the Messiah coming on a cloud.

The high priest expressed his outrage by tearing his own robe as he charged Jesus with blasphemy. Jesus had made himself the Son of the Blessed One, claiming universal authority. At this, "they all concurred in the verdict 'guilty,' with its sentence of death." Jesus was then spat upon, blindfolded, and mocked in his role of prophet. Yet there must have been some problem because the Sanhedrin did not put Jesus to death. Some scholars think that the Jewish council could not agree about his legal guilt. Instead, they unanimously agreed to turn Jesus over to Pilate, the Roman governor, whom they hated, and let him decide. This dishonesty was their sin.

In a body, the assembly rose up and led Jesus to Pilate, who, reluctant to get involved in Jewish religious disputes, sent Jesus to Herod when he learned that Jesus was a Galilean. The priests followed. Before Herod, who was pleased at the prospect of a "magic show,"

The *Sanhedrin* was the Supreme Council of the Jews presided over by the high priest.

Mark 14:61

*The "clouds of heaven" are a biblical image of Christ's Second Coming.*

Mark 14:64

See Luke 13:32

Jesus remained silent. He had no respect for "that fox" who, at the whim of his unlawful wife, had murdered John the Baptizer. To mock him, Herod dressed Jesus in a magnificent robe and sent him back to Pilate. That day, as if to symbolize the joining of all forces against Jesus, Pilate and Herod, who had been at odds, became friends.

## Pilate and Jesus' Kingship

The *Praetorium* was the governor's palace.

Luke 23:2

Before Pilate at the Praetorium, the council charged Jesus with three things that would worry a Roman ruler: he had subverted the nation by stirring up rebellion against Caesar, opposed the payment of taxes to Caesar, and made himself a messiah-king who would be a rival of Caesar. This theme of kingship is woven through the trial scenes at the governor's palace. But Pilate saw through the jealousy of the Jewish leaders. "I do not find a case against this man," he told the crowd. "Why do you not take him and pass judgment on him according to your own law?"

Luke 23:4; John 18:31

The priests wanted Jesus out of the way, but they also wanted to keep their hands free of blood. Although their effort to get the Roman governor to pronounce judgment put Jesus in confrontation with the larger world, it did not get them off the hook. It only extended the symbolism of Jesus' death and kingship. Through the centuries it has been the religious leaders who have carried the guilt of Jesus' death, not the Romans.

*These scenes show that it was only a small group of powerful leaders who put Jesus to death, not all the Jews.*

Pilate despised the Jews, but he also feared them. They were forever reporting their Roman rulers to Caesar. He recognized the innocence of Jesus, but his first concern was to safeguard his position. Jesus made it clear that there was nothing to fear from his kingdom, which was not of this world. "Anyone committed to the truth hears my voice," Jesus said. Pilate responded cynically, "Truth! What does that mean?"

John 18:37–38

Pilate heard Jesus' call and tried to free him. He declared Jesus innocent three times, but he was not committed to truth. Although he was intelligent, Pilate was also cowardly and ruthless. Seeing that the leaders were determined to press the issue, he seized every chance to humiliate them. He made them release Barabbas, a real "subverter of the nation." He made them admit over and over that they wanted Jesus killed. He forced them into just what they wanted to avoid—staining their pure consciences with Jesus' blood.

*Barabbas* means "son of the father," another twist of irony.

But in spite of having declared Jesus innocent, Pilate revealed his cruel nature by ordering Jesus to be beaten, saying, "I have not discovered anything about him that calls for the death penalty. I will therefore chastise him and release him." If he hoped to appease the Jewish religious leaders by inflicting this less drastic punishment, it didn't work. At the leaders' instigation, their followers yelled, "Crucify him!"

Luke 23:22; John 19:5

There are no details of the flogging itself, but the Romans were not known for their gentleness. To the evangelists, the scene of the scourging highlights Jesus' kingship. Although it was done to deride him, Jesus was dressed in regal purple, given a crown of thorns and a mock scepter, and worshiped as the King of the Jews.

On hearing that Jesus claimed to be the Son of God, Pilate became superstitiously fearful and returned to speak to Jesus, who now refused to answer his questions. Pilate, the coward, was astonished at Jesus' fearlessness; "Do you not know that I have the power to release you and the power to crucify you?" he asked. "You would have no power over me whatever unless it were given you from above," Jesus replied.

Matthew 27:19

John 19:10–11

As the religious leaders exerted more pressure, Pilate shrewdly shifted the responsibility for Jesus' death to them. Officially seated on the judgment seat, Gabbatha, he asked again, "Shall I crucify your king?" At this the chief priests renounced their proudest religious and national heritage: "We have no king but Caesar."

*Gabbatha* means "elevated place." John 19:15

As Pilate carried out the evil will of his subjects, he washed his hands to symbolize his blamelessness. But he might just as well have issued his condemnation with malice. His halfhearted commitment to Jesus ul-

timately became outright rejection. He ordered the "crime" to be posted in three languages: "Jesus of Nazareth, King of the Jews."

Thus Jesus was condemned at the hands of both Jews and Gentiles. He was sent to Calvary for us all.

*The trials are in Mark 14:53–65, 15:1–20a; Matthew 26:57–68, 27:1–2, 27:11–31; Luke 22:63–23:25; John 18:12–13, 18:19–24, 18:28–19:6*

- The trials of Jesus contain many inconsistencies and surprises. How many do you find in any one of the Gospel accounts? What part of the trials do you think were most trying to Jesus? (Don't just consider physical pain.) Why?
- In a few sentences, describe the character of Jesus and Pilate during the trials.
- In your journal, analyze your own character for flaws that might result in a rejection of Jesus. What means will you take to make consistent decisions for Christ?

JESUS

## THE SEAMLESS ROBE

The meaning behind actions makes all the difference. In 19:23–24, Saint John gives the spiritual meaning of the distribution of Jesus' garments.

*Jesus' clothes seem to be the only inheritance he left.*

He notes that four guards tossed dice for the robe. This could refer to Christ's "inheritance" being distributed to the four corners of the earth. John also records that the robe "had no seam." Jewish tradition associates a seamless robe with high priests and with such great persons as Moses and Adam. Not allowing the garment to be divided suggests that Jesus was the great High Priest of humanity, because Jewish law forbade the tearing of a high priest's garments. John may also be suggesting the cloak of Joseph in the Old Testament, portraying Christ as one betrayed by his brothers and yet their savior.

Leviticus 21:10

See Genesis 37:3

The early Fathers saw in the seamless robe a symbol of the Church's unity as contrasted with the division the coming of Jesus meant for the Jews. John's Gospel mentions this division several times.

See John 7:43, 9:16, 10:19

The "seamless robe of Christianity" was "torn" by the scandalous divisions that occurred when East and West separated and again during the Protestant Reformation. Ecumenists are hard at work today, trying to weave together the tattered strands and restore the unity Jesus prayed for at the Last Supper: "That all may be one as you, Father, are in me, and I in you; that they may be one in us."

*Ecumenists specialize in trying to reunite all Christian churches.*

John 17:21

- What ecumenical endeavors have you been part of? What insights did you receive while participating?
- What spiritual meanings do you discover in other parts of Chapter 19 of Saint John's Gospel?

# THE WAY OF THE CROSS AND CRUCIFIXION

Golgotha is Aramaic for skull; the place must have been shaped like a skull. Calvary comes from the Latin, "place of the skull."

Jesus was stripped of the scarlet cloak and made to carry a crossbeam, the instrument of his death. The quarter-mile journey to Golgotha was all the more humiliating because at Passover the streets were packed. A boy usually preceded the criminal with the name of his crime held high. We know nothing of the size of the plank Jesus carried, the kind of cross he died on, or how he was nailed. It is thought that a small seat, a foot-platform, or ropes may have supported his body, which could not have been held by the nails alone, even if they were placed in his wrists.

The soldiers, who had the right to press Jews into service at any time, enlisted the help of Simon, a Jew from Cyrene, in North Africa, to assist Jesus. This may hint at the weakness of Jesus, but the evangelists make Simon a representative of every Christian taking up the cross to unite with Jesus' redeeming action.

A group of local women wept and mourned over the pitiable condition of Jesus. Thinking of them rather than of himself, Jesus comforted these "Daughters of Jerusalem." If he, the innocent one ("green wood") suffers thus, how much more will they have to suffer in the days of the tragedy of Jerusalem? The Church sees Jesus' words as prophetic of the sorrow everyone must endure to be purified.

Luke 23:31

In the first of the seven last words from the cross, Jesus forgave his executioners in an act of supreme generosity as they nailed him to the wood. The criminals crucified with Jesus were also made into symbols of the responses the Good News called forth: acceptance and rejection. Jesus' promise of the kingdom to the thief on the right—in Jewish imagery, the side of the righteous—also represents God's will to save, even to the last moment of life.

Luke 23:34

Luke 23:43

In compassion, someone offered Jesus cheap vinegar wine mixed with myrrh as a narcotic, but Jesus refused to take it.

Once their work was complete, the guards rolled dice for Jesus' garments, which by law became the property of the executioners. The evangelists saw in this a fulfillment of the messianic prophecy of Psalm 22:19: "They divide my garments among them, and for my vesture they cast lots."

Although the disciples had fled, "the disciple Jesus loved" and the Galilean women, including Jesus' mother, Mary, stood nearby. Tradition regards "the disciple" as John, who leaned his head on Jesus' breast at the Last Supper. In the last Gospel he becomes a symbol of all humankind and, at Jesus' request, John received Mary as his mother. Jesus' use of *woman* to address Mary suggests the woman in Genesis whose child was to crush the serpent's head. Under the cross, Mary's love, sorrow, and submission won for her the title of New Eve, mother of all the living. John 19:26 Genesis 3:15

The passersby taunted Jesus and tossed his teachings in his face. The sky darkened—a symbol of the cosmic struggle between good and evil that was taking place within Jesus. As life ebbed away, Jesus suffered a painful thirst and felt profoundly abandoned by his Father. You know how hard it is to believe in God's love during a tragedy. Someone has said that the most fundamental question of existence is whether God is good, indifferent, or malicious in relation to creation. The great temptation of Jesus was to lose trust in his Father.

His friends dispersed, his work a shambles, his every breath coming harder, Jesus had reason to doubt. Crying out for water, his words—"I am thirsty"—have been interpreted as his great desire (thirst) to save humanity and to bring to them the rivers of salvation. The words of Psalm 22—"My God, my God, why have you forsaken me?"—express the mystery of his sense of aloneness: the Son of God feeling deserted by God! John 19:28 Matthew 27:46; Mark 15:34

As Jesus drank the vinegar held up to him in a sponge placed on a spear, he made it clear that he had not lost hope: "Now it is finished," he said. It was a cry of victory—he had accomplished his mission, the redemption of the world. And, finally, he uttered his last words, a prayer of trust: "Father, into your hands I commend my spirit." Then he bowed his head and died. John 19:30 Luke 23:46

The evangelists wrote that Jesus "gave up" or "de- Matthew 27:50; John 19:30

livered over his spirit." This suggests that, at Jesus' death, his spirit—the Spirit of God—was handed over to the world. The death of the Suffering Servant was his victory over Satan. By his obedience, he overcame Adam's disobedience; through his goodness, evil was conquered forever.

■ What marks of loving concern do you recognize in Jesus during his last hours? What other lessons do the way of the cross and the crucifixion hold?

## Aftermath

God accepted his Son's offering. As Jesus was swept up into union with his Father, his Father poured himself out on the world in the gift of the Spirit.

Matthew 27:51

The evangelists surround the crucifixion with signs of Christ's glory. The Temple curtain that only the high priest could go past is said to have been torn from top to bottom to symbolize that God was available to the entire world. There were earthquakes, which, in the imagery of the Old Testament, were caused by God's footsteps. God's power walked the earth in the risen souls of the Old Testament saints who emerged from their graves, freed for paradise by Christ's action. The centurion, a Gentile, declared Jesus "the Son of God," foreshadowing the conversion of non-Jews.

A *centurion* was an officer who commanded a century (100 men) in the Roman army.

*The legs of the crucified were smashed with a mallet to hasten death, which sometimes took three days.*

John recorded that instead of breaking Jesus' legs, a soldier pierced Jesus' side with a lance. This symbolized that sin had cost Jesus a broken heart and fulfilled an ancient prophecy, given in Exodus 12:46, that no bone was to be broken in the Jewish paschal lamb. The blood and water that flowed out can be explained medically, but John identified them as signs of the salvation available through Christ's new Spirit-filled Body, the Church. Water suggests baptism, through which we are born into the Church. Blood refers to the Eucharist, through which the members of the Church join in fellowship through, with, and in Christ.

With Pilate's permission, Joseph of Arimathea and

Nicodemus, members of the Sanhedrin, took down Jesus' body. The Galilean women helped and observed the place of the grave. Because Jewish law forbade leaving the dead unburied over the Sabbath, they wrapped him in a fine linen shroud, according to custom, and laid him in a new rock-cut tomb nearby on the outskirts of town. Since the Sabbath sunset was fast approaching, they could not anoint the body. To shelter the tomb from animals, they closed its entrance with a stone. The two Marys returned home to prepare spices and ointments, intending to finish their labor of love after the Sabbath.

*The concern of these two council members shows that not all Jews, and not even all Jewish leaders, were opposed to Jesus.*

## THE CROSS OF JESUS

The New Testament makes the crucifixion the central symbol of Christianity and the turning point of the history of the world. In about A.D. 55, Saint Paul wrote to the Galatians: "I have been crucified with Christ, and the life I live now is not my own; Christ is living in me. I still live my human life, but it is a life of faith in the Son of God, who loved me and gave himself for me." The cross "crosses out" the notion that we are saved by our good deeds, as the leaders of Judaism taught. Jesus cancels sin, no strings attached. When he forgives, he erases sin completely. In the parables of the Good Shepherd and the Merciful Father (Prodigal Son), Jesus had spoken of God's tender concern. In the crucifixion he lived out that concern.

Galatians 2:19–20

People find it hard to believe in totally generous love. In rejecting Jesus, they reject the God who accepts sinners. The challenge of being a Christian is to receive the gift of God: to let yourself be loved despite—or rather, because of—your sins and to let that love shape you.

- ■ Read the passion narrative of any one evangelist. List the sufferings Jesus endured. Why do you think he had to undergo so much?

## SUMMING UP

1. *Words to know:* Gethsemane, (Jesus') "hour," hour of darkness, remorse, repentance, Sanhedrin, clouds of glory, Praetorium, Barabbas, Gabbatha, Golgotha, Calvary, Daughters of Jerusalem, seven last words, New Eve, centurion
2. What prophecies did Jesus make on the way to his prayer in the Garden of Gethsemane? What was Peter's boast? Why is Gethsemane an appropriate name for the garden in which Jesus prayed?
3. How did Jesus show distress in the Garden? What did he suffer? What warning does he issue to his Apostles?
4. How would you describe Jesus when he was apprehended in the Garden? What do you think was his greatest suffering at this time?
5. What is meant by the biblical image of Jesus' passion as "the hour of darkness"?
6. What did Peter's actions at the arrest show about him and his understanding of Jesus' mission?
7. Why did Peter deny Jesus?
8. Why did the Jewish leaders bring Jesus before Pilate? What was the symbolic significance of his being officially tried and condemned by Rome?
9. How is Jesus' kingship highlighted during the trial before Pilate?
10. In what ways did Pilate try to free Jesus? How did he gradually force the Jews to take more and more responsibility for Jesus' execution? Why wasn't he completely successful?
11. Why didn't the evangelists put the judgment of Jesus into actual words?
12. Why are the passion narratives so long?
13. What is the point of the episodes in which Jesus meets the Cyrenean and the weeping women?
14. Whom do the criminals who died alongside Jesus represent?
15. What is the meaning of the scene between John, Mary, and Jesus?
16. What was probably Jesus' greatest temptation while he was on the cross? How did the evangelists bring it out?
17. Explain in your own words the meaning of Jesus' last two words on the cross (John 19:30; Luke 23:46).
18. What meanings can be seen in the way the evangelists reported Jesus' death?

19. What signs did the evangelists use to confirm the importance of Jesus' victory?
20. What is the significance of John's "eyewitness" account of the piercing of Jesus' side?


## Think/Talk/Write

1. What significance do you see in Jesus' choosing the three Apostles who had seen his more glorious moments to witness him in his agony and human weakness? What parallels can there be in this for all Christians?
2. The religious leaders of Israel seemed to reject Jesus for motives of faith. What did they put their faith in? What did Jesus call them to believe?


## Activities

1. Hold a debate on this topic: The kingdom of Jesus is not a purely spiritual one of interior conversion. It affects and is affected by the condition of other people in the world.
2. Write a poem or original paragraph on any aspect of the passion.
3. Compose a Bible service based on one or more scenes from the passion.


## Scripture Search

The evangelists made an effort to declare Jesus innocent even as they told of his death as a criminal. How are each of these persons used to suggest that Jesus was not guilty?

> Pilate (Luke 23:4, 6–7, 14–15, 20, 22–25; Matthew 27:24)
> Herod (Luke 23:15)
> Pilate's wife (Matthew 27:19)
> The political rebel crucified with Jesus (Luke 23:41)
> Judas (Matthew 27:4)

## THIRTEEN

What do you believe about Jesus' resurrection?

What did the witnesses experience?

What was the risen Jesus like?

What did the resurrection mean to the Apostles?

What do you believe about your own resurrection?

Why should you believe in the resurrection?

*Father, all-powerful and ever-living God,*
*we do well always and everywhere to give you thanks*
*through Jesus Christ our Lord.*
*We praise you with greater joy than ever in this Easter season,*
*when Christ became our Paschal sacrifice.*
*He has made us children of the light,*
*rising to new and everlasting life.*
*He has opened the gates of heaven*
*to receive his faithful people.*
*His death is our ransom from death;*
*his resurrection is our rising to life.*
*The joy of the resurrection renews the whole world,*
*while the choirs of heaven sing forever to your glory:*
*Holy, holy, holy Lord.*

(Easter Eucharistic Prayer II)

# He Is Risen

I wish to know Christ and the power flowing from his resurrection; likewise to know how to share in his sufferings by being formed into the pattern of his death. Thus do I hope that I may arrive at resurrection from the dead.

(PHILIPPIANS 3:10–11)

## WHAT DO WE BELIEVE ABOUT THE RESURRECTION?

The crucifixion had been shocking for the Apostles, testing their faith and hope beyond their strength. The strong fishermen were "grieving and weeping." They had given all—their jobs, their families, their hearts—to follow him. And now what?

The *first day* is the day following the Sabbath.

Early on the first day of the week, the rumors began—wild tales circulated by the women who had gone down to anoint the body, something about the body being gone. "Ridiculous! Their sorrow must be getting to them," said the Apostles. Still, some memory must have stirred in Peter and John, for they set out to see for themselves.

See Luke 24:11

John 20:9

It was true! The tomb was empty. But they returned because "as yet they did not understand the Scripture." The great moments of life—forgiveness, birth, death, love—take time to absorb. How much longer, then, to absorb the fact of resurrection!

- How would you react to the news that someone you loved had come back from the dead?
- What do you believe about the resurrection?

## AWARENESS OF THE RESURRECTION

No one actually saw Jesus rise. The most tremendous event of history took place "in the silence of God," as Saint Ignatius of Antioch expressed it. But something happened that first day to rouse the hearts that were sunk in grief. It was more than just an empty tomb with burial linens folded neatly to one side. It was a revelation from God.

*Since no one witnessed the moment of the resurrection, the Apostles needed faith, just as we do. Jesus did not show himself to anyone except the believers.*

That revelation called the Apostles to a mission. They renewed their faith, prayed, and came out of hiding changed men. It also produced a number of stories that center on two things—the empty tomb and Christ's appearances.

The earliest written tradition of the resurrection is found in Paul's letter to the Corinthians. No mention is made there of the women's discovery. Paul's converts may not have been familiar with the details of Easter morning. But all four Gospels begin with evidence of the divine presence at the tomb. They then record the personal appearances of Jesus to his witnesses in what have come to be called the appearance narratives.

1 Corinthians 15

The evangelists use earthquake, light, and angel imagery to express what was beyond expression: the encounter with God. The stunned reactions of the women and the panic and amazement of Peter and John ring with authenticity. The angels had brought an unimaginable message: "He is not here. He has been raised up." No one was surprised at the inconsistencies among the reports of that momentous experience.

Luke 24:6

Understandably, the first Easter was not the most organized day in the lives of Jesus' followers. In John's Gospel, it is dark when the women depart on their labor

of love. In Mark, it is sunrise. In Matthew, there is one
shimmering angel at the grave. In Luke, two young men
appear in shining garments. Mark has the women resolve to tell no one what they have seen. Mary Magdalene is the first witness in John, while in the other
accounts the women run to the Apostles with the Good
News. The Apostles are told in one instance to go to
Galilee, and in another they are directed to Jerusalem.
The variations reflect the confusion of the occasion.

There were so many versions that the stories could
not be settled into one form as the passion and public
life stories had been. We would be suspicious of doc-
toring if they matched exactly. The varying details also
demonstrate that the early Church based its faith not
on the details, but on the truth of the event itself. The
discrepancies prove that the resurrection story was not
something that had been made up. The resurrection,

after all, came as a total surprise and left everyone distracted. The sense of breathlessness and confusion continues into the appearance narratives. Yet all the accounts resound with one clear message: Jesus was raised from the dead!

## THE APPEARANCE NARRATIVES

The evangelists made the resurrection experiences concrete in the appearance stories. To Mary Magdalene, the other women, the Eleven, the two on the road, Thomas, the Apostles in Galilee, the five hundred at the ascension, and Paul, Jesus made a deeply personal self-revelation that profoundly affected their lives.

Suddenly and unexpectedly, Jesus would be standing in their midst. No longer disfigured but radiant and alive, he was the same and yet, somehow, transformed.

What these experiences were, we do not know. They happened to individuals and groups, but only to those of faith. Jesus' appearances filled the Apostles with terror and at the same time flooded them with joy. He made their hearts burn with faith and left them with a hope beyond all hope. The risen Lord was full of power, yet he was gentle. And he always had some mission for them.

The empty tomb alone might have been explained away, but not these deeply religious encounters. Gradually, the Apostles understood. They were the privileged witnesses of the greatest revelation ever made to the world. The death and resurrection became the cornerstone of their preaching, their fellowship, and their faith. After Jesus' departure and the strengthening by the Holy Spirit, the cowardly group boldly began to proclaim Jesus as the Messiah who fulfilled the Scriptures.

Tradition teaches that all the Apostles except John, who was exiled to the island of Patmos, gave their lives for their belief. It seems unlikely that they would have faced persecution and death so courageously for a story

A *cornerstone* symbolically represents the fundamental basis of something.

Blaise Pascal (1623–1662) was a French scientist and religious philosopher.

they had concocted, especially after they had shown themselves to be so cowardly at first. Pascal wrote: "I really believe those stories whose writers get their throats cut."

- Before reading the accounts of the findings of the empty tomb, make a chart with these eight headings: Gospel, Place, Time (day and hour), Who Discovered the Empty Tomb, Who Was Found There, Individuals Meeting with Jesus, Group Meetings, Mission. In the first column (under Gospel) write these references: Mark 16:1–8; Matthew 28:1–15; Luke 24:1–12; Mark 16:9–13; John 20:1–10. Fill in the charts as you read the accounts. What impressions, feelings, or thoughts do you get from these passages? How do you feel about the fact that there are different versions of the same story? Why do you believe in the resurrection?
- Which witness do you identify with the most? Why?

## THE DIFFICULTY OF BELIEF

Two books written in our own day propose solutions to the incredible story of the resurrection. In *The Passover Plot* by Hugh Schonfield, Jesus is given a potion that causes him to sink into a deathlike trance from which he later recovers. In John Allegro's *The Sacred Mushroom,* Jesus is drugged by a fungus drink that later brings him back to consciousness.

False explanations of the resurrection are not new. From the beginning, people had difficulty accepting it. After all, the Apostles themselves expressed doubts.

- Suppose someone told you that they had just seen John F. Kennedy or Martin Luther King alive. What suspicions would you have? What questions would you ask?
- What emotions are expressed toward Jesus in these passages: Luke 24:11, 24:36–43; Matthew 28:17; Mark 16:14; John 20:9, 24–29.

- What answers to the objections of the first converts do you find buried in these resurrection accounts?

> Someone had stolen the body. (Matthew 28:13)
>
> The Apostles had just made up the story. (Matthew 27:64)
>
> Jesus had not really died, but was only in a coma. (Matthew 27:50; Luke 24:18)
>
> The women confused the tombs. (Luke 24:11–12)
>
> The disciples were the unconscious victims of hallucinations. (John 20:25; Luke 24:37; Mark 6:11, 14)
>
> Jesus was just a ghost. (Luke 24:41–44; Acts 10:41; Luke 24:39; John 20:24–39)

- Do the hidden references to these objections in the Gospel strengthen your faith or weaken it? Why?

## WHAT WAS THE RISEN JESUS LIKE?

If you were to attempt to explain color to a blind person, you might use your other senses: orange is like the roar of a jet; red is a flame; green is like cool water. Even if your comparisons were vivid, there could be no way to bridge the gap between total darkness and the magic, beauty, and brightness of the world of living color. But if the blind person could see for even a few days, how that would simplify your task!

The Apostles were like blind people who had glimpsed the glory of Christ. Their task was to share it with the rest of the world. No words or images could convey something so foreign to human experience. The convictions of the witnesses were beyond doubting, and the miracles they worked in Jesus' name were persuasive. But as the eyewitnesses died and new converts were made, false interpretations of the resurrection cropped up. Some said Jesus' body had never actually left the tomb; their faith is too spiritual, a form of underbelief. Others said he had returned in the very same human form he had had before the resurrection; their faith is too materialistic, a form of overbelief.

Even today these two mistaken positions regarding the risen body of Jesus are held. Of course, no description of this profound mystery can exhaust it, and by considering the misconceptions, you may be able to gain a balanced view.

## The Real Jesus—Not Pure Spirit

Some scholars say that the resurrection appearances were only products of the disciples' overheated imaginations, a form of strong wishful thinking or delirium. They claim that it wasn't Jesus, but the *faith of the Apostles* that "rose," as school spirit sometimes "rises" under the influence of a dynamic student-council leader. According to these scholars, it isn't what happened to Jesus' body that matters, but the *fact* of the resurrection, no matter how it took place.

*Divinized* means treated as God.

There is not a single reference in the New Testament to the rise of the Apostles' faith. It was *Jesus* who rose. The Apostles reported that he was alive and living a new and entirely different existence, one that their rather dull and unimaginative minds could hardly have dreamed up. In fact, they themselves were reluctant to believe. It is exactly what you would expect: no one had ever risen before. Besides, a risen, divinized Jesus would have been against the faith of a good Jew whose faith in one God was so strong. In no way could the Apostles have been the source of the story.

## A Spirit-Filled Jesus—Not the Same

*Literary forms* are a set way of presenting ideas. For instance, a writer who wants to say that life is a search for identity or destiny may have a character go on a journey.

At the other extreme, there are theologians who take every word of the Bible as scientific fact. They deny that the inspired writers used literary forms in their writings. These theologians picture the resurrection as if it were an ordinary physical action, with Jesus laboriously unwrapping the bloody winding cloths, stooping to crawl out of the tomb, and blinking in the early-morning light. Resurrection for them means resuscitation of a corpse: a dead body sitting up and returning to this life as Lazarus did when he came forth from the tomb.

The New Testament writers, however, treated the resurrection of Jesus differently. They didn't describe it. They announced it: "He has been raised, exactly as he promised." They didn't say *how* it happened, only *that* it did. And Jesus did not return to his former earthly existence. His appearance was transformed, his garments shone. He was hard to recognize. He did not walk the earth as we do.

Matthew 28:6

Rather, he appeared in a state of glory. The glory of God in Scripture had always been a revelation of himself. The risen Jesus was revealed as Spirit-filled and Spirit-giving. His body radiated a divine peace and joy at every meeting with his friends. He appeared suddenly, passing through locked doors, and then just as mysteriously he was gone. His presence was unpredictable, and he made himself known only to his chosen ones. It was the God-life which had been hidden within Jesus on earth that was now plainly revealed to those of faith.

## LIFE SYMBOLS

Through the centuries, the Church has tried to express the resurrection of Jesus in many ways. What do the following images convey to you about it?

The liturgy of the Easter Vigil uses new fire, newly blessed water, the prolonged ringing of bells, and the Paschal candle to suggest the new life that Jesus assumed at the resurrection, even though these and other images only faintly suggest what really took place on that momentous first Easter morning.

■ Which of the liturgical images mentioned above strikes you most forcibly as you celebrate the Paschal Mystery every year?

The *Paschal candle* is the candle lighted from the new fire at the Easter Vigil liturgy. It represents the risen Christ.

## A Human Jesus

Yet the risen Christ was continuous with his former existence as Jesus of Nazareth. He was not a pure spirit. In at least two of his appearances, he bore the marks of the crucifixion. He was the same warm human being he had always been, greeting his friends by name, teaching, forgiving, consoling, and caring for them. He even retained his characteristic gestures.

Before the resurrection, Jesus had been truly human with his divinity only dimly revealed at such privileged moments as the transfiguration. The risen Christ was that same human Jesus, but glorified—revealed in body, soul, and spirit as full of heavenly beauty and happiness. He was now visibly both human and divine.

■ What human qualities does the risen Jesus exhibit in the following appearances? What evidences of transformation are there?

> Mary Magdalene (John 20:11–18)
> The gathered Apostles (Luke 24:36–43; John 20:19)
> Thomas (John 20:24–29)
> Two disciples (Luke 24:13–35)
> Ambitious Apostles (Acts 1:3–8)
> Fishing trip (John 21:1–14)
> Forgiveness of Peter (John 21:15–23)

■ Try to imagine that Christ had never risen. What difference would it have made to the Apostles? To the world? In your own life?

## WHAT DID THE RESURRECTION MEAN?

When Jesus died, the Apostles thought everything was over. But in the resurrection they discovered the key to Calvary as well as to Christ's identity and the destiny of all creation. The significance of the resurrection to the Apostles can be summarized in four points. It

Mark 3:22

showed God's approval of Jesus. It revealed Jesus as *Kyrios* or "Lord"—that is, God's unique Son. It launched the Messianic Age. And it established the hope of eternal life for all.

## Approved by God

After the crucifixion, the followers of Jesus must have had doubts about Jesus. After all, their own religious leaders had officially condemned him as a false prophet. And if he were the Messiah, why hadn't God saved him?

The resurrection gave the Apostles all the assurance they needed to go on believing. Jesus' trust in his Father had not been misplaced: God had intervened directly to conquer Satan's mightiest stronghold, death. He made it the gate to eternal life!

In raising Jesus up, God showed his approval of approval on Jesus' mission and preaching. He showed that Jesus' miracles had been of God and not of Beelzebub, as the religious leaders had suggested. He confirmed Jesus' claim that his words would never pass away. He supported Jesus' choice of nonviolence, trust, and service over power and politics to gain the kingdom. In short, he confirmed the Apostles' faith in Jesus as the Messiah, the one who saved the world by giving his life into the hands of sinners. In the resurrection, the Father said, "This is truly my dearly loved Son. Hear him."

■ What significance does God's approval of Jesus have for you?

## Revealed as *Kyrios* (Lord)

As the gladness generated by the resurrection deepened, the Apostles grew in their understanding, especially through prayerful meditation on Scripture. The word *resurrection,* which referred to Jesus' conquest over death, didn't cover all that God had done for him. Jesus hadn't just returned to this life. He possessed a new and entirely different life.

In his first sermon, Peter announced what that life was. First he quoted Psalm 16: "I have set the Lord ever before me, with him at my right hand I shall not be disturbed." Then he applied it to the risen Christ: "This is the Jesus God has raised up. Exalted at God's right hand, he first received the promised Holy Spirit from the Father, then poured this Spirit out on us." *Exalted* here means lifted up to a place of honor. Being seated at God's right hand was the Jewish way of saying that Jesus is equal in power with God.

Acts 2:25

Acts 2:32–33

If Jesus had been given the power of God (in conquering death), he must somehow be identified with God. He shared God's life. It was as simple as that. God "raised Christ from death and seated him at his right side in the heavenly world," wrote Saint Paul to the Church in Ephesus. "Christ rules there above all heavenly rulers; he is above all titles of power in this world and in the next."

Ephesians 1:20–21 (Good News)

The followers of Jesus put the idea of Jesus' sovereignty into a short phrase they could use in their liturgies: "Jesus is Lord!" *Kyrios* ("Lord," or "my Lord") was a title the Greeks used to address foreign gods and kings. The Palestinian Jews applied it to God when Judaism forbade pronouncing the sacred name of Yahweh. When the Greek Christian communities used it for Jesus, they meant that in the Paschal Mystery Jesus was revealed as Lord of the universe or as on a level with God, although he was not the same as Yahweh.

*The Greeks and Romans, who believed in equality, did not use titles of honor among themselves.*

Saint Paul made a careful distinction. Jesus was not "the God" (the Father or Yahweh). For him, there were three: Spirit, the Lord Jesus Christ, and God. By the title of Lord, the early Christians accorded Jesus the same homage they gave to God. Christ's commands were to be obeyed as the word of God, and his commissions were to be taken with utmost seriousness. Gradually, the title was extended to include Jesus as Lord of the living and the dead and of all Greeks and

*See Romans 14:17–18 for one instance among many in which Paul distinguishes the persons of the Trinity.*

Jews. The early Christians also acknowledged Jesus as Lord in the Eucharist.

In identifying Jesus as *Kyrios,* the young Church made Jesus the center of its faith and the object of its worship. It was a startling shift for Jews, who were so conscientious about adoring the one true God. The early creeds, however, show that this is exactly what they did: "If you declare with your lips, 'Jesus is Lord,' and believe in your heart that God raised him from the dead, you will be saved."

■ If the Apostles were preparing you for baptism, could you genuinely say that Jesus is your Lord?

Romans 10:9; Jesus is also named Lord in Acts 2:36; 1 Corinthians 12:3; Philippians 2:11; John 20:28; 1 Peter 3:15

### The Messianic Age

Jesus' resurrection gave the Apostles a new slant on history. As Jews, they believed that history had three periods. From Adam to Moses was the period without the Law. From Moses to the Messiah was the period of the Law. The Messianic Age was to be the period when the Messiah would establish a New Law of justice and peace.

They saw that Jesus was the anointed Messiah who had launched the Last Age of universal peace and order. His death and resurrection saved the world from sin and death by the Law of Love. The Messianic Age that Jesus initiated was not achieved by dominating cultural and political institutions. Instead, although forgiveness of sin was a gift, salvation consisted of a moral regeneration—God's reign of love in all hearts. Since God leaves people free, there would always be those who by sin would put up obstacles to the building up of God's kingship. Therefore, although the kingdom of God on earth had been inaugurated in Christ, it looked to the future for fulfillment. It remained for Jesus' followers, the Church, to work with the Spirit to bring it to completion and so hasten the day of Christ's Second Coming.

The Apostles preached that the Messianic Age is the Age of the Church in which God's New People can enjoy a condition of union with him previously unknown, a union as close as that of the head of a body with its members. This union is initiated and nourished by the sacraments, those actions that Christ and his people perform together. Conversion to Jesus means more than personal intimacy with him. It means becoming involved with his community, especially in the celebration of the Eucharist.

See 1 Corinthians 12:12–13

Jesus' resurrection was not an event of the past merely to be admired. It was a call to action, a call to the infant Church to announce the Good News of the forgiveness of sin bestowed with the gift of the Spirit on Easter night. It was a call to live the Law of Love so that all people might come to see God's goodness in and through Christ. Christians were to become a light to a world still engulfed in darkness.

See Matthew 28:18

■ When did you first become aware that you are living in the Messianic Age? What difference does it make in your life? If you have ever shared your faith with someone, describe the experience.

## TO BE OR NOT TO BE

The earliest writings of the Bible show that before Abraham's time people did not speak of body and soul, but of a whole living person or self. They could not imagine life without a body. In Genesis 2:7 life is described as God's breath, breathed into the nostrils. When this breath was withdrawn, men and women simply returned to dust. So long as the body was in the grave, there could be no resurrection. It would be even harder to think of the resurrection of a decomposed body.

Biblical people do not seem to have been concerned with life after death. For them, survival was closely bound up with the community, and the endless cycle of life and death in nature provided a model for them. In ceremonies of initiation into puberty or marriage, they died to one form of life to enrich their existence by entering a new, more responsible role in the community. In dying they simply made room for the next generation, who carried on their life.

*Puberty* is the age of sexual maturation.

There are many other ideas of the afterlife. In the advanced civilization of Egypt, the soul was thought to leave the body for limited periods of time. The inscription on an alabaster chalice to King Tutankhamen reads: "May you spend millions of years, you who loved Thebes, sitting with your face to the north wind, your two eyes beholding happiness." By properly embalming the corpse and burying it with earthly possessions, including servants, for the next world, the dead person's relatives would prepare the soul to continue its life upon its expected return after thousands of years.

*King Tutankhamen (1355 B.C.) was a king of ancient Egypt. His tomb, opened in 1922, yielded many treasures.*

Zoroastrians (called Parsees today) believe in a three-day judgment after death and a general resurrection after thousands of years. Some Eastern religions believe in numerous reincarnations until the soul is perfect.

*Zoroaster (660–503 B.C.) was a Persian religious leader.*

*Reincarnation* is being reborn in another body.

In *Leaves of Grass*, the American poet Walt Whitman expressed the pantheistic belief that at death we dissolve into the universe from which we arose.

A *pantheist* is one who identifies God with the forces of nature.

256

A 1978 Gallup Poll noted that 47 percent of even those who don't attend any church believe firmly in Jesus' resurrection.

■ Which of the following statements come closest to expressing your belief in the nature of the afterlife?

1. My soul (the spiritual part of me only) will live forever.
2. The body I now have will rise from the grave.
3. Resurrection will occur at the end of the world when Christ comes as Judge. In the meantime, my soul will be in either heaven or hell.
4. In death I (the whole me) will rise to a mysterious life with God.
5. Both my body and soul will rise and live together, although I'm not sure where.
6. I am not sure I believe in an afterlife. I have my own ideas about it.
7. I've never really thought about it.

■ What are your hopes? Which of the following statements comes closest to expressing these hopes? I hope that in death . . .

1. my soul (only) will *leave this world* to live forever in contemplation of God.
2. I (the total person I am) will experience a renewed life that will somehow *interact* both with the world of God (which I don't know much about) and the world I now know.
3. my life will be *accepted* by God as my contribution to his kingdom.
4. regardless of what I have done during my life, *at least my last moment will be turned toward God* so that I can enjoy heaven and avoid hell.

■ Discuss your choices with a partner or a group.

## Hope of Eternal Life

Jesus' resurrection was a source of hope for the Apostles. In it God revealed himself as the God who raised and who will raise the dead. It was a pledge of their resurrection.

Colossians 1:18

The risen Jesus is the promise of our high destiny, the "first-born of the dead." He stands at the end of the journey, already victorious, beckoning all to come to the place prepared for them for eternity. The risen Jesus is the beginning of the New Creation, which will be complete only at the end of time, when the entire Body of Christ—head and members—and all creation share in the restoration of all things in God.

See 1 Corinthians 15:28; 2 Corinthians 5:19

Until that day, Christ's Spirit is ever ready with forgiveness of sin and ongoing grace to help us live this otherworldly life already begun in baptism. "I am with you always, until the end of the world" are the last words of Matthew's Gospel.

Matthew 28:20

If we could not trust God's promise of eternal life and the forgiveness and help we need to attain it, we would be fools to live as Christians, Saint Paul commented. It would be better to take all life's pleasures to the full while we can, living like the pagans who say, "Let us eat and drink, for tomorrow we die." In hope, however, we become an example to the world, especially in time of suffering when, following Christ's example, we surrender to God in trust that the cross leads to eternal life. Christians firm in hope are the hope of the world.

1 Corinthians 15:32

- Think of the biggest need you have. Is it more or less important than the forgiveness of sin? Why? What do you personally hope for from the Lord?
- How do you react to Saint Paul's statement that if you don't believe in resurrection, you might as well live like nonbelievers? Do you think it right for Christians to live life to the full? How can you be a source of hope to those outside the faith?
- What expectations do you have about your body after death? Do you really believe it will rise?

## What Is the Meaning for You?

Two appearance stories serve as models for Christian faith.

The first concerns Thomas. He wasn't rebellious; he was just cautious. For him, seeing was believing. But now Thomas had to throw caution to the winds and acknowledge the human Jesus he had once known as his personal Lord and God. Yet the presence of Jesus helped his faith, because Jesus commented, "You became a believer because you saw me." Thomas' faith came from a direct experience of the risen Christ.

John 20:29

As the foundation stones of the visible Church, the Apostles were special "bridge people," or mediators between the historical Jesus and the risen, or transhistorical, Jesus. Although we don't recognize a Jesus we once knew in the flesh, we can mysteriously touch Jesus by faith in his revelation to his witnesses. If you were to call on Shakespeare to help you write a poem, nothing would happen. But to call on Christ is to encounter a living, dynamic person and to share in his power. The Thomas incident shows that each Apostle in the community needed a personal-faith conversion to the risen Jesus. The same is true for Christians today. Their faith remains a personal, free decision to accept Jesus as Lord.

*Transhistorical* means beyond time and space.

The second "model" story—of the two disciples on the road to Emmaus—shows the ongoing presence of Christ in his community as a source of faith. Jesus gives his Holy Spirit to believers, but not as a private gift to be enjoyed in isolation. Rather, the experience of the risen Jesus is given in his Spirit-filled community where the members are "bridge people" of the risen Lord to one another and to the world.

"Where two or three are gathered in my name, there am I in their midst," Jesus had said. The faith of the two disciples going to Emmaus wavered. Scandalized at the crucifixion, they came together on their journey to talk about it. The story suggests that there are three main ways in which Christians experience the risen Jesus when they gather in community: (1) through the

Matthew 18:20

Scriptures that express the faith of the community; (2) through the breaking of the bread in the worship that Jesus commanded of his community; and (3) in daily encounters with other members of the faith community as all join together to work out problems and share joys and sorrows.

- Read Luke 24:25–27. What does "like a fire burning" mean? If you've ever experienced it, share your experience with someone you trust.
- Read Luke 24:30–31. What do you believe about the Eucharist? What Christian communities do you belong to? How do you make Jesus better known in them? How does Jesus come through for you in the groups?
- Read Luke 24:15–18, 29. Which of the three ways do you most identify with?

## WHY SHOULD YOU BELIEVE?

Probably the first thing to do when thinking about reasons to believe in the resurrection is to consider the alternative. To reject Christ's resurrection is to confine your life to this world. Many people seem to be satisfied with this arrangement. They don't ask too much and they don't get any more than the joy or pain of each moment as it passes. The problem arises when your dreams for a good life run aground. Sickness, betrayal, accident, boredom, and the loss of loved ones can cut a large wedge out of your hopes for something better. The sense of having missed the purpose of it all looms large. As you have seen, Jesus said that to miss salvation is the most painful of experiences—in fact, a living hell. That's not the best reason for looking at a better way, but it's worth thinking about.

To believe in the resurrection is to throw scientific certainty to the winds. What you get in exchange is faith-certainty. Faith-certainty is based on the promise of salvation that God made to Israel thousands of years ago, fulfilled in Jesus' resurrection, and continues to carry out in his Body, the Church.

To believe in the resurrection is to expect absolutely the most to happen, to rule out nothing, to dream the impossible dream. And to live in hope of eternal life is to walk taller now, not only because you have a goal and a purpose, but because through the Paschal Mystery you can transform the bad things, including death, into the material of your dreams.

But even the happy prospect of future life isn't enough. "The heart has its reasons," Pascal said. In the final analysis, there is no other reason for faith in the resurrection than Jesus himself. Only a risen Christ can keep the kind of promises Jesus made—to be your life's companion, your food for the journey, the living voice speaking to you in Scripture, and the unfailing source of the Spirit ever present in your heart. And only the love of the risen Christ can inspire the lasting love you desire, whether it is love of him or love of those you care for in him.

Such faith is the absolute opposite of hell. It is peace and joy. Just before he died, Jesus said, "All this I tell you that my joy may be yours and your joy may be complete." What is the source of this joy? God's goodness. God's love is the message Jesus lived and died and rose to communicate.

John 15:11

The ultimate reason for believing in the resurrection, then, is joy. This joy is Christ's resurrection gift for your journey through life. It will be your heaven when you finally and forever reach home.

- What do you understand by the coming of God's kingdom in its fullness?
- Write five statements that express what you believe about the resurrection. You may include anything about its importance, Jesus' appearances, the tomb, the women, the Apostles, or its meaning to you.
- In your journal, record what the resurrection means to you personally. What new insights did your study of it afford? How does it affect your life on a day-by-day basis?

## SUMMING UP

1. *Words to know:* first day, witnesses, Easter, cornerstone, overbelief, underbelief, literary forms, resuscitation, glorified, *Kyrios,* exalted, Messianic Age, Age of the Church, New Creation, mediators, Paschal candle, general resurrection, reincarnation
2. Describe the resurrection experiences of these witnesses: Magdalene and the women; Peter and John; the gathered Apostles.
3. Name five discrepancies among the resurrection texts. Why don't these dissimilarities disprove the truth of the resurrection?
4. List five objections that were made to Jesus' resurrection. How does Scripture answer each?
5. Why was it hard for the evangelists to depict the risen Christ? Describe the two extreme mistaken positions in regard to the nature of the resurrection.
6. What was the risen Jesus like as far as we can describe him?
7. How did the appearance of the risen Christ settle the dispute between the Apostles who believed in Christ and the religious leaders who didn't?
8. What was the significance of the Early Christians giving Jesus the title *Kyrios* (Lord)?
9. How did the resurrection launch a New Age? What is the role of the Church in it?
10. What hope does the resurrection give us? What means does the resurrection give to attain that hope?
11. How is Thomas a model for believers in the risen Christ? What means of encountering Christ does the story of the two disciples on the road to Emmaus give to members of the Church?
12. What difference does it make whether you believe in the resurrection?

### Think/Talk/Write

1. Why do you think Magdalene, the woman from whom Jesus had cast out seven devils, is the first and quickest to recognize the risen Christ?
2. A college student you know returns for spring break. During a visit to your house, he mentions that one of his professors said that Jesus'

resurrection wasn't all that great. After all, he said, Jesus had raised ordinary people like Lazarus and the widow's son from the dead, and both Peter and Paul had also raised the dead to life, so the resurrection did not really reveal Jesus' divinity. Respond to the professor's views.

## Activities

1. Five hundred million cells of your body are renewed every day and every seven years your entire body is completely different, yet you remain the same person. Incorporate this information into a news feature in which you explain the connection between these facts and the risen Jesus.
2. Find a psalm you think particularly appropriate to the resurrection. Study its moods, eliminate verses that do not develop the theme, and conduct the class or a small group in a choral recitation, using variations in pitch, pace, and volume to dramatize the meaning. Psalm 9 or 18 may suit your purpose.

## Scripture Search

A. The Old Testament contains texts that suggest a coming resurrection. Tell how these passages do that: Ezekiel 37:1–14; Psalm 16; Daniel 12:1–3.
B. While the Gospels tell the story of the resurrection, the Acts of the Apostles and the Pauline Letters interpret the meaning of the event.
   1. Write one sentence summarizing what each of these passages says about the event: Acts 1:1–5; 2:24, 26; Romans 3:23–26; 6:3–11; 1 Corinthians 15:1–8, 35–44; Ephesians 1:3–10.
   2. One of the most important chapters on the resurrection is 1 Corinthians 15. It can be divided into three sections: (a) witnesses to the resurrection, 1–11; (b) our resurrection, 12–34; (c) the risen body, 35–38. Read section (a) and either section (b) or (c). Write a report that includes a brief summary of what is said as well as your personal reaction to either the entire passage or to any part of it.

**FOURTEEN**

Does a person's name really have a special meaning?

What can you learn from the titles of Jesus?

Was Jesus always aware that he was divine?

Who wrote the creeds?

What contribution have the councils made to our understanding of Jesus?

Who is Jesus to you?

*Though he was in the form of God,*
*he did not deem equality with God*
*something to be grasped at.*
*Rather, he emptied himself*
*and took the form of a slave*
*being born in the likeness of men.*
*He was known to be of human estate,*
*and it was thus that he humbled himself,*
*obediently accepting even death,*
*death on a cross!*
*Because of this,*

*God highly exalted him*
*and bestowed on him the name*
*above every other name,*
*So that at Jesus' name*
*every knee must bend*
*in the heavens, on the earth,*
*and under the earth,*
*and every tongue proclaim*
*to the glory of God the Father:*
*Jesus Christ is Lord!*

(Philippians 2:6–11)

# Who Is Jesus?

At Jesus' name every knee must bend in the heavens, on the earth, and under the earth, and every tongue proclaims to the glory of God the Father: Jesus Christ is Lord!

## EXPRESSING THE TIMELESS TAKES TIME

John 19:34

Saint John suggests that at the instant of his death Jesus was glorified by the Father and sent the Holy Spirit into the world. But then, in the same Gospel, Jesus announces to Mary Magdalene on Easter morning, three days later, that he has not yet ascended to the Father, and he gives his Spirit to the Apostles that evening. Saint Luke, on the other hand, marks the coming of the Spirit on pentecost, ten days after Jesus' "ascension," which took place forty days after the resurrection.

*At the time the Apostles lived, people believed that heaven was "up." Actually, there is no human way to describe heaven.*

These apparent contradictions only show that God is not bound by time. Once Jesus died, time no longer existed for him. His redemption of the world was a single event that broke through the boundaries of time and space; it reached back to the beginning of creation, and forward to include the final person at time's end. But Christ had to adjust his appearances to people still governed by time. What God accomplished in the blink of an eye, the Apostles needed a period of weeks,

266                    JESUS

months, and even years to grasp. In fact, the Church today is still grappling with the mystery of Jesus.

How do you express eternal events in the language of time? Saint Luke made a stab at solving the problem by dramatizing the different phases of the mystery of the risen Jesus in several separate events. Today you know these phases as the resurrection, ascension, and glorification of Jesus, and pentecost, or the sending of the Holy Spirit. These events revealed Jesus' true identity.

■ What effect does knowing that all the Church feasts are only aspects of the one mystery of Christ have on you?

Acts 1:9

## THE ASCENSION

The Acts of the Apostles reports that Jesus appeared to his Apostles "over the course of forty days." (Forty days is a symbol in the Bible that indicates an especially sacred time of history.) During this time, Jesus promised that the Apostles would soon be baptized with the Holy Spirit. Then, Saint Luke reports, "he was lifted up before their eyes in a cloud which took him from their sight." The ascension is a way of saying that Jesus discontinued his visible appearances. The cloud into which he disappeared is a biblical symbol regularly used to indicate the divine presence. Its position in the sky suggests Jesus' exaltation at the right hand of the Father. The Apostles returned to the cenacle with Mary to ponder the meaning of all that had happened and to pray for divine guidance.

A *cenacle* is a small dining room, usually on an upper floor.

Since childhood, you have been taught that Jesus is divine. But to the Jewish community, which believed strongly in one God, there was no thought of such an idea at first. They saw that Jesus had been "approved" by God in the resurrection and that God had worked powerfully in him, but it took a while before the idea that Jesus was the unique Son of God really sank in.

## THE SPIRIT AND THE FIRST PROCLAMATIONS

It was in the deeply religious experience of pentecost that the gathered community of Jesus' followers realized who Jesus was. At the same time, they understood that it was their mission to preach the revelation they had received. As the Holy Spirit continued to enlighten them, they tried to express their growing understanding of Jesus' identity in words they could easily remember and repeat. These became the *titles* of Jesus and the *creeds* used in their sermons, letters, and Gospel accounts.

*Christology* is the area of theology that studies the Person and attributes of Jesus, especially the ways in which he is both human and divine.

You have already seen that from the first writings of Paul to the last evangelist, the Church's Christology underwent a rapid development under the mighty impulse of the Holy Spirit. Finally Jesus was declared the only-begotten Son of God from all eternity. It is this faith that has been handed down to us.

*Doctrines* are official statements of belief that are taught.

As the Church absorbed new members, each generation and region added new insights to its grasp of Jesus' role in the world. *Church councils* were called to formulate doctrines about the sacred mysteries revealed in Jesus. In this chapter you will explore this growth in the Church's understanding as reflected in the titles, creeds, and councils so that you can clarify and deepen your own faith.

- By which title do you most often address Jesus? Why?
- What is your favorite line in the creed? What doctrines have you been taught about Jesus? Which do you feel are most important? Why?

## EARLY CHRISTIAN FAITH

### What's in a Name?

The average American adult is said to possess at least ten identifying numbers.

- How important is your name to you? How do you feel when people mispronounce or misspell it, call you belittling nicknames, or address you either too familiarly or too formally? Why?
- What numbers have already been assigned to you? Which will be added as you grow older? How do you feel about being known by a set of numbers?

If you are like most people, you aren't happy to be only a number. You like your name and you want it spelled and pronounced correctly. Your name gives you a sense of uniqueness and identity. Your name is a bridge. It gives people power over you and reveals something about you to them. The way others use your name reveals something about your relationship with them, too. When people address you, they ask for a response. You cannot remain indifferent to their call to relationship.

By studying the names and titles given to Jesus by the Christian community after his resurrection, you can learn what Jesus came to mean to his followers and enrich your own understanding of him. It can put into perspective the many facets of Jesus' personality and mission you've learned about so far. You can also see how the mystery of Jesus continues to unfold even today.

A *title* is an official name given a person by virtue of role, rank, or office, or as a mark of respect.

- Does the name you personally give Jesus make any difference? Why or why not?

# THE JESUS PRAYER

The experience of thousands prove that tranquilizers, saunas, and fun vacations are not the cure for the hectic pace of modern life.

■ Have you ever felt that you were going crazy? What do you do at such times?

Catholics have rediscovered the Jesus Prayer, a kind of Oriental mantra or prayer formula that has the power to still your body and open your spirit. It originated with a simple Russian peasant who had lost his family and home in a fire. To keep from despair, he became a pilgrim in search of someone to teach him the secret of continual prayer. One day he met an old monk who, in response to his request, put him in a bare room and told him to repeat the following sentence five hundred times: *"Jesus, Son of the living God, have mercy on me, a sinner."* The next day he was told to repeat the prayer a thousand times, then two thousand times, then three thousand times. Much later, the man found that almost without conscious effort, from deep within, the words simmered, so that he was praying while he carried on other duties.

Each repetition of the Jesus Prayer is an act of worship. Some people shorten the prayer to *Jesus, have mercy on me.* The first three syllables are said while breathing in, the next three while breathing out, and the final one finishes with a brief pause between breaths. Or you may simply repeat the name *Jesus* until you experience his presence and power.

Many have testified to the increased happiness and peace the Jesus Prayer puts in their lives.

■ Take apart the four phrases of this ancient prayer. How does it sum up the life, message, and reality of the Gospel?

*The most famous Oriental mantra is Om, pronounced so that the m is prolonged.*

## Jesus' Names

Like us, Jesus was known by a number of names as he went through life, and these names are revealing.

His personal name, Jesus, was common in his day because many parents had a devotion to the great Israelite leader, Joshua. As you have learned, it is a shortened form of "Yahweh brings salvation." The early Christians recognized that this name was prophetic of Jesus' mission—to be the "Savior." The evangelists note that it was given him by an angel, a name with such power that just pronouncing it in faith can bring salvation. *Jesus,* or *Jeshua,* was the name Mary and Joseph and his relatives and friends called our Lord when he was growing up. Although now you often hear the two names *Jesus Christ* used together as if *Christ* were Jesus' last name, Jesus was probably not called *Christ* during his life. This title, which means "the Anointed One" or "Messiah," was applied after the resurrection.

Luke 1:32. *Jesus* means "savior."

Like other Jewish males, Jesus was ordinarily known as the son of Joseph, his supposed father. Probably because of the early Christian community's conviction that Jesus was conceived by the Holy Spirit, Mark's Gospel refers to Jesus as "the son of Mary." This is unusual, because in the Jewish culture people were not identified by their mothers. Jesus was also referred to as "the carpenter" and the "carpenter's son" because of his trade.

Luke 3:23; Matthew 13:55; also see John 1:45

Mark 6:3

Mark 6:3; Matthew 13:55

Once Jesus had begun his public life, he was addressed as rabbi—master or teacher. He taught the crowds as the rabbis did, although there is no evidence in the Gospel that he was trained by a rabbi for his office. Most probably, because of his teaching mission, the people called him *Lord,* or *My Lord,* in the way we politely use sir or ma'am.

But since Jesus' true identity was not clearly known until after his death, it was the titles given him by the post-resurrection followers that reveal what he became to them.

- How do you feel about the fact that it took two or three generations for the early Church to grasp who

Jesus is? How long do you think it takes most individuals today? You may want to speak from your own experience.

## The Titles Jesus Received After the Resurrection

### Lord

As you learned in your study of the resurrection, the first title the early Christians applied to Jesus was *Kyrios,* or *Lord.* Peter, and especially Paul, use it frequently, citing Old Testament texts that employ *Lord* to refer to God. By this title, Jesus was put on a par with God, not under him, as *son* implies. It was a title of majesty, declaring that Jesus had been given supreme authority over all people, living and dead, and that as the risen One he had a vital influence on the lives and conduct of his followers and was worthy of adoration.

See Acts 2:21; 4:12, 29–30, 31; 5:41

### Servant of Yahweh

Another ancient title used by the Apostles was *Servant of Yahweh.* This title originated with Isaiah when he tried to understand the sufferings of Israel in Babylon. He portrayed the ideal Servant of God, the perfect Israelite, as someone who is obedient to God's will even in the midst of overwhelming suffering. This "Suffering Servant" was a new revelation because it introduced the idea that Israel's salvation would be achieved through suffering. It also introduced the idea that someone could suffer in place of others. "Because he surrendered himself to death and was counted among the wicked . . . he shall take away the sins of many, and win pardon for their offenses."

Isaiah 53:12

The "Servant of Yahweh" prophesied by Isaiah was to be a mediator, someone who, like Moses, would bridge the gulf between God and humanity. But unlike Moses, who was not called to suffer for his people, this Servant would be sent "as a covenant of the people" by suffering which he did not deserve.

Isaiah 42:1

Isaiah 42:6; also see Isaiah 53:9–11

From this prophecy of Isaiah, the Apostles drew their understanding of how Jesus could be the Messiah and still have suffered so cruel a death. Whenever they said Jesus had fulfilled the Scriptures, it was usually a reference to the Suffering Servant foretold by Isaiah. Through these important prophecies, Mark could present Jesus as the Messiah more by his suffering than by his resurrection, to which his Gospel devotes very little space.

See 1 Corinthians 15:3–4; Luke 24:25–26; Acts 8:32–35; 13:13, 26

- What limitations did Christ take on when he became a human being? What does Jesus teach about the requirements of those who aspire to be spiritual leaders?
- What do you think of the Christian belief that others can be saved by the suffering they offer in union with Christ?

### Christ (Messiah)

But it was the Greek title *Christ,* or *Messiah,* that came into greatest use and stayed with Jesus to our own day. Originating from the Hebrew *Maśiah,* it literally means "the anointed," and expresses the Christian belief that Jesus is the Messiah promised by God to Israel.

Acts 2:36, 17:3; also see Psalms 2:2 and Acts 4:27

It seems, from certain texts, that Jesus might have already been recognized as the Messiah during his lifetime. But he always avoided publicizing his messianic

Acts 10:37 and Mark 8:29

character and corrected the people who professed their faith in him as Messiah. He insisted that his real role would be one of humility, service, and suffering, rejecting the contemporary notions of miracle worker and warrior-savior.

Yet despite all his precautions, it was as Messiah-King that Jesus was crucified. That title identified Jesus with the promise made by the prophet Nathan to David: God would establish a mysterious and everlasting dynasty. When some of the Davidic kings turned out bad, Israel begged God to send them an anointed one worthy of David's name. And when the monarchy was completely crushed in 586 B.C., the people's anticipation was heightened. They called on God to send a Messiah who would bring all other nations to the worship of Yahweh. There was no hint that this savior would be anything but political and Jewish, and there was certainly no thought of a *divine* savior.

But the Apostles had a hard time selling the title because Jesus' earthly career was in no way glorious, regal, or victorious. He had established no kingdom. Israel had not been delivered—in fact, before the last Gospel was written, Jerusalem had been demolished. And the Gentile nations had not been brought under Israel's rule to worship Yahweh. Modern Jews still voice these objections.

For some time, the Apostles tried to get around these objections by explaining that Jesus would be the Messiah at the time of the Second Coming when the whole world would see his power and glory. Peter said, "Reform your lives! . . . May a season of refreshment be granted you. . . . Jesus must remain in heaven until the time of universal restoration."

Another view was that Jesus was to be a purely spiritual Messiah, with his reign visible only in heaven. But the apostolic preachers weren't satisifed with either of these interpretations. By further meditation on Scripture, they broadened the Jewish notion of Messiah to include suffering. The idea of suffering was strictly a Christian interpretation, which made it possible to

Isaiah 9:5

Acts 3:19–21

Acts 3:18, 17:3; Luke 24:26, 46

274

JESUS

preach that Jesus was a Messiah not only in his passion but also in his lowly birth.

To Christians, *Christ* is a title proclaiming belief in Jesus as the one approved by God and sharing his power and glory in a risen, Spirit-filled life. It does not refer to the historic Jesus of the past, nor even so much to Jesus in his Second Coming, but to the risen Jesus mysteriously alive and active in his community of followers.

*Persecuted Christians used either the symbol of a fish or ICHTHUS, which is Greek for "fish," as a code for Jesus' name.*

Gradually "Christ" became joined to "Jesus" as an additional name, and both Mark and Matthew open their Gospels using both names. The title *Christ* even came to replace the name Jesus at times.

Of all Jesus' titles, "Christ" is the most important. It identifies him as the Messiah who was promised and actually sent to the world. It also forms the root of the name "Christian," the title by which Jesus' followers became known in the city of Antioch.

Acts 11:26

■ Where in the liturgy of the Eucharist are the two important titles Lord and Christ used?

■ By what name do you call Jesus when speaking of him to others? Jesus, Christ, our Lord, the Lord? What does each mean to you? How do you address him in your prayer?

### Son of David

Another title that suggested messiahship was Son of David. The people who addressed Jesus in this way in the Gospel could hardly have known Jesus' family background as they called out to him. They may have used this title because they recognized Jesus as the kingly Messiah foretold by the prophet Nathan. Or the evangelists may have put these words into their mouths because, by the time the Gospels were written, they had come to understand that Jesus fulfilled the Scripture as David's descendant.

Matthew 9:27, 15:22, 20:30, 21:9

Writing for Jewish converts, Matthew uses the title "Son of David" at least seven times, but the other evangelists use it as well. Most often it is on the lips of those

Matthew 9:27

who call out to Jesus for a cure: "Son of David, have pity on us."

In the genealogies, two evangelists show that Jesus did indeed have a legal claim to the Davidic throne through both Mary and Joseph. Nevertheless, it was more by his quality of leadership than by his lineage that the people recognized his potential "kingship." The crowds were constantly ready to make him king. Saint John says that after the multiplication of the loaves, Jesus "fled back to the mountain alone" to escape the crowds, and at his triumphal entry into Jerusalem, they also had intentions of crowning him. In riding into the city just before his death, Jesus mysteriously allowed the people to acknowledge him as king. To fulfill the messianic prophecies, he came on a humble donkey—hardly the transport of a king! In his ascension, Jesus is revealed as King of creation and Lord of heaven and earth. His rule, however, remains one of service and humble love.

Matthew 11:8–10

*In Israel, the horse was the symbol of the conqueror. (See Matthew 21:5; Isaiah 62:11; Zechariah 9:9.)*

- There are two kinds of leaders: those who command those who serve. Which is preferred by most people? Why? Which do you prefer?
- Read the following section from Psalm 89 as if it were written just for you, as the servant chosen by God (which you really are), and insert your name on the blank:

    I have made a covenant with my chosen one.
    I have given my servant my word.
    I have made your name, ———————— ,
    to last forever, to outlast all time.

    What is God's promise to you? What does it mean to you? Write your thoughts in your journal.

Psalm 89:4–5

### Son of God

As the thinking of the early Christian community matured, the important title *Son of God* came into use. The way its meaning developed is shown in the three different uses of the title in the Gospels.

The Israelites had always thought of themselves as "sons of God," just as Christians call themselves "children of God." People who were especially dear to God were his "sons" in a closer sense, much as Joseph was Jacob's "favorite son." But no prophet, not even Moses, was thought of as a "divine son." The Gospels make use of all three of these meanings.

On the lowest level, as Jesus calms the storm, the disciples exclaim, "Truly you are the Son of God!" Here they only mean to name Jesus as a "Man of God" in whom God works in a special way. After the resurrection, the Apostles recognized Jesus' divinity in this act; but as simple fishermen of Jewish background, they would never have thought of Jesus as actually being divine. Matthew 14:33

On Calvary when the pagan centurion exclaims, "He really was the Son of God," he recognizes Jesus as an extraordinarily good man—a "favorite son" of God, a man in whom God's goodness was shown in an exceptional way. Matthew 27:54

The title is used in its highest sense at Jesus' baptism and transfiguration. On both occasions the heavens open and a voice says, "This is my own dear Son." When they looked back from the vantage point of the resurrection, the Apostles saw in these two events that Jesus had always been not only *a* son of God, but *the* one, only-begotten Son who had a personal relation with the Father. Matthew 3:17; 17:5

This unique sonship is merely implied throughout the Gospels when Jesus casts out Satan, forgives sin, says that his words will never pass away, speaks on his own authority, and brings the Mosaic law to perfection. But in the last of the Gospels, which uses the title twenty-five times, Jesus is the Son in a uniquely divine sense. He gives believers the "power to become God's children." In John, the title is never applied to anyone but Jesus, and only in John does Jesus state directly that he is the Son of God. John 1:12

John 10:36

In the other titles, Jesus is revealed in relation to what he did for us. The title *Son of God* probes the mystery of Jesus himself. By it we enter into the life of the Holy Trinity, into Jesus' divine personhood, and into the mystery of his being both divine and human.

■ What does being a son or daughter of God (because Jesus is our brother) really mean to you?

*Prophet*

Although the title *prophet* later lost its popularity, it still clarifies certain important things about Jesus. From the beginning of his public ministry, the crowds recognized Jesus as a prophet. We read, "Fear seized them all and they began to praise God. 'A great prophet has risen among us.'' Others said, "He is a prophet equal to any of the prophets." At first it was Jesus' miracles that created this impression. Later the Samaritan woman accepted Jesus as a prophet because of the authority with which he answered her questions on doctrine and his knowledge of her secret sins.

Although Jesus applied the title to himself when he said, "No prophet gains acceptance in his native place," in the parable of the Tenants in the Vineyard, Jesus makes himself the "son" rather than one of the "servants" who stand for the prophets. The Sanhedrin condemned him as a false prophet. But Jesus truly is a prophet because he announced God's Word to the people. Jesus, however, is much more than just a prophet. He not only reveals God's Word, he *is* God's final Word spoken to us *in person*.

Modern scholars have raised this question: Did Jesus *know* that he was more than a prophet from the first days of his life? As early as the fifth century, theologians, saints, and scholars offered explanations of how Jesus, as a human being, could know all things, and how, as a divine being, he could grow in knowledge. The fact is that it can't be completely explained. It is part of his mystery.

Some contemporary theologians say it is a perfection, not a limitation, for human beings to acquire knowledge, and that it would not have been necessary for Jesus to have all knowledge in order to fulfill his mission. They think he would be a better human model if he had to grow by degrees in his self-understanding. He would be false to himself if his anguish in the Gar-

Luke 7:16

Mark 6:15
*Like Jesus, the prophets of the Old Testament worked wonders to show God's approval of their message.*

Luke 4:24

Mark 12:1–11

Saint John's title for Jesus as "Word of God who existed from all eternity" is *logos*, the Greek for *word*.

den and on the cross were only *pretended* because he had already experienced the beatific vision and knew the future.

The *beatific vision* is the direct vision of God.

Jesus did in fact show uncertainty about the future when he said no one except the Father knows the day of the final coming, and he truly experienced fear, pain, surprise, and disappointment. And yet Jesus spoke and acted like the unique Son of God when he taught with authority, forgave sin, and predicted his Second Coming. A modern view is that Jesus had deep insight as to who he was, but he needed time for his self-awareness to surface.

The story of a priest-journalist who returned to his high school for a reunion may illustrate Jesus' situation. In an old school paper on display, he read that when he was a sophomore a student reporter had interviewed him about his plans for the future. He was amazed to find that he had said he might be either a priest or a journalist. Having forgotten the interview, he could hardly believe that at fifteen he had possessed so much self-awareness. And although this early awareness had not lightened the burdens of all his decisions and hard work, it must in some way have guided him all along.

Jesus, too, must always have had a deep intuition of his divinity, which came to the surface more and more as he prayed and cooperated with each circumstance his Father sent him.

It seems that we will have to wait until we achieve our own vision of God to know what degree of awareness of his divinity Jesus possessed. In exploring the question, however, you can better appreciate the depth of this mystery—the union of Jesus' humanity and divinity.

As God's Word, Jesus came in person to reveal all that we need to know of God, and yet he does not reveal God completely. God is a mystery far beyond our reach.

■ Which Jesus appeals more to you—the one who knew all things from the moment of his birth or the one who struggled to find God's will in the circumstances of his life? Why?

## Other Titles

Yahweh means "I am who am." See Exodus 3:14; John 6:20; 8:24, 28, 58; 13:19; 18:5, 6, 8.

John 1:18, 14 (Good News)

Many other titles came into use during the period of the apostolic community. Jesus' personal name suggested the use of "Savior," a title that was restricted only to God in Old Testament times. From the ancient tradition of the sacrifice of a lamb as a memorial of the original Hebrew Passover, Christians saw Jesus as the "Lamb of God," the sacrificial lamb led to slaughter to save the New Israel. It was John the Baptizer's role to point him out. In the Book of Revelation, Jesus is depicted as a lamb twenty-eight times.

The Letter to the Hebrews explains Jesus' role as the great High Priest and the Book of Revelation names Jesus the "Alpha and the Omega," the first and last letters of the Greek alphabet. This title is like the expression *A to Z,* and means "encompassing everything." To the author of Revelation, Jesus is the beginning and the end of human history as well as of each individual life. He gives everything its true meaning.

John's Gospel specializes in titles derived from images such as bread, light, door, and shepherd, which have roots that go far back in the Old Testament. But John's way of having Jesus use the expression "I am" implies Jesus' relationship with the great "I am" who revealed his name to Moses as Yahweh: "I am who am." It is a hidden expression of Jesus' divinity.

So, then, the early Church's final proclamation to the world is that God revealed his divinity in the man named Jesus. Salvation comes to us through the God-man, the man Jesus who is God's only Son. John writes, "No one has ever seen God. The Word became a human being and lived among us. The only One who is the same as God and is at the Father's side, he has made him known."

- In your journal, write your three favorite titles of Jesus. Tell what they mean to you.
- How is Jesus different from other high priests in Hebrews 7:26–28 and 7:23–25?

# THE COUNCILS, THE CREEDS, AND YOU

The challenge of "defining" Jesus was not completed when the last title of Jesus had been recorded in the New Testament. After all, no title can capture any person, much less the deep mystery of the God-man. For several centuries, the Church struggled to express who and what Jesus was to the people who lived in the sophisticated Greek world where philosophy was studied by every educated man.

## Councils

During the first centuries of the Church, when philosophical discussions drew the scholars away from the Scriptures and deeper into theory, exaggerations threatened to make Jesus either pure God, putting on humanness as a person puts on clothes, or pure man, and not divine. Through research and the public debates that were necessary to correct these exaggerations in ways that the people of the times could understand, the Church further developed its understanding of the mystery of Jesus.

In the Church councils called to review the issues, popes and bishops, under the guidance of the Holy Spirit, formulated statements that condemned false teaching and defined the Church's faith in both Jesus' humanity and his divinity.

At this time it is more important for you to be aware that many great thinkers have grappled with the problems of Jesus' identity than to study the heresies themselves. Some of the main Christological heresies (opinions contrary to official Church teachings) are the following: Arianism, Nestorianism, Docetism, and Monophysitism. These heresies, their authors, the corresponding teachings that corrected them, and the councils at which the problems were resolved are shown in the chart on the next page

## Christological Heresies

| NAME OF HERESY, AUTHOR | HERETICAL OPINION | CORRECTIVE COUNCIL AND ITS TEACHING |
|---|---|---|
| Arianism Arius, 256–336 | Jesus was created at a particular point in time by the Father and so was not truly God. | Council of Nicea, 325 The Nicene Creed expanded the Apostles' Creed. It declared Christ consubstantial (equal in substance) with the Father. |
| Nestorianism Nestorius, 428 | Jesus was two persons, one human and one divine. Mary is only the mother of the man Jesus, not the mother of God. | Council of Ephesus, 431 Mary is the mother of God, the one Person who is the Son of God. |
| Docetism (from Greek *dokei* "to seem") | Jesus' body was an illusion, not real, because God could not have taken on the limitations of a man and remained God. | Chalcedon, 451 Jesus is truly human and truly divine. |
| Monophysitism ("one nature"— Eutychian) Eutyches, monk | Jesus has only one nature—divine. His human nature was absorbed by the divine. Jesus' body was different from ours. | Chalcedon, 451 Jesus has two natures, one human and one divine. |

It is said that those who ignore history are condemned to repeat its mistakes. The insights preserved in the early Church writings and council documents form a part of a rich Catholic heritage that is perhaps unequaled in the world. Without them, today's Church would be poorer in its understanding of Jesus.

But investigation of the mystery of Jesus is never complete. The scientific methods and archaeological discoveries of our own age have been responsible for new and exciting ways of seeing him through the Gospels. The Church's self-reflection during Vatican II (1962–1965) continued the probe.

■ Which appeal to you more, the titles of the early Church or the doctrinal statements of the councils? Why?

## DEMOCRACY OF THE CHURCH

You hear a great deal today about councils: the United Nations Security Council, city councils, parish councils, and student councils. A council is a group of people meeting to discuss questions that are of concern to them.

Councils are nothing new in the Church. The first Church council was held in Jerusalem about A.D. 52. After hearing heated arguments on both sides, the Apostles decided not to impose the law of circumcision on the pagan converts to Christianity. This important decision opened the door of the Church to the Gentiles. Following the example of the Apostles, the bishops of the entire Church have assembled on the average of about once every hundred years to reach decisions on matters of faith or morals that needed to be cleared up in their time.

One of the more important councils was the Council of Trent (1545–1563), called to clean up the wreckage left by the split in Christian Europe as a result of the Protestant Reformation in the sixteenth century. In twenty-five sessions, this nineteenth ecumenical council made declarations on nearly every aspect of Christian belief and practice: Scripture, tradition, original sin, the seven sacraments, the Mass, and the saints. It had two purposes—to counteract the Protestant revolt and to reform the Church.

An *ecumenical council* is one in which the bishops of the entire Church participate.

In our own times, Vatican II (1962–1965), the twenty-first ecumenical council, was convoked by Pope John XXIII and completed under Paul VI. It was the first council to invite large numbers of representatives of other churches and Catholic laypersons to witness and react to its deliberations.

Pope John expressed the hope that the council would be a new pentecost, renewing the Church's internal energies, reinvigorating its sense of mission to the entire world, and adapting it to present-day needs. He expressed the desire to see a reunion of the separated churches of the East and West. His statement about "opening a window to let in a little fresh air" has become a classic.

Vatican II was the first council ever to be called just for the purpose of renewal rather than to counteract some heresy. Its main focus was to complete the Constitution of the Church begun by Vatican Council I (1870). Only four of its proposed fifteen chapters had been completed by the earlier council, with the result that only the pope's role had been defined.

The Second Vatican Council took a biblical view of the Church as the People of God. It declared that all are called to holiness and have an important role to play in the building of God's kingdom on earth. In line with this principle, the collegiality of the bishops was clarified and Mary was included in the main Constitution of the Church.

In sixteen documents, the council updated the Church in matters of liturgy, ministry, ecumenism, education, the apostolate of the laity, the use of media, and religious liberty. It laid great stress on the Church's mission to the modern world.

More than two thousand bishops representing nearly every part of the world participated in the four sessions, making use of modern equipment for simultaneous translation. In addition, many learned priests acted as advisers (*periti,* in Latin) to the bishops.

- Ask someone older than yourself what changes have come in the Church since Vatican II. What changes have come about in your own lifetime?
- If you were a bishop today, what further changes would you suggest for extending God's kingdom on earth?

A *heresy* is a belief contrary to an official Church teaching.

*Collegiality* is the authority of the bishops acting in a body and in relation to the pope.

JESUS

## Creeds

When you want to communicate something important, you choose your words carefully; likewise, when the Church wants to express its faith officially, it formulates its statements with great precision. These formulas are known as creeds, from the Latin *credere,* "to believe."

The creeds had their origin in the questions asked of candidates for baptism. The apostolic teaching was gradually put together in a statement called the Apostles' Creed, which is still prayed in connection with the saying of the rosary. Beginning with the declaration of faith in a living God, it states the birth, death, and resurrection of Jesus Christ as Son of God and Lord, and it proclaims the coming of the Holy Spirit. This declaration of faith was usually required at baptism and renewed by all at the Eucharistic liturgies, especially at the Easter Vigil when converts were baptized.

The councils that issued official documents to clarify the teachings of the heretics also composed creeds to renew the faith of the people. Creeds such as the Nicean and Athanasian expand the Apostles' Creed. These proclamations of faith that were made up to fit the needs of the times have continued to be formed through the ages. The last one, the Credo of the People of God, was written by Pope Paul VI in 1968.

- For yourself, or as a class, go through one of the creeds you know. What does it say about Jesus? How different is its teaching from what you find in one of Peter's first sermons in Acts 10:34–43?

## And You?

One day while Jesus and his Apostles were setting out for some northern villages, he asked them some very personal questions. "Who do people say I am?" They came up with different answers: "Some say John the Baptizer, others Elijah. Still others say one of the prophets who is to come." This seemed to satisfy Jesus about

Mark 8:27–29

the opinion of the crowds. Then, looking them square in the eye, he asked, "And you, who do you say I am?"

The opinions others hold don't really make the big difference in your life. It's what you personally believe that counts—what you believe when your parents aren't breathing over you, when you are away from your family and friends, when you face yourself in quiet moments, and when you have to go it alone on the last voyage of your life to face Christ himself.

You may know all about Jesus' titles and the creeds and councils, but it doesn't mean a thing unless you yourself take a stand. The decision is yours. No one else can make it for you. Christ asks you the very same personal question: "And you, who do you say I am?"

■ What do you really believe? Who is Jesus to you? In your journal, write a personal creed expressing your faith, or just informally, in your own words, tell Christ who he is to you.

JESUS

## SUMMING UP

1. *Words to know:* ascension, glorification, right hand of God, pentecost, cloud of glory, forty days, cenacle, Christology, title, doctrine, Jesus, Lord, Servant of Yahweh, Christ (Messiah), Son of David, Son of God, prophet, Church council, heresy, Arianism, Nestorianism, Docetism, Monophysitism, creed

2. How can you explain the apparent contradictions in the Gospels regarding the time of Jesus' glorification and the sending of the Spirit?

3. How do the writings of the New Testament show that the early Christians grew in their understanding of Jesus? What was the role of the councils?

4. What were some of the names and titles by which Jesus was known during his life?

5. What was the significance of the first title, Lord, that the early Christians gave Jesus?

6. What new revelation did Isaiah's Servant of Yahweh add to Israel's idea of a Messiah?

7. What made it difficult for the Apostles to convince the Jews that Jesus was the Messiah (Christ)? How did they solve the problem?

8. How did Jesus reinterpret the tradition in Israel that the Messiah would be kingly?

9. What three stages did the Christian understanding of the title Son of God pass through?

10. How is Jesus both a prophet and more than a prophet? Why do modern theologians believe that Jesus grew in understanding his identity?

11. Name some lesser titles of Jesus and briefly explain each.

12. What two basic types of exaggerations underlie the Christological heresies of the first centuries of the Church? What was the twofold role of the councils in the search of Jesus' true identity?

13. What clear official beliefs came out of the three main Christological councils?

14. Name three creeds that have echoed and expanded the fundamental teaching of the Apostles.

### Think/Talk/Write

1. From your watching of TV and films, how would you judge the modern understanding of the sacredness of God's name?
2. Name the positions of leadership in your school, your home, and where you work. Suggest one way that the leader in each of these situations can be a "king" according to the standards of Jesus' kingship.
3. What is the meaning of the name you received in baptism? In what sense are all Christians named after Jesus when they receive a saint's name at baptism?
4. Which do you prefer, *Jesus* or *Christ*? Why? What pictures does each bring to your mind?

### Activities

1. You maintain a self that is recognizable even as you develop. This is sometimes evident by a comparison of your baby pictures with later photos—there is usually some characteristic look or other feature that somehow remains the same despite the changes. Have the class bring in baby pictures and try to identify them.
2. The real source of your individuality springs from deep within. The more like Jesus you are inwardly, the more yourself you will be. From your study this year, how would you describe the inner Jesus?

### Scripture Search

1. Jesus as Lamb of God: Tell what the title of Lamb signifies in these passages: John 1:29; Acts 8:31–35; 1 Corinthians 5:7; 1 Peter 1:18–20.
2. Jesus is Lord
   a. The title *Lord* occurs almost eight thousand times in the Bible. Tell what the sacred writers teach in regard to this title in these passages: Romans 10:9, 14:8–9; 1 Corinthians 11:26ff, 12:3; Acts 2:36; 2 Corinthians 4:5, 10:8.
   b. Read Philippians 2:6–11 and summarize its teaching.

# HANDBOOK

# The Times of Jesus

The Word became a human being and lived among us.

(JOHN 1:14)

**In five minutes, answer as many of these questions as you can.**

1. Scripture says that we see now (by faith) as in a glass (mirror) "darkly." Why weren't things seen clearly in the mirrors of Jesus' day? (1 Corinthians 13:12)

2. Did Jesus speak Greek? Could Jesus read?

3. How did the four friends of the paralytic get him up to the roof so quickly? (Mark 2:1–4)

4. What's the difference between the tunic and the cloak mentioned in Matthew 5:40? Why would a cloak be needed in a land where the average temperature is 72 degrees?

5. What would people be doing up on the roof at the Second Coming? (Mark 13:15)

6. What was the bushel that you weren't supposed to put your lamp under? What lamp was Jesus talking about? (Matthew 5:15)

7. Most houses in Palestine were primitive structures put together haphazardly with stone and mud. What was the "upper room" in which the Last Supper took place? (Mark 14:14–15)

8. What was Gehenna, referred to in Mark 9:45?

9. Why would a man carrying a pitcher of water in the crowded city of Jerusalem at the time of Passover be easily identified? (Mark 14:13)

10. Why would anyone force you into service for one mile as Jesus said in Matthew 5:41? What did "pressing into service" mean?

*Grade yourself. If you knew:*
- **10** *Ph.D. in ancient Jewish culture.*
- **9** *Master's degree, at least.*
- **8** *Bachelor's degree.*
- **7** *A devoted Jesus fan.*
- **3–6** *Not bad, but you need to bone up.*
- **1–3** *Jesus came for your kind. This chapter should be a help.*

# CONTENTS

INTRODUCTION/293

GEOGRAPHICAL FEATURES/293

Palestine
Jerusalem
Galilee
Nazareth
Samaria

THE SMALLER WORLD/296

Family Life
Prayer
Shelter
Meals/Food
Clothing
Personal Habits
Social Life

THE LARGER SCENE/302

Language
Time
Money
Measures
Economic Classes
Political Situation
Political Authorities

THE RELIGIOUS SCENE/307

Judaism
Religious Authorities
The Temple
Religious Parties

SUMMING UP/311

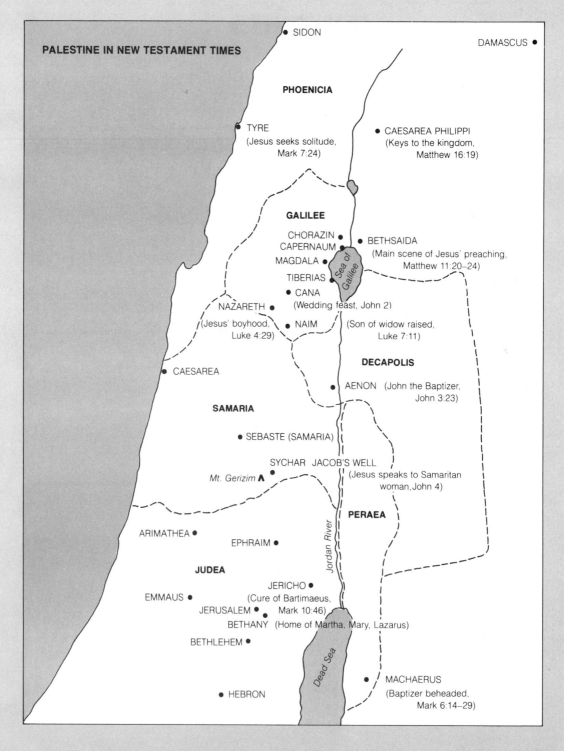

PALESTINE IN NEW TESTAMENT TIMES

SIDON

DAMASCUS

PHOENICIA

TYRE
(Jesus seeks solitude,
Mark 7:24)

CAESAREA PHILIPPI
(Keys to the kingdom,
Matthew 16:19)

GALILEE

CHORAZIN
CAPERNAUM
MAGDALA
TIBERIAS
CANA
(Wedding feast, John 2)

BETHSAIDA
(Main scene of Jesus' preaching,
Matthew 11:20–24)

Sea of Galilee

NAZARETH
(Jesus' boyhood,
Luke 4:29)

NAIM
(Son of widow raised,
Luke 7:11)

CAESAREA

DECAPOLIS

AENON    (John the Baptizer,
John 3:23)

SAMARIA

SEBASTE (SAMARIA)

SYCHAR   JACOB'S WELL
(Jesus speaks to Samaritan
woman, John 4)

Mt. Gerizim ∧

Jordan River

PERAEA

ARIMATHEA

EPHRAIM

JUDEA

JERICHO
(Cure of Bartimaeus,
Mark 10:46)

EMMAUS

JERUSALEM

BETHANY   (Home of Martha, Mary, Lazarus)

BETHLEHEM

Dead Sea

MACHAERUS
(Baptizer beheaded,
Mark 6:14–29)

HEBRON

# INTRODUCTION

Because they do not understand the outdated language, many people have trouble reading the Bible. Today, there are translations on the market that practically do away with this problem.

Although most of the references in the New Testament are universal enough to be understood by everyone, some of the examples that Jesus uses in his teachings are built on customs and habits that have long since become outdated.

A quick reading of this handbook will enlarge your grasp of both the smaller world that shaped Jesus during his childhood and youth and the larger scene he faced when he left home to fulfill his mission. Familiarity with his environment and times will make him come alive for you as you follow his journey through Palestine.

For a more complete explanation, John McKenzie's *Dictionary of the Bible* and Henri Daniel-Rops' *Daily Life in the Time of Jesus* are invaluable resources.

# GEOGRAPHICAL FEATURES

## Palestine

A commonwealth under Roman occupation after 63 B.C. when Pompey conquered it, Palestine consisted of Jewish Judea with Jerusalem as its center; Galilee; heretical Samaria; and other non-Jewish (Gentile) regions. The Greek federation of Decapolis (Ten Cities) lay to the east of Galilee, and the Canaanite region of Syrophoenicia lay to the west. The Sea of Galilee was north of the country; the Dead (Salt) Sea was south of it. The Jordan River ran from north to south and connected these two bodies of water. It gave rise to summer brooks (wadis).

About the size of Vermont (ten thousand square miles), Palestine had a population of about two million at the time of Jesus. Rainfall was twenty inches along the coast but diminished to one to two inches in the Jordan Valley and in southern Judea. There were two seasons, winter (wet) and summer (dry). The sirocco—hot westerly winds—destroyed crops at the seasons' change. Heavy morning dew, cool nights, and snowcapped mountains were other features of the land. Originally inhabited by Canaanites, who were known for merchandising, it was the Land of Canaan—the Promised Land given to Abraham and his descendants.

## Jerusalem

Located in Judea, Jerusalem—the Holy City—formed the pulsing heart of Jewish life. Already identifiable in Abraham's day, it was not occupied by the Israelites until David captured it to make it his headquarters and the political capital of Israel. Because of its position on two hills, it formed an excellent defense and was known as the Mount, or Citidel, of Zion.

Jerusalem was also known as the City of David because it had become the nation's religious center when David had the Ark brought to it. After Solomon built the first Temple, it became a place of Israelite worship, for the Jews believed that the Lord was there in the place he himself had chosen. To them, Jerusalem was the meeting place between God and men.

After their return from Exile, the Jews celebrated Yahweh's praise of Jerusalem with psalms and feasts. Jesus "went up to Jerusalem" in his infancy, in his youth, and at the beginning and end of his career. From its beginning, his life points to Jerusalem as the city of his destiny. He loved it and wept over its future destruction, but he also knew that the prophets had been stoned there. It was by Jerusalem that Jesus was finally rejected and outside its walls that he was killed. The city was destroyed by a counterrevolutionary siege under Titus in A.D. 70. The kingdom that Jesus had inaugurated was to become the New Jerusalem, the city of moral perfection, of which the old city had only been a shadow.

## Galilee

The California of Palestine, Galilee was the "land of happiness." Compared with hot, dry, barren, rocky southern Judea, there was enough rain in Galilee for lush subtropical foliage, fertile soil, sunny blue skies, rolling hills, and the clear, fresh water of the Sea of Galilee (also

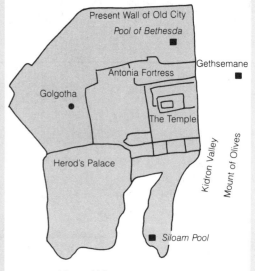

**JERUSALEM IN NEW TESTAMENT TIMES**

Present Wall of Old City

*Pool of Bethesda*

Gethsemane

Antonia Fortress

Golgotha

The Temple

Herod's Palace

Kidron Valley

Mount of Olives

Siloam Pool

Hinnom Valley

JESUS

known as the Sea of Gennesaret, Chinereth, or Tiberias). Many cities, one of which was Capharnaum, dotted its shores. Its surface, almost seven hundred feet below sea level, covered an area roughly eight miles wide and thirteen miles long. Galilee's beauty was enhanced by snowcapped Mount Hermon to the north, the mountains of Samaria in the south, the Sea of Galilee to the east, and the Mediterranean seacoast on the west. Two important trade routes crossed through it, making it the "region of the nations."

## Nazareth

This small Galilean village, twelve hundred feet above sea level, was located midway between the Sea of Galilee and the Mediterranean. Here Jesus spent the greater part of his life, first with Mary and Joseph, and then in his public ministry until his rejection. In the Gospel, Jesus is called "Jesus of

Nazareth" eight times and "the Nazorean" twelve times. His teachings are heavy with images of nature drawn from the local Galilean scene:

*Trees.* Oaks, terebinth, pink-flowered tamarisks, mustard, laurel, willows, sixty-five-foot-tall junipers. Much brushwood. Most useful trees: olive and fig. Abundant vineyards.

*Flowers.* Crocuses, tulips, hyacinths, narcissus, gladiolas, crimson wild lilies, probably anemones.

*Grass.* Several varieties, including couch and meadow grass, dandelions, thistles, and reeds.

*Animals.* Wild: bears, porcupines, antelope, gazelles, jackals, foxes, wolves, leopards, lynx, hyenas, lions. Domestic: sheep, goats, donkeys, hens, geese, oxen, swine (not kept by Jews), pigeons, camels. Other: crows, sparrows, vultures, rats, owls, fish (carp and twenty-six other varieties), asps, cobras, vipers, adders, lizards, edible locusts, centipedes, butterflies, wasps, mosquitoes, flies (*Beelzebub* means "Lord of the Flies").

## Samaria

Samaria was once the northern capital of Israel during the latter days of the monarchy. After their deportation by the Assyrians in 721 B.C., only a few Israelis were left. They eventually worshiped at their own temple in Gerizim. The Samaritans fought the rebuilding of the Temple in Jerusalem after the Babylonian release. This together with their intermarriage with foreigners and the fact that they had preserved only the Law but not the prophets in their Bible, caused them to be regarded as heretics by the Jews.

## Family Life

The family was the backbone of Jewish society. Betrothal (engagement) was legally arranged by the father, the head of the house, who held strict rights over his wife, children, slaves, and property. Although the betrothed couple were bound to strict fidelity to each other for about a year before their marriage, often they did not see each other until the wedding. After a year of betrothal, the bridegroom came in procession to claim his bride. They were married at an elaborate ceremony followed by days of celebration.

Families were large, in response to God's command to multiply and fill the earth. There was more rejoicing at the birth of boys than at the birth of girls, and it was the boys who received formal education. At an early age, they were sent to the synagogue where, seated around the local rabbi, they learned the Scriptures by recitation.

Unlike some of their neighbors, Jewish families did not live in clans in Jesus' day, but only in couples—for example, Joseph and Mary, Zebedee and Salome, and Zachariah and Elizabeth. Four men are described in the Gospels as "brothers" of Jesus: James, Joses (Joseph), Simon, and Judas. Eastern Orthodox Christians believe that these men were children of Joseph by a former wife and were probably jealous of the achievements of a younger half-brother. There is nothing in the New Testament to support this view, which had its origin in the third century. Since the Refor-

mation, the most common view of Protestants is to regard these men as Mary's younger children by Joseph.

From very early times, however, the Church has proclaimed Mary's perpetual virginity. It sees the Greek word for *brother* as more specific than the Hebrew, which extended to cousins and other male members of a tribe. Further, in other New Testament passages, James is clearly called the son of Alphaeus, and the mother of James and Joses (Joseph) is named as another Mary. Finally, in John, why would Jesus have given his mother into John's keeping if she had younger sons to provide for her?

Women owed their husbands fidelity, served them at table, performed the household duties, drew the water, reared the girls, and sometimes watched the flocks. Thought of as weak, women were not required to observe the entire Law of Moses, and in many instances were actually protected by it. They never went out in public without covering their heads. Although they were not taught to read or write, women were encouraged to ponder and pray over the Scriptures they heard read in the synagogue and recited in prayer, in order to be able to help their sons understand it and to urge their husbands to observe it. The mother, especially of sons, was queen of her home and commanded respect. She performed a variety of functions in the family religious celebrations, although she took no active part in synagogue or Temple services.

The men trained their sons, supported their families, led family prayers, and assisted in the synagogue.

## Prayer

The whole of Jewish life was interwoven with prayer. Prayers preceded all meals, and the *Shema Israel*—the main commandment of the Law—was repeated three times a day.

*Shema Israel*

> Hear, O Israel! The Lord our God, the Lord alone! Therefore, you shall love the Lord, your God, with all your heart, and with all your soul, and with all your strength.
>
> (Deuteronomy 6:4–5)

There were special days of fast, and every Sabbath was announced by a trumpet call. When entering or leaving the house, the family reverently touched the mezuzah, a small case nailed to the right doorpost of the house. It held the Commandment as a sign that the house and its inhabitants were dedicated to God. Clothing, fringed in accord with the prescriptions of the Law, was consecrated to God. At prayer, each man wore small boxes (phylacteries) containing the Word of God strapped to his forehead and arm.

The Jews traveled great distances to observe the Passover in Jerusalem, and everyone who lived within reasonable distance made a pilgrimage to the Temple in Jerusalem for the three major feasts. Weekly Sabbath services, held at the local synagogue, included the recitation of the *Shema* and a series of Eighteen Blessings, one reading from the

Torah and one from the Prophets, a homily, and a priestly blessing.

The Sabbath was a day of prayer and strict rest observed to honor the Lord of creation. Thirty-nine types of work were forbidden. For example, on the Sabbath a faithful Jew could not tie or untie a rope, put out a lamp or light a fire, sew two stitches, write two letters of the alphabet, use medicine, walk more than three thousand feet, filter wine, wear hair ornaments, or go out while wearing an artificial leg! It *was* permitted, however, to assist at a birth. Washing the dead was allowed, but not embalming.

Birth, puberty, marriage, and death were accompanied by sacred rites. Even the poorest families hired flute players and a mourner to accompany a funeral procession. The dead were embalmed and laid in stone sepulchers, which were washed (whitened) from time to time to honor the dead.

## Shelter

Because lumber was scarce, homes were constructed of stones gathered from the fields and held together by mud and straw. Walls were frequently no more than lean-tos set up against limestone rock. Tree trunks served to support a flat roof; it was made of slightly sloped beams interwoven with reeds and was reached by means of outside steps. This multipurpose roof area was used for sleeping at night, occasional dining, visiting, drying clothes, and quiet meditation. Below the roof was the stone structure of one room divided into a cooking area and winter sleeping quarters. A cave in the rear provided a

shelter for animals, since most families owned at least a goat and a donkey. Because houses had a single, low door and lacked windows, the interior was always dark. A metal lamp that burned olive oil was kept lit on a lampstand or in a niche all day, permeating everything with its slightly rancid odor. Floors were pounded dirt.

A wooden chest, a spinning wheel, a wooden bushel (a bowl-like measure for grain), and a table were the standard furnishings. The poor slept on rollaway mats, either on the ground or on the roof. When people began to place tents on their roofs, enterprising carpenters learned to build a structure atop the roof to form an upper room, called a cenacle. In one of these chambers, which were sometimes rented out to guests for dining, Jesus and the Apostles celebrated the Last Supper.

Each dwelling opened onto a court. Narrow, irregular alleys or streets separated the houses, and a wall enclosed the entire town. The narrow town gate was closed at night and sentries were posted by it to keep watch. Most people worked small plots of ground either near their houses or outside the town. Since there was no plumbing, waste materials were buried. The large and overpopulated Jerusalem had a city dump, Gehenna, whose constantly burning refuse lighted and fouled the countryside.

## Meals/Food

The Jews liked eating in the open air. Only the wealthy had dining rooms. Cooking was done outdoors or, in the event of rain, under a lean-to. To eat, the people sat cross-legged on the ground around a table, although better homes had fixed benches. Chairs were rare, found only in the homes of the wealthy. As a mark of prestige, the leader of the synagogue service sat in a special "Chair of Moses." But even strict Jews imitated the Greco-Roman custom of stretching out to eat on couches covered with cushions.

The women ground grain on a millstone and worked the heavy dough with oil in kneading troughs every few days. The raised barley bread of the poor was baked as rough, round, flat cakes in small ovens placed on outdoor fireplaces formed by hollowing out the ground and lining it with stones.

Honey was used instead of sugar and was more important than milk. The Jews liked their food highly spiced. Goats' milk that was "hardened" into a kind of yogurt was kept in the coolest corner of the cave portion of the house; when it was shaken in skin bags, it produced cheese. Meat or eggs were rarely served, although a sheep or lamb might be slaughtered for a feast. Fish, usually salted or dried, was common. Olives were used for many things; in addition to being eaten, their oil was used for cooking and lamps and as an ointment. There was a wide variety of vegetables, especially beans and lentils, but also greens, onions, garlic, parsley, and cucumbers. Fresh fruits included apricots, pomegranates, and melons; raisins, dates, and dried sycamore figs were mixed with walnuts and coated with honey to produce a candied dessert. Wines—sweet and dry, but always red— were served watered or honeyed. Shekar was a beer made from fermented grain.

Bread was the staple of the two daily meals, one eaten early, before the day's work, the other late in the evening. Cheese or fish and vegetables rounded out the meals, to which guests were often invited, because the Jews were a sociable people. Certain foods, such as pork, were considered "unclean." On the Sabbath, only a noon meal, prepared the day before, was served.

Flat metal plates with turned-up edges, along with large metal cups, served as dishes. Knives were used, but not forks or spoons. Stone water jars stood against the wall ready for hand-washing and, after a journey, foot-washing before meals. During meals there was to be no reaching out or greediness, and it was the height of rudeness to refuse food that was offered.

The master of the house served everyone at the table in a strict order of precedence. Guests were seated according to rank, the priests and rabbis taking the first places and those of priestly or other aristocratic families being seated next. Within a single household, the firstborn son was seated and served first, the males of the current or main wife ranking before half-brothers, whose position was further determined by age.

## Clothing

Men wore a sac or sackcloth—a kind of loincloth—under a straight but billowing shirtlike garment called a tunic that was fringed at the bottom and reached well below the knees. Worn during the day for work, it was removed for sleeping. A belt held in the tunic, whose many folds of material formed pockets that could hold knives, tools, and other articles. Workers could tuck their shirts into their belts and so "gird their loins." Men wore turbanlike head coverings tied at the forehead; these coverings were never removed, even in the Temple. Women also wore tunics and cloaks, but theirs were more highly decorated. Sandals with rush soles were worn everywhere except in the Temple, where it was required to remove them. A large cloak was worn for formal occasions and when speaking to important personages, but it could also be used as a blanket during a cool night on the roof, as a saddle for a donkey, or even as a carpet. For prayer, male Jews covered their heads with a shawl.

## Personal Habits

The Law laid down strict requirements regarding what made one unclean or unfit for worship. To touch the diseased or dead made people unclean, as did eating animal meat that had not been bled, having sexual relations, or dealing with non-Jews. Many kinds of uncleanness could be purified by washing. The Jews were a people of great personal cleanliness. Foaming soap was used for personal bathing and washing clothes, and scented herbs were used to overcome perspiration odors in the hot climate. Both women and men dyed their hair and wore jewelry on their hands, arms, and legs. Women wore makeup, curled their hair, and wore wigs. They used polished-metal mirrors, which reflected indistinct images.

## Social Life

Friendliness and a spirit of community characterized Jewish social life. Although the Jewish people did not attend the circuses or other public entertainments that were common throughout the Roman Empire because they were forbidden to mix with the Gentiles, at home they played games similar to checkers, and children played hopscotch. Men enjoyed wrestling.

People greeted one another on the streets with *Shalom*—"Peace and all blessing"—and kissed one another instead of shaking hands. The local well or spring was a meeting place for the exchange of gossip; it was run by a master who appointed the hours when the women might draw water in pitchers and jugs, which were carried on the head. Men sold their produce and crafts in crowded stalls in markets, or bazaars, just outside the city walls.

Because making graven images was strictly forbidden, the Jews did not produce artists or architects. Reading, writing, geography, and history were learned only through studying the Torah, and young Jews were not introduced to the literature of Greece and Rome.

## Language

Although Rome ruled Palestine, Greek was the language of the land. Roman soldiers, including the centurions who were stationed locally, spoke Latin. Hellenism, or Greek influence, made inroads into the people's lives, and several of the Apostles from Galilee had Greek as well as Aramaic names because they dealt with the Greek world. The Aramaic *Mattayah* was corrupted into the Greek *Mattaios* (Matthew), and John took the Greek name Mark. The Apostles Philip and Andrew were known only by their Greek names.

Judea was most Jewish in its population and practice. Samaria was schismatic—that is, it was Jewish, but the people worshiped in their own temple on Mount Gerizim. Galilee, through which passed the great trade routes between Egypt and the East as well as those between Damascus and Arabia, was the richest and most cosmopolitan region. In Judea, Aramaic was the most widely used language, while Greek was as important as Aramaic in Galilee. Just as for centuries Latin was the official language of Christian liturgy, so Hebrew was reserved for Jewish scripture reading and worship.

Jesus and his Apostles may have been trilingual, speaking Aramaic among themselves (it was a language in its own right, not a dialect of Hebrew) as well as Hebrew and *koine* (common) Greek, which was used universally. There is no record of the presence of a translator when Jesus spoke to Pilate, who possibly communicated with him in Greek. The inscription on the cross was written in three languages—Latin, Greek, and Hebrew—so that it might be read by all who came to Jerusalem for the Passover.

Aramaic words that have come down to us in the New Testament include *Abba* (familiar form of *Father;* Mark 14:36), *Aceldama* ("field of blood" or Potter's Field because it could provide potter's clay; Acts 1:19), *Golgotha* ("skull": a place of skulls, a place of execution, or resembling a skull; Matthew 27:33), *corban* (nonblood offerings given in sacrifice; Mark 7:11), and *mammon* (wealth or profit coveted to such an extent that it gets in the way of love of God, or money gained from self-centered motives; Matthew 6:24, Luke 16:9, 11, 13). There are also Aramaic sentences in the New Testament: *Ephphatha* ("Be opened!"; Mark 7:34), *Talitha koum* ("Little girl, get up"; Mark 5:41), and *Eloi, Eloi, lema sabachthani?* ("My God, my God, why have you forsaken me?" Mark 15:34).

## Time

The Jews' day began and ended with sunset. Their time references were not scientific but imprecise; thus, although there were always twelve hours between sunrise and sunset, the length of the individual hours varied according to the seasonal changes in the amount of daylight. As a rule, reference was made to the four main hours: the first hour (6:00 A.M.), the third hour (9:00 A.M.), the sixth hour (noon), and the ninth hour (3:00 P.M.), with the two following hours included in each. The night hours were known as *watches*, based on the sentries' three-hour turns at every city gate.

The week began with the first day (Sunday) after Sabbath. The days were called by number. The third day, for example, was our Tuesday. The Sabbath began at sunset of the sixth day after a period of preparation (Friday) and ended at sunset the next day (Saturday). Thus the "three days" Jesus was in the tomb could have been as few as thirty-six hours if he was laid to rest about 5:00 or 6:00 P.M. on the fifth day (Friday) before the beginning of the Sabbath, and rose at 5:00 or 6:00 A.M. of the first day (Sunday).

Each of the twelve months began at the new moon, with a thirteenth month added every two or three years. The first month was called Nisan and occurred at the spring equinox, during our March or April.

Years were counted either from the founding of Rome or from the first year of the current ruler's term. Thus, according to Roman chronology, Jesus was born in year 747 after the founding of Rome. It was not until the sixth century A.D. that the Christian calendar, which marks Jesus' birth as the starting point of the Christian era, came into existence. The monk who arranged the calendar made a miscalculation, however, and Jesus was probably actually born in 6 B.C.

## Money

Money from three sources circulated in Palestine, and the following coins had the same value:

Imperial: Roman, 4 denarii
Provincial: Greek, 1 stater
Local: Jewish, 1 shekel

Roman and Greek money was coined in gold, silver, copper, bronze, or brass and bore a likeness of the ruler. Jewish money was stamped with fruits, vegetables, or names, but not with anyone's likeness (in obedience to the first commandment). A half-shekel was one didrachma or two denarii. Five silver shekels were equivalent to two weeks' pay. Twenty-five denarii was the daily wage of an unskilled laborer. A talent of silver was worth six thousand drachmas or fifteen hundred shekels or staters. The widow's mite was probably a *lepton*, a Jewish coin worth 1/128 of a denarius or a drachma—perhaps less than the Roman *as*, or penny, which would buy two sparrows.

## Measures

The following measures were commonly used in biblical times:

    ephah (dry measure) = 22 liters or quarts

    cubit = 21.6 inches

    fathom = 6 feet

    furlong = 202 yards

    mile = 1,000 paces or 1,618 yards

A Sabbath day's journey (the total amount of travel allowed on the Sabbath) was two thousand cubits, a little over half a mile.

## Economic Classes

Although the Jews were theoretically a democratic society—King Herod, who was only half-Jewish, and his court were never accepted—the wealthy members of the priestly families formed the social aristocracy. However, they were not the primary leaders of the people. Since the Jews esteemed the Law so highly, it was the masters of the Law—the lay scribes and Pharisees—who exerted the greatest influence over the thinking of the common people.

There were two classes, the rich and poor. The wealthy who owned land or businesses were urged to give alms. (In the parable of Lazarus and Dives, Dives—Latin for "rich man"—is an example of this class.) The poor engaged in agriculture, the crafts, and unskilled labor.

The craftsmen, fishermen (unless, like the sons of Zebedee, they owned large fishing operations), carpenters, and smiths were better off than the others. Joseph, a cutter or worker of wood, would have had a shop for selling his plows, yokes, and cabinets in the local bazaar. He also cut down trees and constructed the frames for supporting the flat roofs of local houses.

The peasants, or unskilled laborers, tilled the soil of wealthy landowners, who usually lived in Jerusalem. From the yield of fruits, vegetables, or grapes from these plots, they had to pay rent to the landowners, taxes to the government, and a Temple tax that came to 22 percent of what remained. A sudden drought, plague, or illness usually meant starvation for the peasants, but because manual work was held in high regard (even the rabbis practiced trades), they were respected and socially accepted by the rich.

Social outcasts were either people of mixed blood, like the Samaritans, or Jews who had taken on Greek ways. Tax collectors were in the same despised class as prostitutes, or women of the streets, and other public sinners. Orphans and other unfortunates without families, including the sick, the crippled, and the aged, were at the mercy of society because there were no hospitals or welfare institutions. At the very bottom of the social totem pole were the untouchable lepers. With all these as well as the "average poor"—with whom he identified—Jesus was successful in his appeal.

## Political Situation

The Jews chafed under Roman occupation even though, in practice, Rome seldom interfered in Jewish affairs. Although they were exempt from military service because their laws forbade them to have contact with Gentiles, the Jews were required to follow Roman edicts and decrees, which were generally posted on public buildings, and to pay 25 percent of their income in taxes to Rome. Taxes were estimated by census and were collected through speculators, the Jewish publicans. The contract was awarded to the highest bidder, who could keep the profit—whatever he collected over and above his bid. The Jews despised these Jewish publicans, whom they considered traitors. Military troops guarded the large cities and, as an example of the ever-present oppression suffered by the people, Roman soldiers could force any Jewish male to carry a burden a mile. For this purpose, stone markers measured the miles along the road.

## Political Authorities

The following rulers were active before, during, and immediately after Jesus' lifetime.

*Augustus, Caesar Octavianus,* grand-nephew and adopted son of Julius Caesar, was the first Roman emperor (30 B.C.–A.D. 14). He was a handsome man who was careful of his appearance and always tried to improve his mind by reading. He bragged that he had found Rome in bricks and left it in marble. He was ruler at the time of Jesus' birth in the 747th year of the founding of Rome (6 B.C.).

*Tiberius, Caesar* succeeded his step-father, Augustus, as Roman emperor (A.D. 14–37) when Jesus was twenty years old. Jesus died during his reign.

*Herod the Great* became king of Judea (37–4 B.C.) through his friendship with Marc Anthony. He was a great builder and began remodeling the Temple in 19 B.C. (it was not completed until A.D. 67). Married ten times, he was subject to insanity in his last years; he executed his own sons and attempted to commit suicide. He was king when Jesus was born, and, according to the Gospel, ordered the slaughter of the innocents.

*Archelaus,* the favorite son of Herod the Great, was eighteen when he was made ethnarch of the best section of Palestine—Idumea, Judea, and Samaria—when his father's kingdom was divided in 4 B.C. Continuing his father's cruel practices, he stirred the anger of the Jews, who reported him to Rome. Augustus had him exiled in 759 (A.D. 6) and replaced the ethnarchy with the office of a procurator who was directly responsible to the Roman administration.

*Herod Antipas* was made tetrarch of Galilee and Perea when the kingdom of his father, Herod the Great, was divided. He married Herodias, the wife of his still living half-brother Philip. At her wish, he had John the Baptizer beheaded. A spy for Tiberius, for whom he built the city Tiberias on the shore of Galilee, Herod Antipas was mistrusted by Roman officials, including Pilate. He was the ruler when Jesus died, and was banished in A.D. 39.

*Philip* was the third son of Herod the Great and tetrarch of the region east of Galilee. He died in A.D. 34.

*Pontius Pilate,* the fifth Roman procurator of Judea (A.D. 26–36), sentenced Jesus to death to satisfy the Jewish leaders.

*Annas* and *Caiaphas* were high priests, not to be confused with chief priests, who were heads of the many priestly families in Jerusalem. Only one high priest sat in office during Jesus' later years. Annas, who was the father-in-law of Caiaphas and a former high priest, retained great influence in Jewish government at the time Jesus was tried.

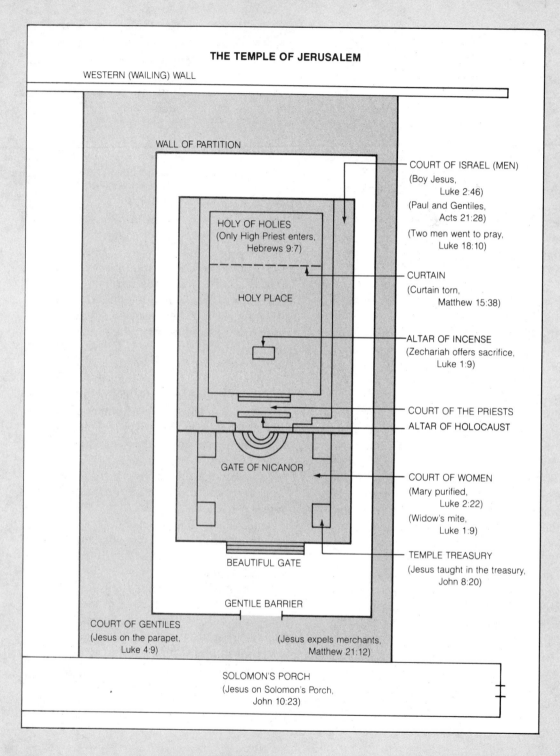

# THE TEMPLE OF JERUSALEM

WESTERN (WAILING) WALL

WALL OF PARTITION

HOLY OF HOLIES
(Only High Priest enters,
Hebrews 9:7)

HOLY PLACE

ALTAR OF INCENSE

GATE OF NICANOR

BEAUTIFUL GATE

GENTILE BARRIER

COURT OF GENTILES
(Jesus on the parapet,
Luke 4:9)

(Jesus expels merchants,
Matthew 21:12)

SOLOMON'S PORCH
(Jesus on Solomon's Porch,
John 10:23)

COURT OF ISRAEL (MEN)
(Boy Jesus,
Luke 2:46)
(Paul and Gentiles,
Acts 21:28)
(Two men went to pray,
Luke 18:10)

CURTAIN
(Curtain torn,
Matthew 15:38)

ALTAR OF INCENSE
(Zechariah offers sacrifice,
Luke 1:9)

COURT OF THE PRIESTS
ALTAR OF HOLOCAUST

COURT OF WOMEN
(Mary purified,
Luke 2:22)
(Widow's mite,
Luke 1:9)

TEMPLE TREASURY
(Jesus taught in the treasury,
John 8:20)

## Judaism

The "trinity" of Judaism is expressed in the saying, "*God* created the *People* by his *Torah*." That the one God made a covenant with the Jews and gave them the Law is the very heart of the Jewish faith. The Torah, which we call the Pentateuch, is the first five books of the Bible; it is credited to Moses. Because the traditions of the Chosen People were threatened during the Babylonian Exile, those who returned to Judea in 538 B.C. placed great emphasis on the Law. Orthodox Jews—those who remained strictly faithful to the tradition—settled around Jerusalem, although more Jews lived outside Palestine in Jewish settlements throughout the empire. Despite the influence of foreign neighbors, the unity of religious belief and practice that resulted from the renewal of fidelity to the Law prevented Judaism from being absorbed by the Greco-Roman culture. Orthodox Jews were suspicious of Galileans and despised Samaritans, and kept strictly to themselves. But when the national-liberation movement came to a head in A.D. 66, it was in Galilee that revolution broke out, thus bringing about the destruction of Jerusalem and crushing Jewish hopes for independence. Except for a very brief period in the second century, the Jews were not to have their own land again until the establishment of Israel in 1948.

## Religious Authorities

The strong religious convictions of the Jews, amounting almost to rigidity, kept the Romans from interfering in their religious affairs. The Sanhedrin was the Jewish supreme council, composed of seventy-one men of three classes:

- High priest, the head priest who presided over government, with God as its head
- Elders of the chief families and clans, chief priests, former high priests, and elders of the four high priest families
- Scribes, members of the Pharisee sect

Strictly speaking, the Sanhedrin held authority only in Judea, but it was known to extend its power to the diaspora, those countries outside of Palestine where the Jews lived. As the national court, it made legal decisions in religious and secular affairs, maintained its own police, and had power to convict, except perhaps in cases of capital punishment, which may have been reserved to royalty or to Rome.

## The Temple

The one Temple of Jerusalem was the center of the Jewish nation and, to the Jewish mind, the center of the world. The Jews believed that it rested over the foundation stone around which the flat earth had been formed in a sea of surrounding water. Under the Temple flowed the River of Life, giving water that sprang from the Source of all life—the one true God himself. They believed that God's presence rested over the Temple.

Supported by the Temple tax, the Temple was the scene of daily morning and evening sacrifices attended by large crowds who milled around its many courts. During the most sacred feast of Passover, nearly a million people passed through its precincts. Jews visited the Temple for private devotions. There was a tight system of priestly duties that involved twenty-five thousand in its service. Levites (members of the priestly family of Levi) served as cantors, providing all the music for worship. Gentiles and women were strictly forbidden in certain areas.

The local synagogues were houses of prayer for each town, and were the only fine buildings to be found outside the cities. Each was built around a special sacred cupboard, the Ark, which held the scroll of the Torah, or Law, and a pulpit from which the best-educated person in the town, the rabbi, preached. The men assisted in reading and in commenting on Scripture, but it was the rabbi on whose shoulders the formal education of each generation of boys in the synagogue school rested. Otherwise, education of the sons was mainly the responsibility of the father. The synagogue was the center of Sabbath worship and of Jewish social life.

JESUS

## An Ancient New York

Jerusalem was the New York of Palestine. Always bustling, "at certain times of the year the city's animation increased enormously. These were the periods of the great feasts, the Passover, the Feast of Weeks, the Day of Atonement, and that happiest of them all, the Feast of Tabernacles. During these seasons prodigious crowds of pilgrims filled the city; . . . a great many had to sleep outside the town in the suburbs, on the hills, in tents or in huts made of branches, or just under the open sky, as Jesus and His disciples did in the garden of Gethsemane. The crowding was unbelievable—vast throngs of men and of animals too, for at a single Passover it could happen that two hundred thousand lambs would be brought. This was the time when the inhabitants of Jerusalem might see their brothers from the whole of the diaspora, Jews from Babylon with their trailing black robes, Jews from Phoenicia in tunics and striped drawers, Jews from the Plateaus of Anatolia dressed in goat's-hair cloaks, Persian Jews gleaming in silk brocaded with gold and silver. All these people crowded into the court of the Temple. . . . It was a fair, yet a pious fair, an astonishing hurly-burly."

From *Daily Life in the Time of Jesus* by Henri Daniel-Rops (New York: Hawthorn Books, Inc., 1962), p. 115.

## Religious Parties

In biblical times, religious parties functioned something like political parties. Although politics were involved, their different platforms stemmed primarily from differences of religious interpretation

*Pharisees.* Called the "separated ones"—probably because they rejected the political ambition of the priestly classes—and mentioned a hundred times in the New Testament, the Pharisees were the largest religious group. Chiefly middle-class laymen, they were associated with the synagogues. Their emphasis on strict observance of the Law resulted in the setting up of countless extra rules to guarantee that the Law would not be lost. They subscribed to oral tradition as well as to Scripture and thus believed in angels, the resurrection of the dead, and a final judgment, none of which could be "proved" from Scripture alone. Although they despised Roman occupation, they were not politically active in opposition to it. It was some members of this group whom Jesus criticized for substituting legalism—excessive strictness in keeping the Law—in place of sincere love of God.

*Sadducees.* A small group consisting of the priestly class, the Sadducees were powerful political leaders who served in the Temple in Jerusalem. Because they believed in a strict interpretation of the Torah, they rejected the doctrines of the Pharisees, who exerted a greater influence among the people. As members of the wealthy class, the Sadducees were mediators between Rome and the Jews, and accepted Roman rule as a means of gaining privileges for the nation. This party died out after the destruction of Jerusalem in A.D. 70.

*Essenes.* The discovery of the Dead Sea Scrolls in 1947 turned up a good deal of new information about the Essenes. They were one of several groups who departed from established Judaism and Temple worship to follow the prophets in seeking a more spiritual religion. Like monks, they lived lives of penance in desert communities, expecting the Day of the Lord at any moment. John the Baptizer may have been influenced by them.

*Zealots.* These dagger-carrying members of a radical national-liberation movement believed that only by conquest of Rome would the messianic kingdom be established in Israel. Driven underground during Jesus' life, the Zealots gained enough strength by A.D. 66 to originate the revolution that led to the complete destruction of the Temple and of Jewish nationalism.

JESUS

## SUMMING UP

*Geographical Features (pages 293–295)*

1. *Words to know:* Land of Canaan, Mount Zion, New Jerusalem, "region of the nations," Nazorean, viper
2. Draw a rectangle. Place the four main regions of Palestine in it. Add the two bodies of water and the Jordan.
3. Name five features of the climate, including the sirocco.
4. Why is Jerusalem called (a) Mount Zion, (b) the City of David, and (c) the Holy City? What is the New Jerusalem?
5. Name an animal, a plant, or an object that could symbolize Galilee. Explain why you chose it.
6. What was one custom regarding names in Jesus' day?

*The Smaller World, 1 (pages 296–299)*

1. *Words to know:* betrothal, cenacle, shekar, *Shema Israel,* mezuzah, phylacteries, Sabbath
2. If the underlined word makes the following statements false, substitute the correct word. Otherwise, write True.
   a. Betrothal was the ceremony that admitted Jewish boys to adult status in the faith.
   b. The mother was forbidden to participate in family religious celebrations.
   c. Women did not learn the Law in formal classes.
   d. The Jews had many cookouts.
   e. Barley bread was served at every meal.
   f. A devout Jew recited the *Shema Israel,* the heart of the Law, all his life.
   g. The Sabbath was a day of rest which was safeguarded by two hundred rules.
   h. At prayer, the men wore the mezuzah strapped to their foreheads and arms.
   i. The people honored their dead by placing flowers at their graves.
   j. Families within reasonable distance went to Jerusalem to worship three times a year.

*The Smaller World, 2 (pages 298–301)*

1. *Words to know:* lean-to, bushel, "unclean," sackcloth, tunic, *shalom,* bazaar

2. Tell how five of the following figured in Jewish culture:

| | | |
|---|---|---|
| "unclean" | *shalom* | chairs |
| scented herbs | village | roofs |
| jewelry | bazaars | eating habits |
| circuses | Gehenna | mezuzah |

3. Match the numbered words with the lettered statements.

a. Place for keeping animals  
b. Source of light in the house  
c. Source of safety for the village  
d. Place for keeping tools, sleeping, visiting  
e. Place of garden plots  
f. Winter sleeping quarters  
g. A food included in every meal  
h. The only cutlery that was used at meals  
i. Place where people went barefoot  
j. Worn on formal occasions  
k. Upper room  

1. bread
2. cave
3. cenacle
4. cloak
5. fish
6. gate
7. knives
8. lamp burning oil
9. outside city
10. roof
11. Temple
12. tunic
13. under the lean-to
14. wall
15. window

*The Larger Scene (pages 302–305)*

1. *Words to know:* Hellenism, Aramaic, Hebrew, *"Talitha koum," "Eloi, Eloi, lema sabachthani,"* the ninth hour, the third day, shekel, denarius, talent, peasant, publican
2. What three languages were used in Palestine? How were they used?
3. Which region of Palestine was most cosmopolitan?
4. Draw the face of a clock and indicate the four main hours in the Jewish day.
5. How many months were there in a Jewish year?
6. What were a shekel, a talent, and a mite?
7. What is meant by a "Sabbath day's journey"?
8. What was the difference between the social aristocracy and the wealthy class?
9. What three kinds of work did the poor engage in?
10. Draw a totem pole on which you mark off the various classes of Jewish society at the time of Jesus.
11. How was manual work looked upon in Jesus' day?
12. What two duties did the Jews have toward the Romans? How did the Romans harass the Jews?
13. Who were the political and religious rulers associated with the life of Jesus?

*The Religious Scene (pages 307–310)*

1. *Words to know:* Judaism, Sanhedrin, Temple, Passover, Levite, synagogue, Pharisees, legalism, Sadducees, Essenes, Zealots
2. What is the Christian equivalent of the Jewish Torah?
3. What three points compose the "trinity" of Judaism? What does each point mean?
4. What was the difference between a synagogue and the Temple?
5. What was the holiest day of the Jewish year?
6. Who were the "separated ones" and what did they believe?
7. What was the monastic community that had a more spiritual ideal of the kingdom than the "establishment" in Jerusalem?
8. What was the philosophy of the Zealots? How do you think they would have regarded the other three parties? Match these positions.
   Pharisees          endured them as not wrong, but not aggressive
   Sadducees             enough in politics
   Essenes            laughed at them as unrealistic dreamers, escapists
                      despised them as traitors to Judaism's best interests
9. Draw a square to represent Rome. Line up the four religious parties according to their closeness to the Roman government.
10. What was the main commandment of Israel? How were the people constantly reminded of it?

*Scripture Search*

Consult your handbook and the map on page 292 as well as Mark's Gospel to find the answers to these teasers.

1. Where did John baptize? (1:5) From where did Jesus come? (1:9)
2. What economic class did James and John come from? (1:19–20)
3. Where did Jesus begin preaching? (1:21)
4. How did the paralyzed man get through the roof? (2:4)
5. How do you know that Levi was well-to-do? (2:14–15)
6. Write the place names in 3:7–8 on a rectangle that represents Palestine.
7. Why does 3:31 *not* prove that Jesus had some brothers?
8. What birds might find shelter in the type of plant described in 4:31–32?
9. How big was the lake mentioned in 4:35–41?
10. Why did Jesus teach in the synagogue? (6:2)
11. Where would Jesus find a place like the one described in 6:32?
12. What was the purpose of the rules mentioned in 7:3–4?
13. Was the woman in 7:26 a Jew or a pagan? How do you know?
14. What kind of bread would Jesus have been talking about in 8:14?
15. Was the action of the people in 11:8 and 14:3 usual or abnormal? Why?
16. What coin is being referred to in 12:15–16 and in 12:42?
17. What is the name of the prayer Jesus quoted in 12:29–30?

# Acknowledgments

The authors wish to thank Sister Mary Raphaelita Boeckmann, S.N.D., Superior General, Rome, Sister Mary Christopher Rohner, S.N.D., Provincial Superior of the Sisters of Notre Dame, Chardon, Ohio, and Sister Margaret Mary McGovern, S.N.D., High School Supervisor of the Chardon Province, who supported and encouraged the writing of the Light of the World Series.

Humble gratitude is also due to all who in any way helped to create the Light of the World Series: parents, teachers, co-workers, students and friends. The following deserve special mention for assisting to plan, organize, test or critique the series: Notre Dame Sisters Mary Dolores Abood, Ann Baron, Karla Bognar, Peter Brady, Mary Catherine Caine, Virginia Marie Callen, Deborah Carlin, Naomi Cervenka, Reean Coyne, Mary Dowling, Dorothy Fuchs, Kathleen Glavich, Margaret Mary Gorman, Jacquelyn Gusdane, Mary Margaret Harig, Joanmarie Harks, Nathan Hess, Sally Huston, Christa Jacobs, Joanne Keppler, Owen Kleinhenz, Jean Korejwo, Leanne Laney, William David Latiano, Aimee Levy, Nadine Lock, Mary Ann McFadden, Inez McHugh, Louismarie Nudo, Donna Marie Paluf, Helen Mary Peter, Phyllis Marie Plummer, Eileen Marie Quinlan, Patricia Rickard, Mark Daniel Roscoe, Kathleen Ruddy, Kathleen Scully, Dolores Stanko, Melannie Svoboda, Louise Trivison, Donna Marie Wilhelm, Ms. Laura Wingert; Ms. Meg Bracken; Sister Mary Kay Cmolik, O.F.M.; Mr. Robert Dilonardo; Rev. Mark DiNardo; Ms. Linda Ferrando; Mr. Michael Homza; Sister Kathleen King, H.H.M.; Ms. Patricia Lange; Mr. James Marmion; Mr. Peter Meler; Rev. Herman P. Moman; Rev. Guy Noonan,

JESUS

T.O.R.; Ms. Nancy Powell; Ms. Christine Smetana; and Ms. Karen Sorace.

The following high schools piloted materials: Bishop Ireton H.S., Alexandria, Virginia; Clearwater Central Catholic H.S., Clearwater, Florida; Elyria Catholic H.S., Elyria, Ohio; Erieview Catholic H.S., Cleveland, Ohio; John F. Kennedy H.S., Warren, Ohio; Notre Dame Academy, Chardon Ohio; Regina High School, South Euclid, Ohio, St. Edward H.S., Cleveland, Ohio; St. Matthias H.S., Huntington Park, California.

The following parishes piloted the Parish School of Religion abridgement: Corpus Christi, Cleveland, Ohio; St. Anselm, Chesterland, Ohio; St. John Nepomucene, Cleveland, Ohio; St. Thomas More, Paducah, Kentucky.

Special appreciation to Sister Mary Roy Romancik, S.N.D., for management of all production and testing as well as for careful reading of the original draft. Her suggestions resulted in the reworking of many sections.

Deep appreciation to Mrs. Anita Johnson for research; to Sisters of Notre Dame Mary Linda Mary Elliott, Regien Kingsbury, DeXavier Perusek, Seton Schlather, and Robert Clair Smith for special services; and to typists Sisters Mary Lucie Adamcin, Catherine Rennecker, S.N.D., and Josetta Marie Livignano, N.N.D.

**Pictures**

Cover photograph and all chapter openers are by Lee Boltin; After Image 89, 300; Alinari 244; Michael Amster 297, 298; Art Institute of Chicago 249; Marshall Berman 19, 269, 270; Brown Brothers 154; CARE 67; Bob Combs 40, 153, 170, 176, 245, 261; Contemporary Christian Art Gallery 9; Randy Copperman Collection 109; Damascus University 29; FAO 77; Fine Arts Gallery of San Diego 224; Philip Gendreau 23; Glencoe Library 38, 55, 112, 113, 130, 166, 175, 210, 213, 237, 252, 280; Glennstock 10, 43, 119, 137, 185, 189, 195, 207, 250, 279, 301; Tony Heim 295, 298, 308, 309; Israel Government Tourist Agency 74, 155; Israel Museum 56; Louvre 223; Magnum 310; Iris Malinsky 197; Ger. S. Manetas & Sons, Athens 60, 61, 62, 64, 93, 259, 267; Stephen McBrady 13, 18, 255; Metropolitan Museum of Art 146; Monkmeyer Press Photo Services 144, 186, 199, 286; Neysa Moss 159; Mt. Wilson and Palomar Observatories 98; Museum of Historic Art, Princeton University 232; National Gallery of Art 51, 92, 98; Oriental Institute, University of Chicago 79; Steve Padilla 96; PIX 284; Red Cross 171; Religious News Service 134, 156, 168, 191; Robert Rubenstein 38; Marilyn Sanders 51, 179; Paul M. Schrock 16, 53, 103, 129, 151, 164, 260, 272; Skirball Museum 303; Special Olympics 193; D. Stevens 228; Stockmarket 15, 17, 30; Bob Taylor 35, 135, 173, 247; University of Colorado Library 80; Yerkes Observatory 45, 66.

JESUS

# Index

Apostles, the Twelve, 115–119, 205, 223, 245,
    248, 259, 266–267
Appearance narratives, 245–246, 259–260
Assertiveness, 131, 144–145
Augustus, Caesar, 89
Baptism, 111, 190, 258
Bethlehem, 95, 99
Birth announcements, 90–92
Bible, the, 29, 38–45
Caesarea Philippi, 207
Capharnaum, 149, 164, 295
Chosen People, the, 75
Christ, the, 34–35, 50–52, 251, 259, 271,
    273–275
Church and Jesus, the, 178, 254–255, 260–261,
    268
Compassion, 137–143, 145–146, 157, 170
Conversion, 110–111, 254–255
Cross, the, 190–193, 196, 199, 208, 210,
    222–223, 234, 237
Cyrus of Persia, 78
David, King, 77, 79, 81, 149, 274, 275–276, 294
David, Son of, 275–276
Disciple, 114, 116
Essenes, 310
Eucharist, the, 129, 213–214, 226, 236, 255
Evangelists, 49–51, 56–57, 59–67
Exile, the, 78
Exodus, the, 39, 72–74, 172, 196
Ezechial, 79
Faith, 10–15, 33–35, 52, 178, 242–246, 260–261,
    268–269, 285–286
Francis of Assisi, Saint, 155–156
Gallilee, 110, 113, 149, 294–295
Gehenna, 187–188, 299

God, Son of, 64–66, 124, 179, 206–207, 209,
     211, 252, 267, 268, 276–278
God's Plan, 17, 20–21, 33, 35, 124, 152–153,
     170, 188–189, 194
Good News, the, 33–34, 50, 54, 89, 95–96, 98,
     114, 159, 170, 188–189, 237, 254–255
Gospels, 42–43, 50–53, 54–67
Hebrews, 75
Heresies about Jesus, 281–282
Herods, the, 89, 99, 230, 304, 305
Hidden life, the, 101–102, 109–110
Holy Spirit, the, 33, 39, 52, 55, 80, 112, 179,
     196, 217, 236, 245, 266–268, 281
Incarnation, the, 87, 93
Infancy narratives, 87–92, 95–96, 98–103
Inspiration, 38–39, 54
Israelites, 75
Isaiah, 81, 96
Jeremiah, 78, 81
Jerusalem, 95, 99, 207, 210–212, 293–294, 309
Jesus, 9–15, 17, 18–19, 23, 34–35, 60–67
  Authority of, 143–149, 172–173, 205
  Historical Jesus, 29–30, 54–55, 125–128,
       172–173
  Personality of, 127–136, 227
  Preaching of, 113–114, 143–149, 150, 152, 153
  Word of God, 36–37, 66, 88
Jews, 75
John the Apostle, 33–34, 114, 117, 207–208, 209,
     225, 227
John the Baptizer, 81, 91, 110–111, 128, 167
Josephus, Flavius, 29
Kingdom of God, the, 110–111, 113–114, 147,
     149–151, 159, 171, 178–179, 254–255
Kyrios (Lord), 252–254, 272
Last Supper, the, 212–217
Lamb of God, the, 195–197, 213–214, 216, 226,
     236, 280
Languages of Palestine, 302
Light of the World, 22–23
Maccabees, the, 78
Magi, 98
Man, Son of, 136–137, 227
Mary, Virgin, 92–94, 97, 99–100, 235, 296
Messiah, the, 51–52, 60, 81, 88, 90, 95, 99, 102,
     149–150, 179, 206–207, 209, 228–229,
     245, 252, 254–255, 271, 273–275

Messianic secret, 176–177
*Metanoia*, 110–111
Moses, 73, 76
Moses, the new, 61–62
Mystery, 17, 22, 190
Nazareth, 109–110, 295
New Covenant, 154–159, 212–213, 215, 237,
    254–255
Nonviolence, 157–158
Old Covenant, 73–74, 76–77, 78, 196
Parables, 147–148, 153, 177, 194, 206–207
Paschal Mystery, the, 194–199, 212–217
Passion narratives, the, 225–236
Passover, 72–73, 194–195, 210, 212–215, 216
*Pax Romana*, 89
Peter the Apostle, 33–34, 114, 117, 207–208,
    209, 225, 227
Pharisees, the, 310
Pilate, Pontius, 230–231, 305
Preaching of Jesus, the, 113–114, 143–149, 150,
    152, 153
Precursor, the, 91, 110–111
Presentation, the, 100
Purification, the, 100
Rabbi, 61–62, 113, 142–143, 149, 271
Redemption, 100, 186, 190–191, 266–267
Resurrection, the, 38, 175–176, 190–194, 223,
    242–245, 247, 248–249, 258–261, 267
Risen Jesus, the, 247–249, 251–255, 259–261
Sadducees, 310
Salvation, 110–111, 113–114, 184–186, 188, 252,
    260–261
Sanhedrin, 307
Satan (the Tempter), 112–113, 144, 168, 178,
    189–190, 225, 236, 252
Savior, the, 62–63, 184
Sign as Miracle, 165–167, 169, 174–176,
    178–179, 184
Sin, 168–169, 185–188, 205, 237
Suffering Servant, the, 60, 99–106, 193–197,
    235–236, 272
Synoptic Gospels, the, 59, 60–63, 65
Tacitus, Cornelius, 29–30
Teaching of Jesus, the, 149–150, 152–154, 158,
    169–170, 205–206, 213, 215, 217
Temple of Jerusalem, the, 102, 211–212, 236,
    307–308

Temptation, 112–113
Titles of Jesus, the, 268–280
Tomb, the empty, 243–245, 247, 298
Transfiguration, the, 208–210
Twelve, the, 114
Virgin birth, the, 91, 94
Yahweh, 77, 152, 253
Zealots, 310

JESUS